Jobs for the Boys?

Jobs for the Boys?

Women Who Became Priests

Liz and Andrew Barr

Hodder & Stoughton
LONDON SYDNEY AUCKLAND

British Library Cataloguing in Publication Data
A record for this book is available from the British Library

ISBN 0 340 78534 9

Typeset by Avon Dataset Ltd, Bidford-on-Avon, Warks

Printed and bound in Great Britain by
Clays Ltd, St Ives plc

Hodder & Stoughton
A Division of Hodder Headline Ltd
338 Euston Road
London NW1 3BH

Contents

Acknowledgments

As Christians and as religious broadcasters, Andrew and I have been witnesses to a long struggle in the Church of England over whether or not women could be ordained. We attended most if not all of the General Synod debates on the matter over the past three decades, sitting in the public or press gallery, and Andrew was an executive producer responsible for the BBC coverage of the final historic debate, televised on 11 November 1992. In the final decade of the last century of the second millennium the General Synod, the governing body of the Church of England, at long last voted by a two-thirds majority in all three of its houses to allow women to offer themselves for ordination to the priesthood.

We have been witnesses, but not experts. This is not a book for anyone who wants an academic, theological or legal assessment of the Act of Synod and Resolutions A, B or C. Our purpose has been to allow some of the women who have taken on some of the 'jobs for the boys' to give their own vivid accounts of their personal experiences of this seismic change in the order of the church. Some we met were battle-hardened veterans from the earliest days; only the very youngest appear to have walked through an open door, and even they gave us accounts of members of their own congregations who will not receive communion from them – because they are women and not men.

Because we are not experts, we owe great thanks to three people in particular who have helped us frame the stories in this book. With their knowledge of the history of the movement, their experience of the general public's reaction to women priests, and their understanding of the future, their wisdom has been of great guidance to us. We have taken the liberty of quoting them liberally throughout the book, and much of their conversations with us appear in our concluding chapter, 2001–50 AD.

Revd Una Kroll is one of the most determined campaigners for women over the years, who is retired but still licensed to officiate in the Church of Wales. She welcomed us to her medieval anchorage in

Monmouth, where she rises each morning at four to pray for the rest of us. She answered the question, 'Has God always been calling women to the priesthood from the very beginning?' and gave us a clear account of the story of women in the church from the first to the twenty-first century.

Canon Lucy Winkett, a minor canon of St Paul's Cathedral, whose exposure to the public in the television documentary made behind the scenes at St Paul's brought her 2,000 letters, has given us insights into how the general public at large respond to women priests.

The Ven Judith Rose, Archdeacon of Tonbridge, at the General Synod in July 2000 sponsored a Private Member's Motion on the ordination of bishops. It has begun the process of theological debate on the issue of ordaining women to the episcopacy, and she gave us a clear-sighted forecast of the future for women in the church.

Different people helped to point us in the right direction, because with 2,000 women now ordained priests in the Church of England, it at first seemed impossible to know where to begin. Bishop John Sentamu; Bishop Gavin Reid; Archdeacon John Barton; Dr Philip Giddings; Christina Rees, Chair of Women and the Church; Jane Ozanne, member of the Archbishops' Council; Sue Primmer, former diocesan communication officer for the Diocese of Birmingham; and Vin Arthey, television producer and former diocesan communication officer for the Diocese of Newcastle, all led us to some of the remarkable women whose stories are told in this book. Our great thanks are due to them.

I must also thank Judith Longman, who has put up with not one but six delayed delivery dates for the manuscript with patience and fortitude – and is still our friend.

Above all, Andrew and I have gone round the country to meet and talk to twelve extraordinary women and we can't measure the debt we owe them for their powerful stories and the insights they have given us into what it has been like from the inside. Sometimes Andrew went to talk to them, sometimes I went, and sometimes we both went. We are hugely grateful to all of them for their patience as we fiddled around with recalcitrant tape recorders and microphones, drank their coffee, and then sat back and let them do all the work of telling us about their own journeys to priesthood.

REVD UNA KROLL

CANON LUCY WINKETT

THE VEN JUDITH ROSE

Introduction

It is the last morning of the old millennium. The clouds of incense in an Edinburgh church are so dense that the high altar has become invisible. This is Sunday 31 December 2000 in Old St Paul's, a church that takes pride in tradition and where even the switching on and off of electric light is imbued with liturgical significance.

Although I'd had a lifetime's experience working in religious broadcasting and had responsibility for the television coverage of Church of England and Lambeth Conference debates about the ordination of women over several decades, I still did not know quite what to expect when Liz and I began to meet the women who would tell us their stories for this book.

Now, the fog of incense thins to reveal a diminutive human form behind the huge high altar. It is the Revd Bridget Macaulay, arrayed in vestments clearly constructed for a man of substantial dimensions. Bridget is to lead the Anglo-Catholic congregation through the most holy moments of the Mass. As she sings the service in a small, rather vulnerable voice but with great care, it is clear what she means when she describes her role in celebrating the Eucharist as 'speaking the words of truth'. It is difficult to realise that a huge revolution lies behind this small performance.

Kneeling to receive Communion in Old St Paul's from Bridget seems so natural now. Yet I cannot forget Ken, an old and dear friend of ours, who as an Anglican priest came with me to worship in this same church only a few years ago. First he carefully inspected the building to ensure that the Mass would be true to the Anglo-Catholic tradition that lay behind his own vocation. Since the ordination of women to the priesthood, Ken has left the Church of England to become a Roman Catholic priest, and although our friendship is in no way impaired, we can no longer go to the altar to receive Communion together – even at Old St Paul's.

On this last morning before the dawn of a new millennium, it is another diminutive pioneer I am reminded of as I watch Bridget consecrate the elements – Revd Florence Li Tim Oi. In the midst of difficult debates about women's ordination at the 1988 Lambeth Conference, I sat on the grass outside the University of Kent with a tiny old woman who – almost half a century earlier – had become the worldwide Anglican Communion's first woman priest. Yards away from her, relaxing in the sun, was the large figure of a very senior bishop, one of the most formidable opponents of the ordination of women; neither of them made any attempt to approach one another. It was a courteous non-meeting of two disparate worlds.

Florence, who had always obeyed the instruction of her bishop, sought no voice in the main debate, although her very presence was revolutionary, which was why I was filming her for Channel 4. With modesty and in halting English she told the reporter, Ted Harrison, how in the Second World War, newly ordained by her bishop because there were no men priests to do the work, she had served as a priest in Japanese-occupied Hong Kong. It was difficult to edit her contribution for our conference report, not because of her language difficulties, but chiefly because she was so extremely self-effacing. She hardly seemed like the embodiment of the threat to divide Christendom that others were predicting in the debates that day. Could her quiet presence really be seen as something so destructive to peace? And could a door to a future role for women in the priesthood really be opened so gently and so modestly?

It's been a dozen years since Florence Li Tim Oi came to the Lambeth Conference. Since then I have heard many sermons and arguments prophesying inevitable schism. We have been exhorted to join the faithful remnant. Other lay friends, men and women, including clergy wives, told us that they – and we – must leave the Church of England if women's ordination was allowed. They said that priesthood was a sacrament, ordained by God . . . not an equal opportunities issue for women's liberationists. And as journalists, we've sat and listened to uncomfortable debates in the General Synod, which have gone on raging – years after it had been declared that there were no *theological* objections to women's ordination. (A 1935 Commission set up by the Archbishops of York and Canterbury had produced a report stating that there were no theological or biblical obstacles to the ordination of women.)

So what obstacles *did* remain?

It was a damp day, 11 November 1992, when the final stage of this debate was reached. Damp for the large crowd who stood all day outside Church House, waiting for the result of the Synod deliberations. Rarely can there have been such intense press and broadcasting interest in the proceedings of the Church of England, and most of the day's debate went out live on BBC 2. As executive producer I sat in a little cubicle overlooking the debate with John Barton (now Archdeacon of Aston), an experienced broadcaster who was doing the commentary.

To be of any help to an interested but uninvolved general audience, we had to leave our own feelings and hopes at the door. Thinking back, I cannot be sure that I even knew at the time what John's own personal convictions were. We did wonder what might happen during and after the vote, whatever the outcome, and I had to judge the tone and content of John's commentary as the debate evolved to make sure we remained impartial.

The speeches were outstanding and, as is the tradition with the General Synod, the choice of speakers from each side so even-handed that it seemed too close to call when the final speaker sat down. Before the vote, Archbishop George Carey asked the Synod to pray with him. It was a moving moment. He gave no hint of his own position, and when the President made the prophetic-sounding call for the Synod to 'Divide', the chamber emptied, with clergy and laity dividing in what looked like equal number to vote; we were left with a cliffhanger. As the moments ticked by John Barton and I, with nervously inadequate mental arithmetic skills, added and re-added how many votes would constitute the pre-scribed majority. After what seemed like a very long time the tellers approached the platform, each muttering their result and passing over a small scrap of paper. We peered down in vain. We could see the bewigged figure of the church's legal expert, Brian Hanson, and the Secretary General of the General Synod, Philip Mawer, peering at the papers while doing their own sums with what looked like equal uncertainty. At last the figures were passed to the Archbishop, whose face remained inscru-table. He had the composure of well-dried concrete. Up in the com-mentary box our window was steaming up.

At last we were told: the Synod had voted by the necessary majority plus two votes for women to be allowed to put themselves forward for ordination as priests. The vote was to be received in silence. So it was – in the chamber. But from outside the hall there came a thunderous explosion that sounded like a bomb. A huge rocket had been let off by the joyful crowd who had stood and waited outside all that day, as they had on so many other days. Now they started to sing.

The waiting was over. There was much silent hugging in the public gallery. In the chamber members of Synod stood up and quietly dispersed, and although for both sides of the debate this had been a matter of passionate concern, nearly everyone displayed cool reticence and court-eous consideration for one another's feelings. There were a few tears, but no displays of triumphalism. Broadcasters and onlookers could only guess what they were feeling, and what might happen next.

Nearly two years later, in St Mary's Episcopal Cathedral in Edinburgh, I saw for the first time women candidates for ordination come before the then Primus of Scotland, Bishop Richard Holloway, and kneel at the altar. All except one. Behind them up the nave came another figure, a diminutive one, on two sticks. It was Revd Elizabeth Malloch, aged eighty-four, and not at all well, who after a lifetime in education had at last been able to answer the call to the priesthood in her retirement. At her memorial service last year in the same cathedral, Richard Holloway recalled how he felt as he watched her courageous walk down the length of the cathedral. She had been determined not to come to the altar in a wheelchair. 'Perhaps we did bend the rules a little about age limits,' he told us. 'No we didn't, we broke them completely,' he admitted.

Liz and I only heard Revd Elizabeth Malloch preach one sermon as a priest. It was delivered with some difficulty as the cathedral's public address system was on the blink. But it was a sermon we have never forgotten, rooted in Scripture but located in life. Her text was from Matthew 13, the parable of the man who sows his field with good wheat, but in the morning his servants come and tell him that an enemy has sown weeds and tares in his field. He says, 'Let both grow together until the harvest.' Elizabeth said she had been musing for a long time about what lesson could possibly be drawn from this. She came up with a memorable phrase: the wheat is still growing. However many things go wrong, and in the middle of all the horrible and cruel things that happen in the world, and the awful things we do ourselves, the good part of us is still growing. It's a message of hope that we have carried with us ever since. This phrase, 'the wheat is still growing' has come to mind many times while we have been listening to women telling us the sometimes painful and difficult stories of their experiences on the road to priesthood.

This introductory chapter has been finished during a visit to the Crypt of St Paul's Cathedral in London. The visit did not arise from any holy intention, but from the need for somewhere warm to sit on a cold day. Down in the crypt where food is served and souvenirs sold there is a small area where the passer-by can rest without having to pay the customary tourist entry fee into the main cathedral. There are a few monumental tombstones dotted around down there, but I was most curious about the memorials in the floor, which hundreds of visitors walk over each day. Few pause to read the names. In this busy part of the crypt of one of the world's most famous cathedrals we seem to be, in every sense, 'below stairs'. They record the service of Victorian vergers and their families. Here is the wife of Robert Russell Green, 'a verger of this Cathedral' and Mary his daughter, who died aged eleven months, Sarah who died aged two months, and Thomas who died aged two years. And here lies Ann Lamon, wife of another verger, whose inscription reads, 'Her end was peace.' Then there is John Lingard, Dean's Verger for fifty years, and his wife, Ann, and their four children, who all died before their parents did. These are the memorials to long-forgotten friendships and the kindness of people supporting the clergy of the Victorian cathedral, these unregarded records of grief and loss.

St Paul's Cathedral was in the news a couple of years ago when its life was featured in three television documentaries. The first and most memorable looked at life through the eyes of Revd Lucy Winkett, the cathedral's own first woman priest. To the casual viewer, it must have seemed incomprehensible that this sensitive, talented and vivacious young woman had to cope with so much rejection by some of the servers. The cameras watched as she kept calm but tearful as the situation worsened, and an uneasy compromise was sought. Not surprisingly it is said that Lucy Winkett had over 2,000 letters of support from viewers, of which 1,500 arrived during the first week after that documentary was shown.

A recent advertisement in the *Church Times*, seeking to appoint a priest, looked for 'a mature and strong leader with a servant heart'. With Lucy Winkett now properly established upstairs in St Paul's, a priest and holder of the splendidly Trollopian title of Chaplain and Warden of the College of Minor Canons, it strikes me that any and all the women who feature in this book fit that bill perfectly.

ANDREW BARR
NOVEMBER 2001

CANON CATHERINE TRISTRAM

1

Girls Can't Be Cowboys

Canon Catherine Tristram

Non-stipendiary curate, Holy Island

I was invited to speak at our clergy deanery chapter before the vote. They were almost all of them against it, but most of them have always been very pleasant to me, very gentlemanly. I was a deacon, and Denis, my vicar, was there. I spoke about the ordination of women and at the end someone thanked me and then there was a bit of a pause and someone said – do we think that a woman preaching would be in any way substantially different from a man preaching? Whereupon one of the brethren, said, 'Oh yes, I think so. Women would be very diffuse in their preaching. They would go all round the point whereas men, of course, go straight to the point.'

And my vicar said, 'It's the other way round in my parish . . .'

Introduction

AB and LB: On midsummer nights passengers northbound on the London–Edinburgh east-coast express have an almost mystical view across the North Sea towards Lindisfarne (Holy Island) and the nearby Farne islands. Late in the night sky the sun finally sets not in the west, but slowly dips below sea level on the far north-eastern horizon. These are images to raise the spirits of the most jaded city dweller.

Walking gingerly over the level crossing at Beal in Northumberland, pilgrims for Holy Island are likely to be overtaken by television film crews en route to one of today's most popular religious broadcasting locations. Their destination is the setting for the currently fashionable pursuit of searching for 'Celtic spirituality'.

Lindisfarne is said to be 'a thin place' – a place where the gap between heaven and earth seems almost bridgeable. The island attracts its fair share of those who want a 'quick fix' of spirituality, who think they can bring their problems and in some magical way they will be solved here. Much legendary nonsense is written about the lives of those hardy old medieval Christians, the Celtic saints. Walking on Holy Island before dawn on one of the shortest, darkest winter days, with the wind roaring across bleak sand-dunes, you will begin to experience something closer to the real world in which Aidan, Bede and Cuthbert lived out their Christian witness. This is a world Canon Catherine Tristram knows well, after nearly a quarter of a century living and working on the island, for most of that time as Warden of Marygate House, a retreat house where people come to learn and to rest, and leave refreshed.

No one visiting Holy Island can make the journey unless they've first checked the little white Lindisfarne bible of tide tables. Come at the wrong time, and there's a wide stretch of water cutting off the small community and the retreat house of Marygate from the rest of the world. We crossed on a calm spring day, aiming the car between the long straight line of poles planted in the sand marking out a safe passage. The sea, with the tide due back in less than an hour to engulf the road, was a distant glint in the sun.

And there we found Canon Catherine Tristram, known to everyone there as Kate. We were first introduced to Kate by a television producer friend, who admired her greatly as someone who was afraid of the sea, but who had been led by faith to work on a small island surrounded by wild waves. As it turns out, the reality, like some of the wilder legends of the Celtic saints, isn't quite like that.

The story Kate told us, her journey from a wartime childhood playing cowboys and Indians in the West Midlands to a grown-up life on a small island in the north-east, was about a long, still ongoing pilgrimage.

Kate

When I read Columbanus, which I did last year, and the set of thirteen sermons that he preached to his monks in the last year of his life, what does he say all the time, *all* the time? Life is a road. You do not settle down on a road. Nobody stops on a road. They travel over the road towards the homeland.

You can't be a cowboy – you're a girl

The big tragedy of my childhood was that I was a girl and not a boy. I couldn't believe it. I didn't really believe it until I got to adolescence, and then I had to believe it. All the things that I wanted to do when I grew up were things that boys did. I was reading adventure stories about people climbing mountains and I longed to be an explorer. At another point, I longed to be a bug hunter. I wanted to go off and discover creatures that hadn't been discovered before. And so on. I remember squabbling with my older brother. We were playing cowboys and Indians, and we were squabbling about who should be what, and my grandmother, rather squashingly, interrupted us with, 'Kate, you can't be a cowboy, you're a girl.'

And that echoed right through my life. You can't be a cowboy. Poor little child – doomed to be an Indian forever!

Wartime childhood

I was born in 1931 on the borders of Worcestershire and Staffordshire. The nearest town was Stourbridge, in North Worcestershire, which is where I went to high school. When I was eight, the war started.

When I look back, I think there were very useful lessons learnt during the war. I mean, we learnt to do without. But the main thing for me, as a child during the war, was that not a single adult that I ever encountered ever suggested that we might not win. We were all very positive about the war. It was just a matter of when we were going to win it. I remember saying to my mother, 'On the day the war ends, can we have an egg for tea?'

And mother saying, 'I don't think it'll be quite as quick as that.'

Living in the West Midlands, we weren't in the direct line of fire, but we got everything that missed Birmingham and Coventry, so we did get bombs and landmines in the area. We were evacuated temporarily once when a stick of bombs fell along our road – the nearest one was about thirty yards away from our shelter. It fell in the middle of the night and we were evacuated immediately. They were all live bombs, but not a single one of them went off. We had to go immediately out of the shelter to my father's mother, who lived about two miles away, and the bomb-disposal moved in and made them safe or whatever bomb-disposal people do. We were allowed back about three days later. That was the nearest.

Even though we were bang in the heart of the Midlands, I remember Dunkirk Day. I remember people virtually dancing in the streets and saying that all these little boats had gone across and rescued our men. We had the news on almost continuously, and the first man I ever fell in love with was Winston Churchill. I thought Churchill was marvellous. I would have happily died for Churchill.

We carried gas masks everywhere. We sometimes had to wear our gas masks during lessons as a drill, and the teacher came round and put a card on the end of your nozzle, your snout, so that she could see whether it was airtight. You had to breathe in and hold the thing on the end of your gas mask. We also had to practise getting under our desks at a signal from the teacher, in case of a sudden air-raid. We all wore little nameplates, with our name and addresses, on our wrists – and we knew these little wristlets were to identify our body in case we were killed. But I don't remember any of us ever feeling in the least bit frightened. It was quite exciting.

We had a big garden and my father and my grandfather had built an air-raid shelter, which was partly a tool room. My mother's parents both lived with us. The inner room had bunks for my brother and me, and it had two armchairs for Mum and Granny, and the outer room had two armchairs for Dad and Granddad. So that was our arrangement during the air-raids. After the raid was over, we used to go through the garden in the middle of the night and back to our rooms in the house.

The tin hat

My brother was two years older and he was quite a leader, so we were the leaders of the gangs of local children. We formed good gangs. We didn't destroy anything, and we didn't attack anybody, but we called ourselves 'The Gang'. We had one or two fights with rival gangs, but only pretend fights – throwing green apples at each other and that sort of thing. Not anything serious. Nobody was hurt. At the beginning of the war, we turned The Gang into a kind of home guard, and we all polished our bicycles like anything, to be ready when Winston Churchill wanted us to take a message.

I was the only girl in our gang – but I was very much a tomboy as a child. One day, as part of our war effort, my brother and the other boys dug a big pit in our garden and they fetched out my father's old tin hat. My father had fought in the trenches in the First World War but he was too old for the second and, in any case, as a mathematics teacher he was in a reserved occupation. So he had this tin hat for during air-raids, doing his ARP work. My brother and the other little boys thought that this tin hat should be tested, to make sure it was all right. So I had to crouch in a big hole that they had dug in the garden with the tin hat on my head, while they threw half bricks at it from quite a distance. Afterwards we had to explain to Dad where all the dents in his tin hat came from.

I was never hurt. We had a lot of adventurous play. We lived in the country, so we had very extensive playgrounds. We could go anywhere and we did. In those days children could have what would now be called dangerous toys. We all had bows and arrows. We all had sheath knives, which we wore on our belt and learnt to throw. Throwing our knives was quite a sport, and my father had an air rifle, which he taught both my brother and me to shoot with.

So I don't know quite how we survived our childhood, but we did survive it, neither of us being hurt and no child in the neighbourhood being hurt. My parents believed in freedom and my mother bit her lip and conquered her nervousness and just waited for us to come back in again, alive or dead as the case might be. But that was the sort of childhood . . . if you say was it happy – yes, it was happy, and my brother was my best friend during the whole of our childhood.

Non-religious upbringing

Both my parents were teachers. My father taught maths in a boys' school and my mother was a primary teacher, mainly specialising in what we used to call ESN children – educationally subnormal children.

My family was totally non-churchgoing. I remember when I was about eight taking myself off to two or three Sunday schools, presumably with my little friends of the time. One was a Wesleyan Methodist Sunday school, another was a primitive Methodist Sunday school and the third was the local Church of England Sunday school. I didn't go for very long at a time to any of them. I didn't feel I was learning anything and by the age of ten, I gave up going. My parents made no comment on this at all. They allowed me to go. They allowed me to stop going.

That was the only religious teaching that I had in childhood, apart from what I got in school. I went to an ordinary state primary school and then to the state high school. So, of course, we had Scripture and the thing that I think was important was not anything that was taught us, because I don't remember most of it, but the fact that in those days we did an immense amount of learning by heart. My memory is that we learnt the Twenty-third Psalm in the reception class of primary school. It might have been the second year, but it was very early on.

I can remember to this day the beautiful pictures that formed in my mind from the Twenty-third Psalm. I can remember the still waters and the green meadows, and even the valley of the shadow of death, because my childish picture was of myself walking through a very stony valley accompanied by a shepherd's crook bobbing up and down beside me. I knew that you couldn't see God, so there was an invisible presence, and the shepherd's crook bobbed along the valley of the shadow of death. I can remember the table spread with the most luxurious fabric I could imagine – black velvet – and the single silver chalice cup in the middle of it. Those lovely pictures formed in my mind and I haven't ever forgotten them. But in terms of a living faith, it didn't mean anything to me for many, many years. We did a lot of learning by heart and later on I was grateful for that. So that was my religious upbringing.

I think my brother kept up the family tradition of non-churchgoing all his life. He became an artist, and emigrated to Australia.

First Christian stirrings

By the time I was in the sixth form, though, I was getting quite interested in Christianity. I was in the sixth form for three years, taking A levels and university entrance, so I didn't leave school until I was nineteen. In my last year at school I took myself off on a kind of church crawl – Sunday by Sunday visiting the various kinds of church that there were in our town. I got to know a little bit about Baptists and Methodists, and I went to a Roman Catholic church – and that really did blow my mind. I'd never experienced anything quite like it. I thought it was marvellous. We're talking still about the 1940s, so it was the Latin Mass of course.

I was very much attracted to the Roman Church in terms of liturgy. I don't think that the actual worship of the Methodist and Baptist or C of E really appealed to me at all, though I did hear some good sermons. I was never into hymn singing. I think in the Roman Church, I felt the seriousness of the devotion to the altar. This was worship with a focus to it, but I didn't understand any of the theology of it at all at that stage. I knew nothing really.

So I built up a little experience of what different churches were like. I did it alone, or sometimes with different friends from school. Again, my family made no comment when I went out in the evenings on my bike to visit the local churches. And I didn't turn myself into anything like a committed churchgoer. It was just exploration. I was the sort of kid that wanted to know about things and why things were and how things were and what there was to know. I was into things like philosophy. At school we were reading bits of Plato and I wanted to know why people believed what they did believe.

I didn't believe myself, and I didn't at that point make any efforts to join a church or become a regular churchgoer.

Workers' Educational Association

Another thing that had an influence on me at that time was the Workers' Educational Association (WEA). They used to put on all sorts of courses for evening classes. Our principal history teacher, who I admired and liked a great deal, suggested to some of the sixth-formers that there was a good course that we might like to go to, called 'Makers of the Modern World'.

The person leading it was from Birmingham, a man called Gordon Stuart, a very good man. We learned all about Freud and Marx, and people like Albert Schweitzer. It was an extremely good course, one evening a week during the winter, and I thought it was fantastic being introduced to all these people.

But I was also aware that Gordon Stuart was a Unitarian minister, and I became clear what that was. He believed in the moral teachings of Jesus, but he didn't believe in things mainstream Christians believe – he didn't believe Jesus was part of a Trinity, or rose from the dead. I'm sure that it was important that I was introduced to all these 'Makers of the Modern World' through a man who had, as it were, basically a religious approach to life, even though it was not orthodox Christianity. He was a very good man and I think that was very important. But when I did later become an Anglican, I had to account in my own mind for the fact that Gordon Stuart had managed to be the man he was, and a Unitarian.

So these were all things that happened during the sixth-form years and certainly inclined me towards an interest in religion, though it still didn't turn me into a churchgoer.

The Man Born to be King

I suppose I ought to mention one other thing that happened before I left school. Oxford and Cambridge entrance exams were in November, and by December I knew that I'd got in to Oxford. My parents were so pleased – it seems silly now – they bought me a very special Christmas present, which was my very own first little radio set. It was long before the days of portable radios, and it had to be plugged in, but it meant that I was free for the first time to go up to my room and listen to whatever I liked. I could listen to something that the family was not listening to downstairs.

I don't know what it was that made me tune into it, but I listened to Dorothy Sayers' radio plays, *The Man Born to be King*. It was the second time they were being broadcast, because they went out for the first time during the war, but I hadn't heard them then. It was a continuous series every week on Sunday nights, and I listened to these and for the very first time in my life, I found the life of Jesus interesting and significant. Apart from what we'd learnt at school, I really didn't know the Gospel stories. This put the whole Jesus story together for me for the first time.

Some people said it was blasphemous. Dorothy Sayers wrote in the front of the second edition about all the desperate attempts that had been made by some people to get the plays stopped during the war. They said things like, 'Singapore's just fallen, take these blasphemous plays off the radio before we lose something else!'

They thought God was punishing us for listening to it. The things they objected to were having somebody acting the voice of Jesus, and saying the things that he said. And they objected to the crucifixion scene with the soldiers using rough language. She didn't use any *rude* language, but she did use rough language. Dorothy Sayers wrote rather sarcastically, 'I suppose, since the creed says so and the Bible says so, we have to accept that he was spit upon and flogged and nailed to the cross – but no doubt it was done in the most gentlemanly manner!'

Because my bedroom was directly above our large living-room/ kitchen, I didn't want my parents to hear, through their ceiling – my floor – what I was listening to. So I put my radio on top of several cushions, masked it with a blanket and listened to *The Man Born to be King* with my ear next to the set. I was doing them an injustice, but I was so new to it all, I didn't want to have to discuss it. It was my secret.

But listening to *The Man Born to be King* – I think that probably was a stage on the way.

Somerville College, Oxford

In 1950 I left school and went to university to read history. We had had a very good history teacher at my school and I was enthusiastic. I went to Somerville College, Oxford, and it was Oxford that really affected my conversion to Christianity.

For the very first time I met people, whose minds I respected – both the dons and fellow students – who were Christians. I could talk about it all for the first time. I could ask questions and discuss it and also, of course, I found things to read. We had no religious books at home.

C. S. Lewis was very much about in Oxford in my day, and I joined a philosophical club that used to meet every week called 'The Socratic Club'. This was a club that discussed philosophical/religious questions. The dons sat in the middle and discussed things together at their level, and we undergraduates sat round the outside and listened, and took in whatever we could. *Very* occasionally a brave undergraduate asked a question.

So I was going and listening to these arguments and at the same time I was starting to read. C. S. Lewis was president of the club and he used to turn up – not every week but sometimes – and all sorts of interesting people were speakers. I read everything C. S. Lewis wrote or had written by that point. His writings don't appeal to me now, and as a man he did not appeal to me even at the time, because he seemed exceedingly aggressive as a person and appeared deliberately to set out to floor people.

However, it all brought me into the orbit of people who thought religiously. I didn't go to church in Oxford a great deal at that stage – but I know that I was moving towards seeing the religious question as being the most important question in my life.

Death of a stoic

In the summer term of my second year, my father died suddenly. He had concealed the fact that he was ill. I suppose if you ask me what my father's creed was – he was a stoic. We didn't know until shortly beforehand when my mother, realising that he was getting thinner and thinner, insisted on having the doctor.

X-rays proved it was cancer of the lungs – but it was much too late to do anything. He was in hospital for only three days before he died. He must have been in a lot of pain. We think that he probably knew what it was, though it was not mentioned between my parents and neither parent mentioned it to either of us children. But after he died, when we came to look at his papers in his desk, absolutely everything was in perfect order. There was nothing whatever for us to do.

Now, I can't tell you really how that affected me. I loved my father very much. I don't think that I turned to religion for relief from it, because I was already turning to religion. I think it freed me, though. I loved him and I respected his opinion. I would probably have felt it quite hard to become a member of the church during his lifetime. This is me looking back on it all now. It wasn't a conscious thought, 'Now I can join the church.' But he wouldn't have approved, I don't think. On the other hand, I think he would have approved of his daughter sticking to her guns and doing the thing that she thought was right. But it would have caused some rows at home, probably. Anyway, we don't know because he did die, and one thing that that did was to bring me in greater touch with Christians who wanted to try and comfort me and help me.

So it was towards the end of that term, the third term of my second year, that I decided that I would go ahead and commit myself to Christianity. By that time, I'd seen enough of churches to say to myself, 'Well, if I'm going to be anything, I'm going to be an Anglican.' We're talking about confirmation now. So I went ahead and I was confirmed during the first term of my third year.

A real 'spike'

I came into the Church of England at the absolute top. I was a real 'spike'. Like all other undergraduates, I went everywhere, exploring, investigating, sermon-tasting, worship-tasting and everything-tasting. Sometimes I went to St Aldate's, where the sermons were excellent; sometimes to St Mary Magdalene's, and others high and low; but the Church of the Cowley Fathers was the one I liked best. That was where I used to go for High Mass on a Sunday morning and that became the high spot of my week.

One of the people that I met when I was moving towards confirmation said to me, 'Now realise what you are doing. It means that you'll be in church at least once every single Sunday for the rest of your life, and that you will pray at some point every single day for the rest of your life.'

I came into the notion that it was a highly disciplined life to be a Christian. You committed yourself to all these things.

I think I would say that I've lived a committed life since I first became a Christian. I was twenty-one when I was confirmed. I was an adult, making a real commitment for life. That was how I thought of it and that was how I have lived it, and I have never had times in my life when I didn't go to church on Sunday. I've had times in my life that have been more prayerful and times that have been less prayerful, like anybody else – the ups and downs of the emotional life – but never when I've actually withdrawn my membership.

In those days, Anglo-Catholicism – which I would have reckoned I belonged to – was very much into religion as a matter of the will and not of the feelings, and therefore you *will* to serve God. You show that by going to church, and if you don't feel like it, too bad, you still go. That was the way I was brought up in my first Christian years at Oxford.

It has seen me through some good and bad times, but I have never been able to think otherwise. Why should I not go to church just because I'm feeling rotten? I'm feeling angry with God, I'm feeling fed up with the way things are, but I will go to church. I'll take my body if I can't do anything else. If I can't take my heart and my mind, I will still take my body and that's an indication of at least the desire to worship.

I have kept to that.

Brain versus voice

At the end of that term, hard on the heels of my confirmation, I decided that what I wanted to do after getting my history degree was stay on at Oxford, if I could find any possible means, and do a degree in theology. I wanted to go on learning and I felt that I owed it to myself to learn the Christian faith at the deepest and most academic level that I could possibly do. And where is better than Oxford? Stay on and do your theology there.

So I did. But I didn't qualify for another grant.

To finance myself for the first term, I went and lived as a companion to an old lady. She was the widow of a professor of Chinese. She had children but they were all away doing their own thing, and she liked to have a student in the house. She gave free board and lodging to a student who would live in her house, cook her evening meal for her and occasionally accompany her to meetings that she wanted to go to. My old school, Stourbridge High School, also gave me a small bursary to help pay the fees. But at the end of the first term, the poor old lady went into hospital and eventually died, so that was the end of that. I was flung out onto the world again.

My mother, bless her, didn't understand what it was all about, this theology business, and of course my father was dead. But my mother was a working teacher and had her own income and so she said, 'I will give you the rest of this year. I can at least do that. I'll give you the next two terms.'

So I went and found myself lodgings and Mother gave me enough money to cover the fees and my living expenses. Then in the summer term I became aware that the one and only scholarship for graduate women to read theology was being offered.

So I applied. You had to go for interview, and when I turned up there were about ten other people waiting to be seen and I thought it was hopeless. When I went in, the interview was with the whole of the Senior Common Room of St Hugh's College, who were offering the scholarship, and a theological adviser, Austin Farrer. I found myself sitting at one end of the table, with all the dons of St Hugh's College sitting at the other end in their gowns.

They asked me all sorts of questions and I heard myself giving them all the wrong answers. For instance, they said to me, 'Are you dependent upon getting this money?'

My brain said to me, 'Yes. Go on, tell them you must have it.' And I heard my voice saying, 'Oh no, whatever you decide, I shall finish the course somehow.'

They asked me this and that and the other. Austin Farrer asked me something about the Son of Man passages in the Book of Enoch and I told him it wasn't a fair question because I hadn't studied that yet. We were all getting into a lather.

I came out – and I'm not a crybaby, but I went home to my room and alone, I cried for three solid hours. It had just been so awful.

Then a day or two later, came a letter which said I'd got it. I went to see my New Testament tutor, who had been doing a little bit of inquiring behind the scenes. He told me that they had not intended to give it to me at first, because there were other people better qualified on paper, and they must just have liked me. So that dealt with my financial problems for the rest of my course.

In 1955, with a BA in theology, I wanted to be ordained

In my year in the theology school there was me and a couple of hundred men. There were no other women in my year. That didn't bother me particularly; I was used to being the only girl in the gang.

In 1955, I became a BA Theology. But then, of course, I had to decide what to do. I longed to be ordained. That was what I wanted. I wanted to serve God within the church as a minister. I think it would be true to say that at any point in my life, if ordination had become possible, I would have left whatever I was doing, to become ordained.

But it wasn't a living hope. Nobody in my environment was talking about it, not even the most enlightened. Nobody was even discussing it. I didn't even know there were such things as deaconesses. I had never heard of any and never met any. Nobody mentioned them to me.

Bedford High

As I had been brought up in educational circles, I decided to teach. I was happy to go into school and teach what they used to call 'Scripture'. In those days, graduates could go and teach without a postgraduate teaching certificate. Your degree made you a qualified teacher.

I went for interview at Bedford High School, an independent, all girls school – part boarding, part day, but a very good school. The headmistress said to me, 'Don't worry that you haven't got a teaching certificate; we will teach you everything that you need to know on the practical level here.' And they did.

At the age of twenty-four, I became the Head of the Religious

Education Department at Bedford High School. And for the next five years I taught Scripture to girls aged between ten and eighteen, up to O and A levels. I think I was a successful teacher and I liked the kids.

The 1960s – moving north-east

I think, because I'd loved those WEA classes back in my sixth-form days, I'd got it at the back of my mind that I would really like to teach older people, and so when a job appeared at St Hild's College, Durham, I applied for it and got it.

St Hild's College was a strange mixture. It was an extremely agreeable mixture, but it was unusual, because St Hild's, and the men's college next door, Bede College, were both halls of residence for university students doing any old degree that Durham University offered, but they were also teacher training colleges.

I was lecturing in theology and also involved in the practical side of teacher training. For my first twelve years in St Hild's, I was living in the college, part of the residential community. You don't really – at least I didn't – make connections with the churches in the town, because we were a church college. We had our own chapel, our own chaplain. We were a little bit apart from the parishes of the town.

I enjoyed enormously being in Durham and being at St Hild's. The work itself was very productive. We had great freedom in those days – in the 1960s. In fact, I always think of the 1960s with great affection. I was twenty-nine in 1960, and my own thirties corresponded with the 1960s and it was just wonderful. It was so expansionist, so unlimited somehow; and we did very interesting experimental work in the college with students, experimenting in methods of teaching children. We were absolutely into what we called 'modern methods' and 'activity methods' and all the rest of it. Quite out of fashion now, but great fun at the time.

They were interesting times really, the 'sixties'. The day that *Honest to God* came out – having read the thing in the *Observer* the day before – I was hotfoot up to SPCK in Durham. Had they got a copy? No.

'Really, truly, please?' So she produced one from under the desk. I read it on the day it was published and I thought it was terrific.

Getting active – out every night

I was at Durham at St Hild's until 1978, for eighteen years altogether. After twelve years, I bought a house in the nearby village of Lanchester, the reason being that my mother was not able to continue to live alone, so she came to live with me. During that year, unfortunately, she was diagnosed with Alzheimer's and it progressed fairly fast, and she soon had to go into a nursing home.

For the remainder of my time teaching in Durham, I was living in

Lanchester by myself. That was when I decided to join the parish church. Quite quickly I became a very active laywoman. I was reading the lessons, and I was soon on the PCC and then I was onto the deanery synod. Then, because I was on the deanery synod, I was also on the Board for Mission and Unity. And because I was on the Board for Mission and Unity, I was put onto the Northumbrian Industrial Mission. And because I was on all these things, I ended up on the Bishop's Council, when John Habgood was Bishop of Durham.

For the next five years I was out almost every night at some meeting or other. I had a very full experience of being a layperson on all these committees and getting a lot of experience of how the church works administratively and organisationally.

So little do people know the way their lives will turn out

I didn't like Holy Island at all the first time I came, in 1961. I was brought by a friend, who said I must see it. We came one day in the summer, soon after I'd arrived in the north-east, but it happened to be a miserable, wet day and we couldn't find anywhere open for a cup of tea. Everything looked a bit dreary and dismal and the rain didn't stop. We went into the church and even that looked dark and dismal.

I said to my friend as we drove back off the causeway, 'Thank goodness I need never go there again.'

So little do people know the way their lives will turn out.

St Aidan's Weekend

I did come back, but much later. I was, by the way, rising through the grades of lecturer. I became a senior lecturer, a principal lecturer and eventually head of department, which was the highest grade. I became head of department in 1973.

My department offered a course on the coming of Christianity to the north-east, about the early years of Celtic Christianity, and we based the students for a week at Alnwick. Bringing them over to Holy Island for one day of that course in 1973, we realised that Marygate House had opened. They defined it as a place where people can meet, and they didn't say whether it was to meet God, meet the island, or meet each other.

It had actually opened in 1970, and was offering accommodation for individuals and groups on retreat, and was always open for educational groups with their own programmes to carry out. My colleague, who was the church historian, said, 'I've heard good things of this place, we might like to bring the students here next year.'

He wrote off and got the information and the following year, he – but not I – came up with a group of students. That was in the summer of 1974.

Now, that was a rough summer for me. That was the summer that my mother had to go into a nursing home. My friend, this colleague, said, 'You've had a bad time, you've not been away anywhere on holiday. Elizabeth and I – that was his wife – are going up to Holy Island for a week at the beginning of September, which sounds rather interesting. Why don't you come with us and at least see something other than home?'

So I came in September 1974 for what they call the St Aidan's Weekend. It was a study weekend. They had a good speaker, speaking all about St Aidan and the early years of the monastery here. This was all news to me. In my teaching, I was doing mainly biblical studies. That was my speciality, not church history, because even though I had a degree in history, I'd rather abandoned that. But I was really set on fire by this weekend.

So the next year, when it came round to the St Aidan's Weekend – so called because St Aidan died on 31 August and the St Aidan's Weekend is always the nearest weekend to that – I came by myself for the St Aidan's Weekend.

I liked the island, I liked everything. And they got to know me a bit. They asked me to lead the third one, the next one, in 1976.

Because the other speakers had spoken about things in their own particular experience, I thought I would do something of a historical study about St Aidan and that particular period. I called it 'St Aidan and Liberation' and so I came and I led that weekend, and it went off very well. I came back to stay for one or two other weekends, and I was beginning to form a connection with Holy Island.

Meanwhile, back in Durham . . .

Meanwhile, back in Durham, in 1975, the two colleges – St Hild's and Bede, the men's college next door – amalgamated. It was a forced amalgamation. Neither faculty wanted it, but the government imposed it on us, creating a very large college – the college of St Hild and Bede – with some 1,100 students.

I became the Head of the Religious Studies Department for the joint college. So that was a big job, big department, and all the students in the college at that point did some religious studies, because it was a church college and we required it of them. So there was a lot of work, but at the same time we realised that even this amalgamation wasn't going to be the end of it. Right through the 1960s if you were in teacher training you were told, 'Expand, expand, expand, take more students', and then in 1970 you were told, 'Stop expanding', and then, almost immediately, 'Start to contract, start to shrink.'

So now the thing that had been our greatest joy became our greatest problem – the fact that the two colleges were already half in the university.

Some of our people were university people, some were teacher training people.

In 1977, the government found it expedient to get rid of more teacher training places by pushing our two colleges wholly into the university. The new college of St Hild's and Bede was going to become simply halls of residence for the university, and the large teaching staff – eighty-six of us – was going to be disbanded. Half of us would get jobs in the university, and half of us would be made redundant.

I wasn't over-worried for myself because I'd had a successful career up to that point and I thought I would get offered a job in the university. It would be a different job, but I'd be all right. So I wasn't worried, but at the same time, everything was very disturbed all around us, and there was real kerfuffle going on. This was a most miserable time because, as you can imagine, lifelong friendships were broken as people wondered who was going to be made redundant and who wasn't and so on. It was a dreadful, dreadful time.

A pure joke

I was at home one Wednesday in June 1977, marking exam papers. The post arrived and I saw there was a letter from the Warden of Marygate House. I'd written to book myself in for a weekend, so I assumed this would just be the reply for that, and I made myself a cup of coffee and sat down to read her letter. I must have told her something of what was happening in Durham because she made the kind of joke that you do make to comfort people in that situation. She wrote, 'Never mind – if the worst comes to the worst, we can always give you a job here!' Meaning it as a pure joke.

The heavens opened. In that split second, I simply knew that I'd got to leave Durham and come here. It wasn't a rational decision at all. I had not planned it. I just knew that that was what was going to happen.

I sat turned to stone in my chair at home for a while.

There was nothing for a person of my type to do at Marygate House in those days. It changed later, but at that point there was nothing for me to do here. I was forty-six. I'd got nineteen years of my career ahead of me, and I was going to come here, a lifelong academic, a lifelong teacher – to do what? There was no teaching here. I wasn't domesticated, and the only thing I could have done was the washing up.

I wanted the first person I met to say, 'Don't be stupid!'

After a bit, I recollected myself and I thought, 'Well, got to do something about this. I'll drive into college and speak to the first member of staff that I meet and tell them this, and they will tell me not to be a fool and I'll forget about the whole thing.'

So I drove into college and the first person I met happened to be the chaplain. I said to him, 'Oh, Jeff, I've just had the most stupid idea. I've thought that I will leave Durham and go to Holy Island!'

But instead of saying, 'Don't be stupid', he said, 'Well, why not?' Which he wasn't meant to say at all. He was so nonplussed, he just found himself saying it.

I told another colleague, a priest who was in my department – and a good friend of mine – and he put on a mock pompous voice and said, 'I think you've had an Abrahamic call!'

Then I told my closest woman friend, Lilian Groves, and she said, 'Don't be stupid!'

No way back

That was on Wednesday. I thought about it until Friday and then I went to the principal of the college and I said to him, 'I'm withdrawing from this whole business of applying for new jobs and I'm going to Holy Island.'

He said, 'You're not.'

'Yes, I am.'

'No. You're not.'

'I am. I shall at least have to investigate it.'

I came back to my house from the college and rang up Joan Harris, the warden, and said, 'Joan, you know what you said in your letter about giving me a job if I wanted one? Could it become real if I did want one?'

She more or less fell flat on the floor. She said, 'Well, you'd better come up and talk about it.'

So she looked in the bookings for that weekend and there was – of course – one room vacant. I said, 'I'll come tomorrow.'

So that Saturday I came up and I talked to her, I talked to the other people who were working here, and I talked to Denis Bill, the vicar at the time and one of the founding fathers of Marygate House. They were all completely astonished, but when I went back home again on the Sunday, it was more or less fixed.

I mean, it was fixed for me from that split second on the Wednesday. I just knew. I went back to see the principal and said, 'Yes, I'm withdrawing from this whole process, I'm going to Holy Island.'

He said, 'Realise one thing. If you go, there is no way back.'

The future? An absolute total blank

And then, as the news began to break, people began to take different attitudes. Some of my colleagues who didn't know me so well thought that I was really cracking under the strain of everything that was happening and they went to Lilian, my friend, and said, 'Do try and persuade Kate to go and see a doctor, will you?'

But nothing, over the next year, happened to make me change my mind.

Being head of department, I had to give a whole year's notice. The college was kind to me, it gave me the summer term of 1978 as a sabbatical. So I arrived here earlier in the year than I thought I was going to be able to.

I had no idea, no plan of what I was going to do. The future was a total blank in my mind. People back in Durham said, 'Have you got a job description?' No. 'Well, have you got a contract?' No. 'Well, you're an utterly mad woman! What are you doing?'

'I'm going to Holy Island, that's all I know.'

My mother was dying. I knew she was coming to the end of her life. She was alive when I took this decision, but she was dead before I actually moved up here.

I had a house to sell and I was lucky that a cottage came vacant here and I was able to buy it, the one I'm still in. I had had a redundancy package from the college. I must say that I came here with very little money because keeping mother at the residential home had taken virtually everything I had. I came with very little by way of anything saved up. I also came to Marygate with the agreement that I wouldn't cost Marygate anything. I wasn't expecting a salary. Marygate started with almost nothing and it was running on an absolute shoestring. I had my meals here.

So I was very poor, but I was full of idealism and enthusiasm and a 'we must find a way, God is leading us' sort of feeling. I was probably more religious in those early years here than at any other time of my life.

Who shall I be?

I didn't know what God was calling me to, but in a sense I wagered my whole life on the fact that it was a genuine call. As the principal said, there was no way back into the sort of work I'd been doing. I was betting my life on it being a call from God.

And it was weird. That last year at Durham, when I knew I was coming here, but still having to go through the motions down there, I went through moments of total panic. Waking up in the middle of the night and thinking, 'I shan't have a union. Who's going to defend me when I haven't got a union?' And, 'Who shall I be when I am no longer the Head of the Religious Studies Department in the College of St Hild's and Bede? Who shall I be?'

But at no point did I think I'd made the wrong decision, although they gave me lots of opportunities. They were so kind. I came here feeling that everybody had wanted me to stay down there.

A difficult beginning

The first two years were very difficult. Here I was, miles away from anybody that I knew. People here were wondering why I had come. No one belonged to quite the world I was used to. Everyone, it seemed to me, stood back to see what would happen.

Assistant Warden of Marygate

I was going to succeed Joan as warden eventually, because she was over sixty and she was also arthritic. In the meantime I worked as her assistant for a year and a half. I did whatever she told me to. I did the shopping for the house and I did this, that and the other.

When I'd been here about six months and was still wondering what it was all about, the Durham Diocesan Director of Ordination came up here with a group and he said – could the house take a resident student?

He had in mind a young man who had just failed his second year in theology at King's College, London but still wanted to be ordained. He had to leave King's College but the bishop wanted him to go somewhere where he could recover his confidence a little bit, and then go forward eventually to ordination. So we said – yes, we could take that student. And John came. I was supposed to teach him things that he would have done in his third year at King's College, London and rebuild his academic confidence a bit.

That was my first great success. He's a vicar in the Manchester Diocese now, and he comes back most years and brings a group. Of course, he's a middle-aged man now.

And on the heels of that, other youngsters started coming. Joan did all the cooking, but as we expanded, we needed a team. Young people started to come and by the time Joan retired, I had a team of five young people helping in the house.

Joan retired suddenly. She fell in her cottage and broke her hip and had to go into hospital, which pushed everything forward. I took over at that point. Hadn't a clue how to do the finances. Hadn't a clue how to do housework, how to do anything. But I had these youngsters to help me.

For most of the time that I was warden here, I ran it with a group of young people and they were mostly either school- or college-leavers. They were almost always under twenty-three years old, and they came for different reasons. Some of them came because they had come to the end of something and didn't know what to do next – they wanted thinking time.

Some of them came because they wanted tuition. With my background, I could teach up to A level in religious studies and history. We had boys who wanted to be ordained and couldn't take the first step until they got their two A levels necessary for college. We did the whole course here and then sent them down to Durham to take their exams, and a large number of them are now ordained.

Sometimes they came for other kinds of teaching. I had four people together who were specifically here to do New Testament Greek. Two of those were girls, who had already got degrees and if they could get their Greek, they were going to be allowed to go into the second year of a theology honours course. The other two were boys who were on a theology course already, but doing so badly at their Greek, that their universities had told them to go away, and only come back when they'd learnt it. So I had two highly resistant boys and two highly intelligent girls. One of my girls got 100 per cent in her Greek. When the second girl got only 99 per cent I said to her, 'You utter disgrace, you absolute – however did you come to lose a mark?' She said, 'Well, I didn't think I did, but the tutor did!'

Both of those girls are now ordained and doing extremely well. Heaven knows what's happened to the boys.

Many young people came also because they had had troubles and breakdowns and needed a place and time to recover from their problems.

The human chain
People said to me – When your young people leave, how do you get new ones? Where do you look? And I used to say, 'Upwards!' I don't know how it was, but they came and came and came. Obviously there was some kind of human chain of communication. One person told another person, who told another person. But sometimes I had more young people than I could take.

I usually had a team of between five and eight young people. They were students, but they did all the work of the house. When Joan first retired and I had my first meeting with the five young people who were here, I said to them, ' I can't look after this house, I'm not domesticated. I can't cook or anything like that.'

They all said, 'Don't you worry. We can do it.'

None of these students had any vocation to domestic life. They were all what you might snobbishly call 'professional-type' young people. They were all going on to professional jobs. They weren't going to spend their lives cooking and cleaning, but they cleaned and they did the laundry and they did the shopping and they did everything.

We shall live by faith
I did the accounts. Actually we had a very, very kind man who came and showed me that first weekend a system of doing accounts and I always kept to his system.

When I took over, I realised prices were going up and if we were going to have a fixed charge, we were going to close the door on a good number of people who needed to come. I wanted everybody to be able to come that needed to. We have our own board of trustees. I persuaded the trustees to abolish all charges for staying here, and rely on donations only. The trustees were a bit doubtful, but the young team thought it was marvellous.

I said, 'If God wants to keep us open, we will stay open and if God wants to close us down, why should we want to stay open?' That was our motto. 'We shall live by faith.'

It meant also that all our guests *were* our guests. We never asked for money.

It was sometimes a bit hairy, this.

The miracle of the gas bill

It was March, when the electricity bills came in. They came to £500 and we hadn't got it. I was sitting in the kitchen looking gloomy and the vicar, Denis, walked in. 'What's the matter?'

I said, 'These.'

He picked them up and put them in his pocket and walked out. The next day, at our normal morning Eucharist, our electricity bills were on the altar and Denis prayed that our needs would be met. He gave me the bills back and nothing happened.

One morning I woke up sure that I was going to get the final demand for the bills that day. But I didn't. Then from a totally unexpected quarter, I got a donation of £500. I went straight into Berwick, and paid the electricity bills. That's the only time we've had a miracle, but it's the only time we really needed one.

So that's how the finances were run.

Meanwhile, a different vocation was developing for me

By now I was running weekend courses as well as coaching the resident students. I thought to myself, 'I thought I had given up teaching for life when I came here, but actually this is far more interesting and varied than anything that I would have done if I stayed in Durham.'

And then in 1983, when Denis had been to see me about something else, standing with his hand on the doorknob, he said, 'Have you ever thought of being a deaconess?'

I said 'No' because I never had. I'd thought of being a priest, but deaconesses I knew nothing of.

He said, 'Well, I think you ought to be. And if you don't refuse, I shall go and tell the bishop.'

I didn't refuse because I was utterly astounded. By the time I'd recovered any kind of voice, he'd been down to see the bishop. Then the bishop sent up the head deaconess of the diocese to make sure my arm wasn't being twisted, and lo and behold, later that year, I became a deaconess.

I was not sent to a selection conference. The bishop said, 'She's got a theology degree, so she doesn't need any academic things. She has dealt with students for many, many years so she obviously is OK at pastoral work. Tell her to turn up for the retreat and then for the ordination.' So in December 1983 I became a deaconess in the Newcastle Diocese.

The all-day party

It was an Advent ordination, here on the island. There was a deacon who was to be ordained priest, and a Methodist minister who was to become an Anglican deacon. So there were the three things: a deaconess, a deacon and a priest.

It was 18 December 1983, the darkest Sunday of the year. The bishop had fixed the ordination for nine o'clock in the morning because the tide came up at half past eleven. In the dark that morning, the road was humming with cars coming up from Durham. We were ordained here in my own church. The service was finished by eleven o'clock, and the two other candidates and their guests all immediately went back to the mainland to have their parties.

But I had an all-day party here. The young people were determined to give me a wonderful day. We all came back to Marygate House, including the bishop who stayed for the whole day. We had coffee and then we had sherry and then we had lunch and then we had coffee and then we had tea. None of the guests could get off the island until five o'clock. So we had a wonderful all-day party with 100 guests, and the house was absolutely crammed full.

I had had to put my plans back by a day for my holiday, which I had arranged before I even knew I was going to be ordained deaconess. It was all thrust upon me. So at five o'clock, I went off like the bride without the bridegroom, and I left the youngsters to eat up all the remaining food and close the house for the Christmas holidays. And the next day, I was in Jerusalem on holiday with my friend Lilian from Durham, wondering whether it ever really happened.

I wouldn't mind, provided it was Kate . . .

Once I was a deaconess, I was able to do far more in the church, and preach and help with this and that. Denis and I became great colleagues and great friends, and he very much wanted me to be ordained deacon.

Now, Denis was one who had been trained at Mirfield, brought up in a religious order, and had been much against the ordination of women. But although by then he was getting old, he changed his opinions completely. He moved from saying, 'Oh, no women can't be ordained, it's a ridiculous idea,' to 'Well, I wouldn't mind, provided it was Kate,' to 'I'm in favour of the ordination of women.' He moved all the way – although he was nearly seventy when he retired. I thought that was great.

I remember the second before I walked forward in the cathedral to be made a deacon, thinking to myself, 'I'm a layperson at the moment, in a second I shall be clergy for the rest of my life.'

But in fact, being a deacon made very little change to my life, except I started to wear a dog-collar, and I could take weddings for the first time.

You come along and finish what you began

I was going to be ordained priest in 1994, by which time Denis had retired, and David Adam had come to be our vicar. There were eight of us going to be ordained that night. You know how all the ordained priests stand around with their arms outstretched at an ordination? The bishop said, 'I don't want to be surrounded by a lot of priests. The best thing will be, I want each of you to choose one priest, they will stand in an inner circle and they will actually touch your heads. All the other priests can stand in an outer circle, and just extend their hands.'

I asked David if he would mind if I asked Denis to be the one in the middle circle. He didn't mind, so I said to Denis, 'You come along and finish what you began.' So he did, and I know Denis was absolutely thrilled the night I was ordained priest.

I did feel different afterwards. I felt, 'I don't care how many people argue against the ordination of women; something has happened to me which cannot be now undone. I am different.'

David taught me how to celebrate the Eucharist. He said, 'Now, do it this way, this is the basic Catholic way. If you do it this way, the Catholics won't be able to grumble at you and the Protestants won't be too put out.' So that's the way we both do it.

I celebrated my first Eucharist here on the island, the evening after the ordination. David preached, and Denis, who always did have a lovely voice and still has in old age, sang the Peruvian 'Gloria'. I was quite nervous at the first Eucharist and at the moment when I stood behind the altar, after all the preliminaries, and opened my hands and started on the Prayer of Consecration, my heart almost stopped. It went – whoosh – right in my throat.

Who am I, doing this, that so many saints have done right down through the ages?

The Celtic pilgrimage

All the gifts that I had before have been used here. All of them have been used.

Half my heart is always in Durham. I have many friends there still who I feel speak the same language. But what has developed for me has been different from what it would have been if I'd stayed in Durham, and in many ways it has been a far wider sort of life, an interesting teaching and pastoral ministry I don't think I would have had there.

Since I came to live and study here, the saints have become real, living people to me. A big factor for the Irish Christian monks – people like Aidan – was what they call 'pilgrimage'. Pilgrimage for them meant leaving your own native land, leaving everything that you knew, and going out into the unknown to do whatever God wanted you to do. I was talking to a group of friends about Celtic spirituality and explaining about Irish pilgrimage and afterwards one of them said to me, 'You did that. You came on pilgrimage.'

I hadn't realised it. I hadn't realised that I had, but actually Irish pilgrimage is entirely what I did. I came out and I didn't know why and I didn't know what to do and I didn't know how it was going to turn out.

Two years ago, when I was sixty-seven, I retired as Warden of Marygate House. I was so tired that I thought to myself, 'I will not want to do anything at all except sit in an armchair and read novels.' One morning of sitting in an armchair and reading novels was sufficient to tell me, I did not wish to do that.

I'd received a graduate course prospectus from the University of Edinburgh the previous September but I was so tired, I hadn't even opened it. After Christmas, when I really had retired, I thought I'd look at that prospectus, and I turned the pages, and suddenly there was a course in front of me. I thought, 'That's it, that's what I want to do.' What I wanted was to learn old Irish and medieval Latin and by reading the original texts of the medieval saints, come to a better understanding of how the people lived and thought at the time.

The Edinburgh graduate

When I went to Edinburgh, and was surrounded by these thousands and thousands of youngsters, I felt old. I had never felt old here working with my young team but now I felt old. I am not into computers and everywhere there were computers; even the university library catalogue was on computer. I hate this electronic age.

My real problem, apart from being old, was that I was lonely. I was very lonely up there. The young people I met were nice, but I think they wondered who this granny was. I went to the library and sat down and read my books and got up and went down to the café and had my lonely cup of coffee and my lonely lunch and went home again, never having spoken to a single person.

I loved the actual course. I had wanted to be able to read the original texts, because I reckon that you get nearer to the mind of the person if you can read their original, and now I can. My favourite saint is probably

Aidan, but I got very fond of Columbanus, although I don't think I would have liked him if I had met him in the flesh.

I don't have cosy feelings about the island. I don't think it is necessarily the end of my journey, my final home. I'm a traveller. And when I read Columbanus – now remember, I didn't read him until a year ago – but when I read Columbanus and his set of thirteen sermons that he preached to his monks in the last year of his life, what does he say all the time, *all* the time? Life is a road. You do not settle down on a road. Nobody stops on a road. They travel over the road towards the homeland. The homeland one day will be the life of heaven, but where it is in this life, I don't know.

I didn't know twenty-three years ago and I don't know now.

Revd Jemima Prasadam

2

'God So Loved Lozells . . .'

REVD JEMIMA PRASADAM

Priest-in-Charge, St Paul and St Silas, Lozells

When I first heard that there was a debate over the ordination of women, I think that my first impression was, is it true? Could it be that something religious, something very spiritual could go to the House of Commons? And people who never paid much attention to these things would have the power to decide? I must say, I found it difficult to grasp.

Introduction

AB: Most visitors to Birmingham by car have good reason to say their prayers as they navigate the famous Spaghetti Junction off the M6 Motorway, but once you have negotiated the pasta, an amazing city skyline comes into view. After that the visitor to Jemima Prasadam's parish may need recourse to St Jude once again, as one concrete junction after another is negotiated without any signpost or other visible clue to the whereabouts of her parish, Lozells.

When we set out to have our first look around, Liz was drawing on memories of producing the BBC television programme This is the Day *from Lozells on Christmas morning 1985. Earlier that year there had been the violent 'Handsworth' riots, with the worst damage done to the shops along the Lozells Road. Even at Christmas, mounted police were regularly patrolling the area. When Liz had arrived with the camera crew on Christmas Eve, they found somebody had put a crib inside a burnt-out shop window and a sign that read 'God so loved Lozells . . .'*

Nevertheless Bet Busby, the elderly lady who was hosting the worship programme from her front parlour, was going to share her Christmas celebrations as usual with her friendly next-door neighbours, a Muslim family. They took part in the broadcast on Christmas morning by arriving at Bet Busby's door with the gifts they had made for her.

(Incidentally, the presenter of This is the Day *that Christmas morning was*

Linda Mary Evans who in 1970, when she was only seventeen, had said, along with Una Kroll, that she wanted to be a priest, and had said it publicly. It was thought to be an outrageous thing to do by the church. Linda Mary was ordained priest in the Church in Wales in 1999.)

Liz was wondering not only if she would recognise the Lozells Road again (if we ever chanced upon it) but also how the community was faring nearly twenty years on. We found that what gives Lozells its character today is an unexpectedly vibrant street scene, unusual on an English Sunday. Everyone in the neighbourhood seemed to be out and about, meeting one another and thronging the pavements, and it is clear that many cultures and many races live here. A new mosque is under construction and a sign announces the bank account number into which passers-by may donate money to complete the building. At the end of the road is a new Sikh gurudwara with a beautiful frontage of what looks like polished marble. There are several Pentecostal churches in what once were Church of England buildings, and the name of God is prominent on many shop fascias.

Bang in the middle of the Lozells Road, opposite the Holy Tabernacle Store (closed) and the gents' hairdressers (open and doing a roaring trade on a Sunday afternoon) are the low modern buildings of St Paul and St Silas's Church. Even with nobody there, as on our first unannounced visit, the church makes its mark with a big sign outside: 'Come let us bow down and worship before the Lord our maker.'

We later discovered Revd Jemima Prasadam sometimes uses this as an icebreaker for conversations with the exuberant black youths of the area.

Jemima is Indian and wears a dog-collar with her sari. She is short and very slight and since she doesn't drive, she is best found by walking the streets of her parish and looking for her. Even on a day of thunderstorms she declined a car-lift to return to the vicarage, a fast ten-minute walk from her church. She told me, 'I just keep walking, giving the peace to everyone.'

Lozells today has an ever-changing population and although there may be an atmosphere of carnival on the streets, and in spite of the signs of regeneration since the 1980s, life is clearly still very tough. When Jemima came to the area over five years ago, her own life, too, was very tough. Her marriage had just ended painfully, and she found herself having to make a new life for herself. Jemima's own new start has revitalised a flagging congregation, and in the middle of a community made up of many faiths, Jemima is nurturing a growing gathering unashamed of its clear Christian doctrine, yet offering hospitality to all.

As we so often found when meeting the women who are doing 'jobs for the boys', Jemima has taken on a challenge many good men priests would be defeated by, and sometimes simply by walking around giving the peace, she is making a huge success.

Jemima

The 'Handsworth' riots didn't happen in Handsworth – they happened right here in Lozells Road, where the church is

I live and work in Lozells, a parish of 9,500 people, mainly Muslim. According to the census, one third of the parish is Afro-Caribbean, one third Asian and one third white British, but if you walk along the street of Lozells you will not find many of the latter. It was a puzzling thing for me when I first came to the parish that I saw so few white people, so I set out to walk around and look for myself.

I found that the white British people here are mainly elderly and the majority of them live in their own homes and some in nursing homes where they are literally housebound. There are a few who are active and lively, and you see them on a Saturday morning doing their shopping. They also have other set days – a Tuesday maybe, because of the old Co-op system where you got double stamps on certain days – and they are still used to that.

Some older members of the congregation remember the 'good old days' with great affection. They say that this area used to have all sorts of boutiques that were famous for specialist things, and wealthy people used to come and shop here. They also remember that the parish had very poor people then. Until five years ago, a few people still had outside toilets and no running hot water. So they talk about how the place has changed; and what has happened since the riots fifteen years ago – which are usually called the 'Handsworth' riots, but they did not happen in Handsworth. They happened right across the road from where the church is, here in Lozells Road.

A challenging parish

Until five years ago, there was no regeneration on this side of the parish. The first sight I saw when I arrived was the bulldozers coming and clearing the place. There were hardly any thriving shops, but in the past four and a half years I have seen the whole area come alive.

A lot of people from different and diverse cultures live in Lozells. It is like a melting-pot, with so many people from different parts of the world who have made this their home all living together in quite a small area. There is another interesting factor in Lozells, in that all the subcultures of British society are represented here – single mothers and single-parent families, the unemployed as well as asylum seekers, refugees and people with mental health problems. We are the parish with the highest number of bed-sits in the whole of the city of Birmingham.

The face of the parish changes from week to week, and I am happy I am on foot all the time, 'on patrol'. I am able to tell my colleagues in other parishes and also from the community scene, who are the newcomers to the area, who are the people looking for help, and who are the people that we should be in touch with. It is a very interesting place and gives a lot of opportunities for mission and that is why it is really exciting for me. It is a challenging parish.

How is mission done in a multi-faith and multicultural society?

The PCC is pretty mixed. Very few Asian Christians live in Lozells – most of them are in Handsworth – but we do have one young Asian member. Apart from that most are Afro-Caribbean and white British, and they take on board the issues that face us in the area. Our church building is very congenial for that. We are open to everybody and anybody.

St Paul and St Silas receives many requests from people wanting to visit the parish. Adult education people contact me, and trainee ordinands ask for an interfaith day in the parish, and people from Japan, Denmark, Germany and from Northern and Southern Ireland have been here. There are people who are in touch with us regularly, who come into the area to see how mission is done in a multi-faith and multicultural community.

I think our visitors expect to find Lozells very dismal, with a lot of enmity because so many religions are in the area, and also perhaps it appears our people hardly ever talk to one another. Maybe because this is an inner-city area, they think there is no spirit, that people go about with long faces and there is no joy here. But when they come they are thrilled with our children, sparkling baby eyes all over the place. There are many young people and young children in the area, and that is very much our potential. We may not have detached houses, or even semi-detached houses, but our strength is these young families – young children and young mothers who are slowly recognising that this is the place where they live, and realising that they have to be responsible for its future.

So a lot of people arrive with very set ideas when they look around and meet people, of what it will be like here, but they experience something different and they go away with a joy that was missing before.

Should we call you 'Miss' or should we call you 'Auntie'?

As a church, we are plain and frank with people. We show them that we do not have an ulterior motive of converting anybody or condemning anybody. We do not say that we are better than anybody else, or that we have all the answers. We just say, 'We have something to share with you.' There is a trust and understanding between us, and it took a long time to establish that. We and the people in the community recognise that we are all people of faith; we all believe in prayer and we all believe in God as our Creator. That is the reason we have the lovely text on our notice-board from Psalm 95:5: 'Come let us bow down and worship before the Lord our maker.'

Our common belief in God as our Creator binds people together from all religions. People who stand at the bus stop look at the sign and, because we are on the main road, a lot of teenagers and young people going to the local comprehensive school walk past it and they always tell me, 'Auntie, that is a lovely, lovely verse.'

When I first came here, some teenagers asked me, 'Should we call you "Miss" or should we call you "Auntie"?'

'Well', I said, 'I would be delighted if you would call me "Auntie".'

In India, you always address a person with a title of relationship, and so 'Sister', 'Grandma' or 'Auntie' are familiar titles in our culture. I brought up my children to call everybody 'Auntie' or 'Uncle', and they say that in this country people laugh at them because they had an innumerable number of aunts and uncles. My children were often asked, 'How is it that you come from India and you have all these uncles and aunties?'

But addressing people with a familiar title shows you have an affinity and affection and you care. It is a bonding, and calling one another 'Auntie' or 'Uncle' is a loving way of addressing someone.

Three months turned into five years, and I am still here

A lot of people warned me, when I first came here to Lozells from the St Alban's Diocese that this was not the place for me, because it is very much Afro-Caribbean culture here and one has to be very tough. I am a very slight woman. I do not drive a car and I like to walk everywhere. Even among the PCC, when the appointment was being made, they said, 'Most murders in Birmingham are committed in the Lozells area, and a lot of knifing occurs here too.' So they said that this is not the place for me. They said that they needed a tough man in this parish. They even told me to my face that if I could stick here for three months that would be something, and they were making a mistake in putting me here. But now it's nearly five years, and here I am still.

One evening, one bottle of milk

I was also warned when I came that as this is a dangerous place and that I shouldn't walk the streets by myself after seven o'clock. So I said, 'Right. I won't be foolish. I won't go around looking for trouble.' But I also thought, 'I need to walk and this is where we live and everybody has to share this area. You can't live in fear all the time.' I need to show people this.

One day early on in my ministry an opportunity was given to me, and I had to go out. I was having friends over and I suddenly realised I didn't have any milk. It was a Saturday evening, and the nearest shop was on the other side of Heathfield Road. A lot of young people congregate there, young men who seem so full of aggression. For me, a person comes across a lot of sick and mentally disturbed people during the course of my work, when I faced this big group of young people with so much health and vigour and exuberance about them, the first thought that came to me was just to celebrate. 'Oh, thank God! Isn't this marvellous, all this talent and energy!'

I smiled at them and greeted them. Suddenly their faces changed. I can still remember those faces. They became curious. First of all, an Indian; then a short woman; then a short Indian woman, wearing a dog-collar, coming towards them on the same side of the road. They made way. But one of them looked at my dog-collar and I think the sight of it was too much for him. He asked me, 'Are you a Catholic?' I thought that was an excellent icebreaker for me, so I didn't go past. I stopped, and they all gathered round me and then I said, 'I am a Christian.'

Then suddenly there were all these questions and it was lovely to see curiosity in all these young people and they said, 'This is something new.' And then somebody spoke who seemed to have a lot of grievances against the church. He said he had come into church once, and joined the congregation, but the church hadn't played its part, hadn't done very much for him. I said, 'Maybe in the past that was the impression you had, but now the church is looking for young people like you, and at our church we do all sorts of things that might interest you. But the church often gets a bad press. So please don't let these negative impressions carry on. Let's join hands together and give younger children role models. That's you – there is vigour in you and you have so much that you can offer.'

In that way it is such a wonderful parish. It gives a lot of opportunities and one has to be ready to take them. That was one evening, one bottle of milk. So I kept going to that shop to buy things I didn't need, just to keep up the connection. I was really touched one day when this same gang of youths was smoking and they saw me coming from a distance and they hid their cigarettes. I thought, 'That shows the goodness of their heart.' People really write them off but I thought, 'Lord, thank you for that goodness.'

They didn't have to do that. After all, why did they have to show that respect to me? They call me 'Mama'. Ever since then, whenever they drive past, they beep, 'Mama'. More formal, older people stick to 'Reverend' but I like the young ones who call me 'Auntie' and 'Mama'.

And the children have the benefit

This is such a diverse parish, and people need to get to know one another. People are afraid of each other sometimes, when they don't know about each other's religion or culture and so they have to find a way to make some kind of relationship and a connection, and we offer it here in our church.

We have three Islamic centres in Lozells and two house mosques and there is a big new mosque going up now. We are between two Sikh temples; one is on the estate, and the vicarage itself is next to the Hindu temple and I live opposite the Hindu priest. I can recite Sanskrit, so the Hindu priest and I meet to read the Hindi Scriptures together, and we talk about them, and discuss what we think the text means.

There used to be two huge Anglican churches here, but first of all St Paul's was sold to a black Pentecostal congregation, and later on the second, St Cyrus in St Cyrus Square, was sold to another Pentecostal church. They are both well attended now. Then the PCC felt that our church, the Church of England, should be in the centre of the parish where it could serve the area with a modern building, which is why we have several rooms that are used throughout the week.

In the main church itself the worship area is partitioned off and the rest is used for the Rainbow Playgroup. When we celebrate some of the community festivals, it is usually with wonderful colour – all the colours of the rainbow. Hence the name. We also have a room where young mothers' can meet, since they often feel very isolated. And very proudly the church can say that mothers who have brought their children here, who came as shy young women, now have done courses for which they have gained certificates. We have given them the confidence and the courage to grow has really opened up a new world for them, and their children have the benefit. The playgroup is not just for our own church children – we have Muslim, Sikh and Hindu children. It is such a lovely thing.

Word and sacrament go together

When I came to St Paul's and St Silas's it had a very strong evangelical tradition with a lot of extempore prayer and chorus singing, but without a focus on the Eucharist. The lectionary was something new to the congregation. My first job was to introduce them to the Collect of the Day.

I feel that liturgy is important; it gives Anglican worship its very special character. In worship, every act has meaning. What I try to show them is that in the Eucharist, word and sacrament go together. This is very important, and there is a beautiful harmony when you hold both these elements together. So one Eucharist a month gradually became Sunday Eucharist. We now have the Eucharist in the morning and then in the evening we have Evening Prayer.

When I came, there were no candles, no flowers, nothing at all. And the altar was called the 'table'.

No need to be afraid of a candle

To me symbolism is very important. I introduced the giving of the baptismal candle. As a result, some people told me that they would leave the church, they would walk out. I said, 'Hold on! Just because I am giving a candle to a child who has been baptised, do you think that I am converting this into a Roman Catholic church?'

I handed out baptism service sheets to the PCC, and I said, 'I would like you all to read this and see whether this is what has been approved by the General Synod and whether our bishop is in line with it. If he is not and the General Synod hasn't approved it, then I am doing something totally wrong and I should not be doing it and I want you to correct me and tell me. But if I am the spiritual leader of this church and if this is in accordance with canon law, then I need to teach and say why I am doing it. I am not introducing anything just for the sake of introducing or just because *I* like it, but because of the significance and the meaning behind the act. I want you to understand this. So you don't have to be afraid of a candle.'

There was absolute silence.

Beginning to look at the Anglican Church, how beautiful it is

The early days were very hard because their image of a vicar is very different from who I am and – I am sorry to say – it is a white, British man. Now I don't fit that mould at all. As a woman and a black one, at that, was sometimes hard for some of them to accept me. I am aware of that, and accept that things don't change overnight, so I was patient and I gave them time to get to know me.

Gradually some of the older ones in the congregation began to see and understand the meaning of what I was doing. I wasn't introducing change for the sake of change – that wasn't my intention – and there was no pomp or ceremony about the changes. People realised that what needed to be done had to be done must be done in joyous and respectful worship, to glorify God. And the younger ones began to want to learn also.

So we began to look at the Anglican Church, how beautiful it is, how many strands it has and how they are all valid. So there was no need to criticise anything, but to look instead at our own situation and train our children to see how we can worship God.

My grandfather became a Christian 120 years ago

I was born in South India, in a state called Andhra Pradesh. I grew up in a very big family home, with a lot of rooms. We had paddy-fields and so a lot of workers lived there too. I don't want to use the word 'servants'; we always called them helpers. Interdependence is the note that I remember from my childhood. The beauty of Indian homes, as I remember them, is there is room for the able and the less able, the young and the old. That is why there is assurance for everybody. The Indian home shelters everybody, so there are people who aren't so brilliant, and there are brilliant people too, hard-working people who can cook and do a lot of the work, and others who are less able to do that. But it is still home to each of them.

We always had an open door. It was very hot and our home had a big veranda. We had coconut trees and sweet lime trees. It is a lovely memory.

My mother's father, my grandfather, became a Christian 120 years ago. The way he described it was that he came from light to greater light in Christ. He was the only one in his family who became a Christian.

Because my grandfather became a Christian, all his children and grandchildren were naturally Christians and my mother then had to get married to a Christian. My father was from a different state. My parents' marriage was arranged through contacts and through missionaries. My father came from a Shivite background, so his family's spirituality was based on Shiva, the destroyer, whereas on my mother's side, we come from Vishnu, the protector.

You woke up, and somebody was singing hymns in the house

My father was a health inspector and my mother was the headmistress of the local girls' grammar school. My aunt was the headmistress of a primary school, and one of my uncles was a fisheries inspector. Another uncle had a dressmaking business. His company also made ceramics. I had cousins who were doctors and nurses, so all in all we were a well-known and influential family.

I am an only child, but I have a host of cousins. I grew up in a very strong Baptist background. My father was an Anglican, but I grew up with my mother's family in the heartlands of the Telegu Baptists. Telegu is my mother tongue.

So my education was solidly Bible-centred, and while I was growing up there were a lot of revival meetings that we all went to, and I had a firm grounding in the Scriptures and a great sense of holiness. Family prayers were important. You heard hymns being sung all the time. Because in India people get up very early, my mother and aunties and uncles would be singing early in the morning as they said their prayers. You always hear somebody singing hymns in the house. It was a lovely way to wake up.

They expect vicars to perform magic with their children

I find it very difficult when I came to the West that the vicar and the church are blamed for everything. If parents don't take any responsibility for their children's spiritual growth and God hardly ever springs up in a conversation and then they expect vicars to perform magic with children, just for the forty-five minutes they are in a church, I don't think that's very nice.

When I was young, you watched other people saying their prayers so you prayed; you knelt by your bed and that was the normal way of doing things. There is something that is special about it, personal and also sacred. The church nurtures what starts at home; that is how it is. As children we used to learn whole chunks of Scripture. That is why I still feel that there is a sweetness when you recite Scripture.

But God had other plans

My mother was very much a supporter of Gandhi. She was an educationist and all her thinking was guided by Ghandian principles. To this day I am still guided by Gandhi, who was a very strong influence in our family. We were politically a very active family, especially my cousins, and I was part of the Indian Congress Party and an active member of the Youth Congress in the early days of Independence.

I graduated in 1973 with a BA in economics and politics and then I went and worked for the government, because we had all sorts of projects when independent India was just evolving. The government was launching its five-year plans, and they were taking on younger people, graduates. I went to work on one project as chief project officer and my cousins were expecting me to join them and make politics my career, but a lot of changes were going through me. I couldn't put my finger on it and say what actually those changes were. I did my job, but I knew that there was something else.

My whole family were very prayerful people and I knew my mother always prayed that God should use me, but I didn't know how and in what way. Then I had a letter from the Congress office saying that they were doing an exchange and sending some young people to America, and I was one of those selected. My cousins were very happy, but at the same time I had a telegram from my parents saying that my mother was very ill, and that I had to go home.

I went home, but my mother wasn't there. She was at school. She wasn't ill at all. So then I tried to make sense of what had happened. Surely any parent should be very happy that out of so many, their child has been chosen? But my parents were not happy, so what is it, why? When my mother came home, I asked her and I asked my father too, 'Why did you do this? What was the reason, why?'

They said they were not very happy about all the glamour surrounding my selection. They realised that I had many prospects, from other people's point of view, but I should perhaps ask God what he wants me to do.

I went away, thinking, 'How strange', and I knew that trouble was sizzling within the family because my cousins were very disappointed. They were very much involved with the Congress Party, and it was their dream that I would continue in politics. But God had other plans.

All their hopes were thwarted

I said I would go to America. But all the time I had this feeling, 'Is God saying that I haven't listened to him?' and I was aware that there was something wrong, but I didn't know what it was. I went away from my parents because it was not like God speaking to me in a dramatic way or anything like that. But then, as I read the Scripture and as I prayed about it, 'Lord, is there something that you are saying to me that I am not following?' a Scripture passage, Jeremiah 1, helped me. Jeremiah is called to be a prophet, even though he feels far too young and inexperienced.

I gave my resignation to the Youth Congress. I knew that it was not for me, and that I wanted to study theology. That decision really broke my ties with my cousins. They wouldn't talk to me. All their hopes were thwarted. They asked me what I, as a young woman, thought I could do, because in those days it wasn't open for women to hold any senior position in the church. 'Going to a theological college – so what will she do, come out as what?'

It was a difficult period, but I did three years of theology at the Baptist seminary in South India and got my degree.

An arranged marriage

Then I became chaplain at the American Baptist Mission Hospital in Nellore, which is my hometown, and then, of course, a marriage was arranged for me. That is the normal thing in India, but it is not like the West imagines it to be. In my family you had the freedom to say 'No'.

My husband was a priest in the Church of South India. After we married, we served in various places, before ending up at Serampore Theological College where I too used to teach. While we were there, we were asked if we would come to Wales for a year to serve in Bangor.

Honorary minister for the chapels in the valleys

When I wanted to work as an unpaid curate in the Church in Wales as I'd done in India, the bishop asked me to go to Lampeter University and train for lay ministry. I said, 'Bishop, you are asking me to do this because I am a woman. If I were a man, you would just accept me.'

He said, 'It is difficult at the moment, so think about it.'

I found it difficult to accept it, and my genuine answer was that my twin daughters were teenagers then, and I felt that they needed a lot of support instead of my going away to do a course. I felt that home was my rightful place, and that I could do all kinds of other things, so that is what I did.

When I was in India, I was looked on as a minister, and I used to take services in the Baptist chapel, so when we came to Wales, where they have a lot of Baptist churches, they asked me if I would be their honorary minister. And because I wasn't allowed to do anything in the Church in Wales, I agreed to help them at Sunday services. I worked for three years as an honorary minister in the Welsh Baptist chapels in the Cynon Valley.

I have three daughters, who are all grown up now. The older two are twins. All their names come from Sanskrit. Smitha, whose name means 'smile' is now the head of the department of English in Brasshouse Language Centre. Swapna means 'dream'. She is the younger twin, and I never dreamt of her – she just became reality. She is now a mother herself. Swapna taught in Hong Kong University. And the youngest is Smrita, meaning 'remembrance', and she is now the writer and sub-editor for BBC *Toybox*, a children's magazine. They are all lovely children.

People who have never paid much attention to these things will decide

After our year in Bangor, we went to the Chester Diocese for a few years, then back to Wales, and then in 1983 we moved to Newcastle-on-Tyne. And it was during this time that I first started to think about ordination.

When we were there, I heard that there was a debate in General Synod over the ordination of women as deacons, and my first impression was, is it true? Could it be possible that something so religious, something spiritual could go to the House of Commons, and that people who have never paid much attention to these kinds of matters had the power to decide? I must say that I found it difficult to grasp and take it in.

While we were in Newcastle, I was no longer attached to a church. My husband was with the Church Missionary Society and so we didn't have a parish to run. There was a lot of time on my hands, so I gave my time to the Mother's Union and I served on the CMS Board for Mission and Unity and the Board for Social Responsibility. Then in 1986 Bishop Gill said to me, 'All this work that you are doing at the moment under your own steam, let the church own it. And the way to do that is to go for ordination as a deacon. Have you ever thought about it?'

This was Bishop Ken Gill, the assistant bishop in the Newcastle Diocese, who had served in the Church of South India.

You need a bit of humility

I said, 'Bishop, ordination is not for me because I am already a selector for ministerial training with CMS and USPG. I know about selection conferences and what they can be like!'

He said to me, 'I know now why you say you can't go to this, because you have been a selector and you don't want to be on the other side of the fence. You need a bit of humility.'

It was a bombshell. I couldn't say a word to him and I gazed at the car as he drove off and I thought, 'Go away, run away, leave the drive.' I came back, sat in the chair and I said, 'Dear, oh dear, what did the bishop say to me?'

I was really frightened to go through all this inner process but eventually I rang him and I said to him, 'Bishop, I will face this, I will go. I will do this. Whatever the end result is, I'll go. I'll obey you.'

'Lord, it is your finger which is on the button'

I found it extremely difficult, because the people on the interviewing panel for the diocese were all people I knew very well from the selection boards, and I found it difficult to explain my call to them. It all seemed so artificial. So I just gave very short answers to anything that they asked. I am sure they found it difficult too, but they recommended me to the next stage.

The bishop came to see me again and he said, 'Look, everybody knows you. That is why there was no problem about the first step, but you can't be like that when you go to ACCM. There nobody knows you, and you must be truthful and fair to yourself. You will have to speak up and talk. You don't have to be aggressive but you should remember to sell yourself. Let people know you.' Those were his words.

For a long time I thought about those words. I went to the selection conference, did my best, came away again and then I stopped thinking about it. All that I was thinking was, 'Lord, it is your finger which is on the button and I leave it to you. Whatever you decide, I'll accept, because I have seen your hand in my life at various stages and this is another stage. If this is what you want me to go along with, I will go, and I am sorry if I hadn't seen it before.'

One fine day

One fine day in 1986 there was a letter to say that ACCM had recommended me for training.

I trained for a year at Cranmer Hall, Durham, and was ordained in 1987 as deacon in St Philip's, before moving to Luton to work first as a deacon and then in 1994, after ordination, to priesthood, as a curate in the St Alban's Diocese.

You don't play with holy things, you don't play with God

Bishop John Taylor ordained me at St Alban's Abbey. I very distinctly remember the three days beforehand when we went away on retreat, and while we were pondering and looking at what ordination means, it was an exciting time. I was aware of it, and it was part of me. But I also suddenly realised that with a new life that was beginning, a new world was opening and I was accepting a new responsibility; being a priest is not like playing a game.

To me God is fire as much as he is a loving God, and there are certain inner parameters, and you don't play with holy things. You don't play with God. I think there is a mystery in ordination to the priesthood, in the laying on of hands and also all the prayers of so many thousands and the support and the strength they give. And so I dreaded my ordination.

When everyone arrived for the service, friends and family, and there was so much going on, so much excitement, it was a wonderful thing. Then suddenly I began to shiver and tremble, while we all stood in a semicircle for the oaths. Bishop John Taylor said that there was a lot of antagonism against women priests, and that feminist thinking was being pushed on to us. People were saying that we wanted to have the same power as the men, when in reality we are called to be servants. We are going to be stewards at the Lord's table.

I had very mixed feelings. I really trembled and I prayed, 'At the moment, I feel really afraid of taking this on. Give me the strength.' And that was a most marvellous thing – I found the inner strength to say I could be a channel of grace.

Called to celebrate the life of God with the people of God

I don't think any priest has a magic wand to convert people or anything like that. I very much believe that it is God who converts, it is the Spirit that converts and we are called to our discipleship and to be faithful. As I say every Eucharist, I have a marvellous feeling, but at the same time I am aware that I am dealing with the Holy of Holies. We are called to celebrate the life of God with the people of God.

Some people do have a fixed idea of what the vicar will be like. At my first parish, the church was an old, very large building and it had a big notice-board in front of it. When I first arrived I used to walk past the notice-board to get into the church, and people who might be looking at the notice-board, would say to me, 'Oh, are you looking for somebody? Can I help you?' Or if they saw I had the keys to the church in my hand, they would ask me, 'Are you the new caretaker?'

I would say, 'Yes, I am the caretaker. In one sense I am the caretaker – but I am more than that.'

'What do you mean, you are more than that?'

'I take care of people', I said, 'not just of buildings.'

'Oh, you are a home help?' they would ask.

'Indeed, yes, I am a home help. I fetch prescriptions for some of the elderly ladies when I visit them, and I make a cup of tea for them and sometimes I even give them a massage with my own oils, to give them some relief from pain. But there is another thing I do.'

'So what else do you do?'

I said, 'Inside this building where I am a caretaker, I pray for people – and in their homes where I am a home help, I pray with them.'

My life now . . . sometimes the frowns and hostile looks are hard to take

My space, the time when I can be apart, is at home. I also find it very helpful and uplifting when I have fellowship with the Hindu priest who is my neighbour. It is a sense that we are in it together. In the Sikh chapel, the priest there and I sit together on the floor and share our spiritual journey; that is also very uplifting and very good.

In the beginning it was very difficult here for me, for a number of reasons. In a culture where a number of people are from the Indian subcontinent, many look at me with a lot of uncertainty. To the Muslims, I am not so acceptable, first of all because I am a woman, and second for political reasons, because the majority of Muslims in this country are from Pakistani Kashmir. It is the Kashmir dispute that causes the difficulty.

Being Indian, in their eyes, I am more or less from the enemy's camp, so I have to be treated with a bit of caution, as they do not know where I stand. And because I serve in a white British church, they think that maybe I will drag in some of the women or their young people into the other way of life, which would be too dangerous. So they are very careful with me until they get to know what sort of a person I am. Sometimes the frowns and the hostile looks I get are hard to take, but once they have tested me and got to know me, they take me as their priest.

Now they are not afraid if I take the Bible into their homes. Before, you couldn't take any other Scripture into a Muslim home – the Koran only – but now I take the Bible. The children sit with me and when they are fasting, I fast. I always fast during Lent, but I also fast in Ramadan, because in many Muslim homes here, I am part of their household. So if they are fasting then 'Auntie' fasts too.

I show them what views Christians hold about fasting, and explain that we are not bound by their rules about fasting from sunrise to sunset. I tell them that the main purpose of the fast is discipline and also meditation and prayer. I read the Koran in translation, as I can't read in Arabic, and we talk about much common ground. I have made profound friendships with two of the imams from the mosque.

You are part of our celebrations, so we will be part of yours

As a parish we are looking very carefully at what do we want to do next. What has come very strongly to us is to spread a sense of community, because we have so many refugees at the moment. In the past six months we have been flooded with different kinds of refugees. It is a blessing for us because people trust us and we express our trust and our respect in people.

For the millennium we committed ourselves to doing three things. One was a prayer walk with everybody walking round the parish, praying the Jesus prayer to include Lozells and Birmingham City. But we did not want people to feel threatened, because this is a place where anything can spark off suspicion. So what we did is to have only three people at a time walking together, saying this prayer.

Then the second one was a praise walk, during which we sang many lovely songs, such as 'For I'm building a people of power'.

The third was a candle walk. We distributed 500 of these candles by walking from house to house.

When I first came, people said, 'How do you think we can do anything?' This was because there were only five people including me who were fully employed in the congregation. Some were unemployed; many were pensioners. But the marvellous things that God has enabled us to do are wonderful for us.

For the millennium we were the only parish to invite our Muslim and Sikh neighbours to join us in our celebrations. They all came and they said, 'You are part of our celebrations, so we will be part of yours.'

CANON JANE MILLARD

3

'The Pooper-Scooper Lady'

Canon Jane Millard

Vice-Provost, St Mary's Episcopal Cathedral, Edinburgh

I didn't do anything. I just fell out of a tree and found I was a priest.

Introduction

AB: Look west down Princes Street in Edinburgh, one of the world's most beautiful city streets, and you will see three huge spires. St Mary's Episcopal Cathedral, where Revd Jane Millard works, owes at least part of its architectural prominence to the generosity of two Edinburgh sisters. At the end of Queen Victoria's reign they worshipped in the newly built but incomplete Gilbert Scott-designed building, and the twin spires at the West End of the Cathedral, for which they largely paid, are still known as Barbara and Mary.

Their dark outlines, acting like a long stop at dusk, proudly proclaim Scotland's largest church building, where Jane is Vice-Provost and sometime Chaplain to Richard Holloway, a well-known maverick figure while he was Bishop of Edinburgh and Primus of the Scottish Episcopal Church, part of the worldwide Anglican communion and one of Scotland's smaller Christian denominations.

Worship in St Mary's includes all the traditional liturgies and the cathedral boasts one of Britain's top choirs in the Anglican tradition, supported by its own choir school. The clergy team in the cathedral is led by Graham Forbes, titled the Provost because a dean in Scotland has a similar role to the archdeacon in England.

It is a feature of Edinburgh life that some of the poorest and some of the richest people often live separated by a single street. Despite its imposing exterior, and being situated in one of the more fashionable parts of the city, St Mary's is far more like a family parish church than a grand cathedral. It is home to a wide cross-section of the community, and people from all over Midlothian belong to the cathedral family.

When we asked Jane Millard if she would agree to be in this book, she said, 'I wasn't part of the fight for women's ordination. I didn't do anything. I just fell out of a tree and found I was a priest.'

It was Bishop Richard Holloway who eventually told Jane that she was a 'born priest'. She had lived the life. Dr Una Kroll told us about the medieval nuns, in the twelfth, thirteenth and fourteenth centuries, who had a perception of priesthood in their eucharistic life of prayer and in their apprehension of how the church worked. 'These women didn't overtly speak about priesthood, they just acted in a way that you would expect priests to act.'

Before her ordination, Jane Millard had spent nearly thirty years in Edinburgh, campaigning for and working alongside people struggling to cope with drug addiction, abuse, sickness, crime and poverty, before she 'fell out of the tree' in 1994. Many of her friends are the people that campaigning journalists call 'Edinburgh's underclass'.

Having heard her preach a moving sermon in the cathedral about Milestone House, the AIDS Hospice in Edinburgh, where she was chaplain, I once asked Jane to appear on a BBC Scotland television programme. She told me that she had to refuse, because if her face was seen on television, she would no longer be able to help people with HIV, who all too often need to hide their suffering from prejudiced neighbours. Anyone who she was seen calling on afterwards might be suspected of being HIV-positive. In many years of persuading reluctant people to broadcast, this was the response that most completely stopped me in my tracks.

Most visitors to the cathedral for the daily Choral Evensong are unlikely to uncover Jane's other secret: she is dyslexic, and reading aloud in such formal and public circumstances can turn quite suddenly into a nightmare.

'Very occasionally, I come completely unstuck. I mean, seriously, completely unstuck, but it's only very occasionally. Usually the mouth keeps going and something comes out, even if it's in the wrong order. Very astute people, like the deans and provosts in May last year, do notice something. Two of them approached me after I'd done the reading at Evensong and said that they weren't familiar with the translation. What was I using? I said, 'TJV'. One of them nodded and said, 'Of course' and walked away. The other one nodded but said, 'That's not one I know.' TJV stands for Translation Jane's Version, but it sounds like NIV and RSV and if you say it seriously enough, most people believe you.'

Canon Jane Millard, Vice-Provost of St Mary's Episcopal Cathedral, always strikes me as a reassuring and still centre of calm in the middle of all the chaotic busy-ness of the cathedral. But Jane insists that we call her what she calls herself: 'the pooper-scooper lady'.

Jane

Cool floors, beautiful carpets, and wet earth

I was born in Iran in the days when it was still called Persia. My childhood memories are of gracious living and nannies, and rules about dressing for dinner and being brought downstairs to see the parents. The houseboys and servants were friendly, and my parents were very loving, in spite of the rather formal distance they kept. They were older parents, born just after the turn of the century, so they literally were Edwardians. I had a very fortunate young life in that all the adults were enormously friendly. I was allowed to escape and play in the yard with the houseboy's children, so my childhood was conventional and strict at one end, and completely free at the other.

Other memories are of cool floors and beautiful carpets, the fan going round in the ceiling, and the smell of wet earth. The most evocative memory I have is the smell of wet earth. The kitchen was in a corner of the compound, and they used to tip out the water onto the hard-baked earth outside and now I only have to smell wet earth, and I'm back there, squatting on the ground and playing games in the yard.

Horse daft

My father was a self-made man. Very bright. He had educated himself. He was a very private man, very Edwardian. I was horse daft as a child. Horse daft. I had little buckets all round the house, with pretend feed and things. Yet only after my father's death did I discover that the brush on the hallstand – that had MP on the side of it and that we always used as a clothes-brush – had been his father's horse brush. His father was a mounted policeman, and that was his horse brush. My father never told me.

He was the middle child, his father had died when he was six and he was dumped in and out of an orphanage whenever his mother couldn't be bothered with him. I think he didn't know what a family was really, but he got it dead right for us, and we were always treated with respect. We were always loved. Not in a cuddly way, but in a way of interest and concern.

'Be ye kind to one another'

As far as I remember, we had no religion, no prayers or churchgoing in the family at all. My father was quite strongly *not* a Christian. He had been hauled in and out of the orphanage when he was younger, where religion was overdone. And although I think my mother very much wanted to become a Roman Catholic at one time, she didn't like to, because she knew my father wasn't keen on religion.

As far as I remember I only had three brushes with Christianity as a child, and that was at Sunday school, when we were staying with my grandmother when we came home from Iran. I was baptised but I don't know when; I think when I was quite small at the church where my grandmother lived in Kent. I remember these three Sunday-school visits, and coming home and being asked what I'd learned there. I am not usually good at remembering things, but I quoted, 'Be ye kind one to another.' And that became a standing family joke. Whenever I lose the plot, they say, 'Oh, be ye kind one to another!'

A council of war

I just have one brother, Peter, two years older than me, but in the family we always had open house and friends came in and out, so there was always any number of known and unknown young people around. Then, in the Hungarian uprising, my parents were considering very strongly whether they should take in some refugee children. I remember us being sat round the table, Peter and I, and my father – who wasn't normally a great one for councils of war – saying that he felt moved to invite these children into his home, but he needed to know how we felt about it. They would become part of the family. They wouldn't necessarily be returning to Hungary.

Well, they didn't come. I don't remember what happened in the council of war, or what we said, but later on – after I'd left home – I have often wondered what had happened. Was there something about how my brother and I had responded that had made them think it might not be a good idea?

Both of us have had open house all our lives ever since, and it's strange to think that we must have seemed unwelcoming then. It was coming up for Christmas and I don't know, but I suspect it might have been something to do with our thinking we'd have to share our presents, and that's probably a bridge too far for a child. I'm really quite ashamed, looking back, that we might have deterred them.

Instead my parents endowed something or other for the children to go to, or funded somebody else to take them. They had to give money rather than give a home.

Sailing home

We sailed home from Persia during the war. We came home on the Anglo Iranian Oil tankers, and I remember doing torpedo drill. I remember the sound of the sirens. I knew exactly which boat station to go to. We used to practise this daily. I wasn't frightened, because nobody else was frightened.

Whenever we came back to England, we stayed with my grandmother, my mother's mother, in Kent, but she was frequently bombed out, so it wasn't necessarily always the same house. Granny lost two or three houses in the war. A big family Bible we used to have, and lots of stuff from that generation, were all lost. And my mother's ship went down once when she was coming over, but fortunately I wasn't on that one. It wasn't torpedoed, but it hit some rocks, so we lost a lot more of our stuff. So we don't have many family heirlooms.

After the war we came home to live permanently, and stayed with my grandmother until we could find a house. My grandmother was absolutely wonderful. Eventually we found a house in Surrey. I remember my father commuting up to London every day.

He was always gone early in the morning, so we were almost back to the original Persian pattern of life, where I wouldn't see him till he came home in the evening, and then it was wash and change for dinner. We weren't quite so formal in England as we had been in Persia, but the timing was the same; Daddy coming home, so it was always fearfully exciting at teatime.

Number one flap

My mother, poor soul, having come from a family that was quite large and very poor, was never taught things like cooking, because they couldn't afford to waste the food. And in Persia she'd had servants. So she arrived back in the UK with a husband almost at the top of the tree in a large firm, but she had no idea how to give dinner parties or cook or clean.

She had different degrees of flap. My father would telephone and say, 'I think there are six people coming home with me tonight' and my mother would go into a number one flap, for which we all knew the routine. My brother and I would tidy the house and she would telephone the local shop and we would run down and pick up the things. The local shop lady was lovely and would come up and cook the dinner, because she knew my mother couldn't.

Our house was always a little bit of a jumble. We didn't have any real routine. I'm sorry, looking back now, that I didn't help my mother more, but I wasn't brought up to be domestic either. The only thing I did do was cut the grass and clean the shoes. Those were my two chores, and I still love doing both. My idea of cooking is to tip and pour and shake and see – and rename it if it looks different from last time.

A hole in the heart and a hole in the head

My brother Peter was – and is – extremely clever, one of these hyper-bright people, very, very clever. My father was the same. But I turned out to have what I now know to be a form of dyslexia. People didn't know about it then. I must just have seemed extremely thick, but my parents never made me think I was stupid or slow. I was a bit wild and was often reprimanded for my behaviour, but never, ever made to feel stupid. They were the same with my health. I was never made to feel that I was sickly, although in fact I was a very sickly child.

There'd been a blockade when my mother was expecting me, with hardly any food coming through, so she was badly undernourished, and I was never a healthy baby. I was born with a hole in the heart and a leaky valve. In those days there weren't operations for that, and I wasn't expected to survive.

My father was told that – even if I survived – I would probably be bedridden by the time I was four, and most likely wouldn't live into double figures. But the heart valve must have somehow mended itself. I never even knew there was anything wrong with my heart until years later, when I had a medical at teacher training college, and they picked up a very odd heartbeat. They were amazed, and so was I. My family had simply never mentioned it. My father was so pleased when I became a physical education (PE) teacher.

When I was five, I had glandular fever and was in bed for almost a year, very unwell. I missed almost the whole of my first year at junior school. I then had another episode of illness in my first year in secondary school, so I missed most of that as well.

Nobody seems to have had any idea that I was dyslexic until the eleven-plus, which I failed spectacularly. I scored sixty-four, which was 'educationally subnormal'. The headmaster telephoned my father and said, 'The results are through, but we don't understand your daughter's score.'

They thought this was an interesting phenomenon, because socially I didn't seem as if I was backward. And I wasn't, I just couldn't read. Well, I could read well enough to understand myself, but the words would get jumbled up. They still do. It wasn't a problem for me. I could read the books that interested me, about ponies and things. I was, and still am, fiercely enthusiastic about learning to do things. It never occurred to me that it was important to be good at something. I had no kind of marker of merit in my head. I would try anything. I would launch myself with great enthusiasm into all sorts of things. I didn't know I couldn't read.

Still life

I somehow managed to get into grammar school in spite of failing the eleven-plus. I enjoyed my school days enormously. I had a mixed career. I loved history and English. I absolutely adored poetry. I liked PE. And I came to like art. We had to choose between art, needlework and music, and at first I thought music would be good, so I chose music. I only lasted a couple of weeks before I was thrown out of class for being naughty. I had done – I thought – a very interesting thing.

We used to have inkwells. Some had hinged lids and some had slidey ones. And we had cardboard keyboards, which didn't make any sound and we had to clap rhythms. I thought this clapping rhythms was the most exciting thing, because I was good at that. I didn't know what we were doing most of the rest of the time, because it was all a bit of a mystery and I'm not musical, but I really liked clapping. One day I tied cotton to the lids of all the inkwells, ran the strings under the seat of the desk in front of me to my desk, and when it came to the clapping, off went all these little inkwell lids clapping as well. Which I thought was pretty good. It completely floored the class.

The girl sitting at the desk immediately in front of me was sent out of the room, but it was about a third of the way into the lesson before it dawned on me that she'd been sent out because of the inkwells. I owned up then, but that was considered to be extremely wrong because I should have owned up immediately.

So I was sent off to do needlework, which they'd already begun a couple of weeks earlier, so I'd missed all the beginning. The first thing I did in needlework was to sew, and I did it rather beautifully. I sewed the pigtails of the girl in front of me round the bar of the chair, and when she got up the chair clattered over, she fell off, everyone fell over and she hurt herself. And I was sorry.

So then I was sent to art, that being the only remaining class I could go to. I was asked by this diminutive art teacher, 'What would you like to do?'

I said, 'Well, what may I do?' Everyone else seemed to be drawing pots and apples and things that she had arranged at the front.

She said, 'Do the still life, or something of your own choice, if you've brought something with you.'

I didn't understand 'still life'. I just caught the words 'something of your own choice', so I drew a horse. When she came round to look she was absolutely furious because although I didn't have to paint her apples, I was supposed to have brought along some 'still life' of my own as the something of my own choice. So I was sent to the headmistress's study – one of many trips. But I was allowed to remain in the art class and was only ever expected to draw horses after that, which I thoroughly enjoyed.

Life's always been such a big mystery, because I'm always parachuting in after it's begun.

Being caught by the mystery of music

I used to get the bus to school. And when I was about fifteen or sixteen I lusted after this chap on the bus, who turned out to be the lead bass in a church choir halfway between my home and school. I can't sing a note, but I joined the church choir so that I would be near him. There were professional singers in the choir, and they could carry a duff. I knew nothing. I couldn't read music – but I loved it. The psalms were the biggest revelation to me. There's something about the washing over of the psalm, breathing in and out, and I thought they were fabulous. After a few weeks I'd gone off the lead bass, but had been caught by the mystery of the music.

We can't keep doing this

When the other choristers went up for Communion, they had to step over me in the row and they said, 'Look, you'll have to get confirmed. We can't keep doing this.'

So I was confirmed as a Christian in the then brand-new Guildford Cathedral, by Bishop George Reindorp, along with a great number of other people. I began then to receive Communion at church – but there was no personal commitment from me; it was just so they didn't have to keep stepping over me.

We had a young curate, who one day preached about martyrdom. Some cleric or prominent Christian had recently been killed. And I'm sitting there in the choir, with the sun coming through the stained glass windows, and I suddenly longed to love God enough to lay down my own life. This huge, immense longing suddenly came over me. I could hear the preacher saying, 'But most of us aren't called to be martyrs in our ordinary, boring lives.' He was preaching from a text in Philippians, 'For me to live is Christ, and to die is gain.' And this curate said we'd all got to be faithful Christians, even in our ordinary, everyday, boring lives.

Commissioned to the commonplace

I don't know how you know these things because there is no voice, but the words I heard were, 'You, that is your gift, you are called to the commonplace.' And I'm sitting there in this beautiful aura of sun through stained glass windows, longing to love God enough to lay down my life, and I received the commission to be faithful in the commonplace.

It was a very powerful sermon, and it touched base. I know about the commonplace. I know about building houses out of pine needles in the forest and I know about sitting with people till you learn how they are. And I know now that that calling really was in fact my calling, because everything I have done since has had its roots in very ordinary things. The whole of my ordained ministry is actually very, very low-key, very ordinary, very sweep up the bits.

On from school

After school I wanted to join the WRENS, but my father was not at all keen because he said nice ladies didn't join the WRENS. He thought I should go teaching. So we told the headmistress, and she hauled me in and said, 'Well, the only thing you're fit to teach is PE and I've found you a place at Gypsy Hill College, in South London.' I was quite happy with that. I endured the teacher training, and in my second year I met Geoff.

It happened on 9 February. I can never remember anything, but I do remember that. I had gone with a friend, who played hockey in the English team, to watch an international hockey match in London. When we got back to Waterloo Station I'd missed my train, but a lot of friends from college had just got there, and said that they were all going off to a jazz dance being given by Battersea Tech at Battersea Power Station. I didn't do that sort of thing, but I'd already missed my train, so I went along with them. They were all dressed up in their glamorous party-going gear and I was wearing my hockey-match-watching gear.

At this dance I was pounced on by a chap – I think he was an African. I didn't have the social skills, and was very aware of this, of how to negotiate my way out of dance after dance with this guy, without appearing racist. I didn't have many coloured friends, and I couldn't think how to do it without sounding offensive. I didn't want to hurt him, but I was just about frantic, because I really don't like dancing much, and there I was, dancing dance after dance because I didn't know how to stop. Then out of nowhere, a young man came across the room and said to this chap, 'I'm sorry to break this up, but we've got to go now or we'll miss our train.' And he led me off by the elbow, muttering out the side of his mouth, 'I know you don't know who I am, I just thought you needed a breather.' It was Geoff.

He'd been the driver for his gang of friends, so he wasn't drinking, and he wasn't a dancer either, so he was just sitting watching. He had seen all this going on with me wriggling around trying to get away, and had decided to come to the rescue.

The farmer's wife . . .

If as a child you had asked me, 'What do you want to be when you grow up?' I think I would have said, 'A farmer's wife, on a farm with lots of animals and cart-horses'. I loved being out of doors. If you don't read, you find other things to do, like building pine needle houses in the woods. I didn't really have much ambition. I discovered that I quite liked to be the back marker, the one that provides resource and back up for other people, who actually do the front running. And that's what the farmer's wife does, she looks after everybody.

. . . meets the farmer's son

Geoff walked me back to Waterloo Station after the dance, and asked – would I meet him again and go to a show? We agreed to meet the following Saturday. And the following Saturday I was on the train coming up to Waterloo and when it stopped at the station before Waterloo, I jumped off, thinking, 'I can't remember his name, I don't know what he looks like, I can't remember anything about him. This is stupid.' But as the train was drawing out, I jumped back on further down.

I got to Waterloo, recognised him fine, and said to him, 'I haven't a clue what your name is, I've forgotten.'

So he told me, and that's how we began going out. We'd go up to London. We were as poor as church mice so we walked everywhere, and we spent the whole of that year going up to London and walking round. It only rained on us once.

Geoff – this is the good bit – Geoff was a farmer's son. In the middle of London, I had found myself a farmer's son. They farmed in Somerset, and are the most lovely, Christian family. But Geoff's father got caught in one of these awful things like Foot and Mouth – it was TB – and didn't get any compensation, so he gave up the farm and they moved to Cheddar. So here's me, with my farmer's son, but no farm. Geoff's a mathematician, and numbers are worse than letters with me, so I thought, 'How prudent to marry someone who can add up your milk bill for you.'

We got married as soon as I was twenty-one and had finished my teacher training. We were married from the church in Cheddar because Geoff had farming relatives there who couldn't travel, and my parents had retired to Jersey by then.

The PE teacher

I went for a job teaching PE at a secondary school near Fleet in Hampshire. At the interview they said, 'You're engaged, so there's no point in us employing you because you'll soon get married and have babies.'

People could say that sort of thing to women in those days. I remember saying quite fiercely, 'You've not actually thought that through. My fiancé lives in Hampshire, so it means that I will be coming to live here, and so you won't ever lose me. I'll be staying here, because where he is, I am.'

They were so impressed with this impeccable logic that I got the job.

I became very interested that year in helping children with learning difficulties. There was an 'educationally subnormal' wing – as it was still called in those days – attached to the school, and a lot of these children joined my PE class, and I just loved them. If I had stayed there, I would probably have applied for additional training to teach people with learning disabilities. How do you teach people where you don't have a shared common concept? Trying to find ways to communicate.

Unfortunately, I had been at the school for less than a year when Geoff was headhunted for a job in Scotland, and we had to go. So my theory about staying put because my husband was there didn't quite work out.

The ends of the earth

When Geoff came up for his interview he had said, 'My wife's a teacher, will she get a job?' and they had said, 'Nae problem'. But when I came – having just done a year's teaching and thinking I knew it all – I found that I wasn't qualified to teach in Scotland. I would need a degree. I have never been so shocked in all my life.

We came to Edinburgh in October 1965. I am an ancient person in that my first calling is my marriage. I would have gone to the ends of the earth and back for Geoff, and still will.

It felt like I had done. I had no friends, no job, we had very little money, nowhere to live and my mother died very shortly afterwards. I really didn't like Scotland at all. We came in October, leaving a gorgeous late summer in England. We sent up our clothes and stuff by trunk on the train and came in the car with summer clothes, but the trunk got lost somewhere, so we had no winter clothes and in Scotland in October we were absolutely frozen. Geoff swanned off to work and was quite happy.

We didn't know Edinburgh and we rented a place in Morningside, if you please, where no one spoke to you in those days, in such a lofty district. You'd go in a shop and they'd say, 'Now?'

I didn't know that that was how they say, 'How can I help you?' I used to hate shopping.

I would go to Morningside Library every morning and get out a book. I began to become a full-time reader. I really taught myself to read then. I would read all morning, soup and roll from the Co-op for lunch, take the book back to the library, get out another one, read it, realise I hadn't got anything for tea . . . Geoff would come home and we would eat scraps. And this was my life, day after day.

I signed on the dole eventually. I had to sign on the Professional Executive Register because I was a teacher, and it was such an awful experience. Here were people in their fifties. I was three decades younger than most of them, and it just seemed obscene. They couldn't get a job because of their age, and I remember one of them turning to me and saying, 'You're going to get a job that I could have.' And I think sewn into that moment was the idea that we should manage on one income, because there were so many people who had no jobs.

I began to look for jobs that nobody else wanted – part-time, stupid time jobs – because we had no kids yet. I picked up little bits of fill-in teaching. Forty minutes in the morning and then on the same day, an hour in the afternoon. So they were little bits that other people couldn't be bothered with. I began to get quite a few. And I also enjoyed doing easy, mindless jobs.

And then our children began to arrive, and I was happy.

Open University

In Scotland, as I said, you needed a degree to teach. When the Open University came on stream, with education available for all, I thought – this is fabulous – right, I'll do it. I applied, and on the day our second child was born, Geoff brought a letter into the hospital from the Open University saying I could start the course.

So I began my studies with a toddler and a newborn baby. I really enjoyed the Open University. I did a mixture of psychology and philosophy. You could pick and choose. It's the most amazing system. I even did some technology. I didn't realise a course called 'Human factors in systems failures' was about technology. It was wonderful because it gave you models for looking at things and seeing where they might fall down – soft systems like the National Health Service and cathedral chapters, and hard systems like buildings and cars. I loved that, but I was mostly reading philosophy and psychology. And eventually I learnt to pass exams, a technique that I'd never managed at school.

I didn't get straight 'A's through the course and I did minimum work, not because I'm lazy – although I am lazy – but because it still took me all my time to do the reading. And I had babies and jobs and people to see. My spelling is highly original. I have to have people who understand this.

But I discovered you passed exams by giving them what they wanted and not by what you created yourself. I am a dreamer. I'm a highly creative person, but that's not how you pass exams and fortunately I learnt that. So I passed my Open University exams. I actually got a first, which was an enormous thrill, although in the end, I never took up full-time teaching in Scotland.

The family
We have a very uncomplicated, traditional kind of marriage where I do the washing, the cooking, the cleaning – most of the housework. I bring up the kids.

We've two children of our own, Judith and Andrew, and we acquired two more, a brother and sister, another Andrew and Kirsty, when they were in their early teens; and we have variously looked after friends of the children or the foster children. One boy, Rob, arrived with a tiny kitten and said – could he stay for the weekend? Some time later I was walking the dog in the lane, and this shepherd said to me, 'That's a grand big cat you've got with you.' It was this same 'small kitten', following us. So I went back home and Rob was in the kitchen busy eating something – he's six feet seven so he ate a lot. I said, 'How long have you been with us, Rob?'

He said, 'Oh, about two years, I think.'

Judith, our daughter, will be thirty-two this year, and she's a mum herself now, a single parent. Andrew will be thirty this year, and he's married and works in Edinburgh with Geoff. Kirsty is between my two in ages, and she's a single parent too now, and her brother Andrew is a fireman. The others all just come and go.

I need help

St Fillan's at Buckstone became our family church. The children came with us until they were about nine and seven, when the unholy Christian row to get them to come each Sunday appalled me. I would hear myself shouting at them and thought – you don't go to church like that. Because Geoff was almost always working on a Sunday, they just stayed at home with him.

I began to work with the youth and the Sunday school, and I loved it. I like people, really, but I was terribly shy. To help overcome my shyness, I made the resolution that I would say 'good morning' to somebody every day, whether I knew them or not. I would go down the street and I would say 'good morning' to someone, and that's a habit I've kept.

Then in 1980 my priest at St Fillan's, Douglas Cameron, who's now Bishop of Argyll and the Isles, asked me to do training for the non-stipendiary lay ministry.

I didn't know what he was asking me to do or why, so I said, 'Explain.'

'I need help in the parish. I'm single-handed, I need help.'

So I did it. I wasn't 'called' to it. My understanding of a lay worker was never of someone who did churchy things. A lay worker was someone who cherished and cooked and cleaned and played with the kids, maybe ran Sunday school and the youth club.

AIDS

AIDS came to Scotland in the early 1980s. I joined with a group of about forty others, an ecumenical group, to see what an appropriate Christian response might be. They were mostly priests and ministers, who were all going to do bereavement care and funerals. I didn't have any training for this, as a layperson, so I decided that I would pray for them. Within a week I had three people all needing really practical things, like cooking and cleaning and washing – motherly things. So that's how I got into doing AIDS work.

Geoff validates my ministry, but he's not into the AIDS thing at all. He has never once visited the hospice. But even before the hospice was opened, we began having people with HIV staying at home, and he was quite happy about it. He puts up with all sorts of odd things. He is a believer himself. His ministry is in being supportive to me, in the sense that he allows his home to be used. He financed all my non-stipendiary ministry, which was quite costly when you looked after people who are going to stay with no charge. And he's never, ever, ever questioned that. He has the lovely outlook that we are fortunate.

As simple as breathing and not breathing

I was with someone when he died, because his mother was frightened and didn't want to stay. I said to her, 'Your son has been a delight to you in life; he's going to be a delight in his dying. He's not going to harm you. You don't need to be afraid, don't be afraid to stay.'

So I sat and held their hands. We sat together, in a triangle, and he died and she didn't even know he'd died, he died so gently. I had to say to her, 'I think he's gone.' And it was as simple as breathing and not breathing. There was no alarm in it, no fear in it. It was my first experience of witnessing death, and I wasn't afraid.

Milestone House

In 1986 there was a really bad HIV epidemic in Edinburgh and Milestone House, the AIDS hospice, was opened. By then I had already been working with AIDS patients for some time. Richard Holloway, who had just arrived to be Bishop of Edinburgh, was a trustee of Milestone House, and asked me if I would apply to help out there as part-time chaplain.

So I did apply and was told they didn't really want to give me the job because they didn't think it was suitable work for a woman. But one of my references was from someone with AIDS, about five pages long, saying what a difference I had made in their lives by doing motherly things. So they broke a part-time post into two quarter-time posts, so I had one bit and a Church of Scotland colleague had the other.

Keeping mum

The whole of my AIDS ministry was so ordinary, just helping with everyday things. I was very anxious not to betray the diagnosis of anyone I worked with, because in those days – the mid-1980s – the consequences were quite horrendous. You would get dog's dirt through your letterbox, and lighted rags, or paint daubed on your door. It wasn't safe. So I tried to be very ordinary, somebody who wouldn't look out of place.

But I once betrayed someone's diagnosis quite by chance. There was a family of three sons, and I worked with all three. Two of the boys knew they were diagnosed HIV, but they didn't know about the other one and the other one didn't know about those two, and the mother didn't know about any of them. We all coincided one day, one after the other, in one of their houses and so I was the cause of them all knowing about each other. They each greeted me by name. Then they were all saying to one another, 'How do you know her?'

'She's my cleaner.'

'She's my cleaner, too.'

And the mum said, 'You're not anybody's cleaner. What do you do for my boys?'

So I said to her, 'I love them.' Because that's what I do, when I cook and clean for them.

And of course, in the end they all realised. But that's how it was in the 1980s – you didn't tell even your own family.

Self-discovery

I've discovered quite a few things about myself since working with people with HIV and staying with them through their life experiences. I never realised I could be an angry person until the last twelve years or so. I've always branded myself as too idle to be angry, but I actually get quite steamed up about things now. You have no idea that you can be a scary person but apparently, angry, I can be quite a scary person and I used to frighten people.

I do have quite a sharp sense of injustice and I've always seen it quickly for other people, but I also have it for myself. The vulnerable areas are about attacks on my integrity. I really rise to those – but I've only noticed it recently.

I forgot to tell you

The telephone conversation went something like this.

'This is Richard Holloway. Why didn't you phone me back?'

I am thinking, *Richard Holloway?* 'I didn't know I had to.'

'I left a message.'

'Well, I didn't get it.'

We were both getting quite shirty. He said, 'Well, let's start again.' And he began, 'Jane dear –'

Over the years, I have learned that this usually precedes something that I won't like, but then I didn't know.

'Jane dear, I propose to ordain you as my chaplain to people with AIDS. What do you think?'

This was in June 1990, so he could ordain me as a deacon, which is what he proposed to do. I was speechless.

I can remember him saying, 'Are you still there?'

'Yes.'

'Well, what do you say?'

It was quite late on – twenty past nine at night – so I said, 'Good night' and put the phone down.

He phoned me back and said, 'You don't have to say "yes" tonight. Say it tomorrow. Good night.'

My son came down the stairs. I was still standing holding the telephone – Richard had gone.

Andrew said to me, 'Who's that on the phone? Are you all right?'

'It's the Bishop of Edinburgh.'

To which he replied, 'Oh, yes, he phoned yesterday. I forgot to tell you . . .'

They were dead chuffed, and that was good enough for me

The idea of having a chaplain for my AIDS people was fabulous. I was red hot for that – but not me. I kept telling Richard the names of other people who would be better, but he just hung in. He was not a patient man, but he waited from June till September.

I went to see him and said, 'Will you run this by me one more time?'

So he did, and I said, 'Give me three good reasons why it's me.'

And he said , 'One, to show the church they should be involved. Two, to show the church that they are already involved and that you are just one of many; you are just the one that I'm pulling out. And three, to show your AIDS and HIV people that they can claim the church for themselves.'

I said, 'But that's not what I'm about. I'm your actual skivvy. I'm the pooper-scooper that you get on the greyhound track . . .'

He said, 'And that's exactly what we need.'

The other thing I said to him was, 'If you're dropping me in this, you've jolly well got to look after me.'

So Richard created the post of bishop's chaplain for me. He attached me to the cathedral so that I would have a base. Unfortunately he forgot to mention the fact to Graham, the Provost, so we didn't get off to the best start. But I needed a place to be, while I was learning. Whose work is it you're doing? I was beginning to think it was the gospel of Jane I was doing out there, and not the gospel of God. I believe chaplains should all have a good, firm, liturgical base where they're nurtured and nourished in the faith.

All I am really is a sort of holy-hat bearer, and a general kind of shepherd for the bishop. I find out where the loos are, go to the rehearsal so I know the pattern for service, and can say to him, 'The microphone's over there, switch on, switch off.' It's not really a vital thing at all.

There were people who were jealous, and there were people who were really very cruel. Some people thought I'd ratted on lay ministry, and called me a poacher turned gamekeeper. But the people I worked with, the people with HIV, thought it was brilliant. They were dead chuffed. And that was good enough for me.

Born a deacon

When I was ordained deacon, I was ordained with Brother Timothy in a most powerful and moving service. The cathedral was packed and it felt rather like my wedding. I was just deliriously happy and that sense of astonished joy has never really left me.

The whole of my ordained ministry has been very low-key, very ordinary, very sweep up the bits. For me, it was a blessing having a long diaconate when we as women could not be ordained priests, because that's what deacons do. They're very ordinary and they watch for opportunity, and things happen and then they sweep up the bits left behind when everybody else has moved somewhere else. And I like to think that is progress. I came to the conclusion that I must have been born a deacon.

Working for people with AIDS, and having a long diaconate, were both good because they teach you about powerlessness – about not being without power within powerlessness. About not being without hope in hopelessness. I think the diaconate as a valid order is important, and not just as a transition to priesthood.

I didn't seek to be ordained, but having got there, I thought I would always stay a deacon. Ordination to the priesthood didn't seem relevant to me. I am aware of what a disappointment I was to some of my sisters, because I didn't get all steamed up and wildly excited about it. I didn't campaign for it, and I have never had the longing so I don't know what it is to have that longing denied.

I've always felt that I just fell out of a tree, and found myself a priest.

I tell you – she's going to be a priest
In this province I think we were very wise. We had a moratorium of six months. No ordination for six months, because we had only been approved and recommended to the diaconate, and not to the priesthood. We all went to a panel and talked over how our ministry had been, what was good in it, what would be added to it by being priested. So we talked about all the differences it might make. It wasn't an ordeal. It was a lovely experience. Then they asked each of us, did we wish to be made priests?

I said, 'I don't know . . .'

Bishop Richard was part of the panel and he said, 'Of course, she's going to be a priest.' The others said, 'We're asking her.' And they asked me again.

And Richard said, 'I tell you, she's going to be a priest.'

So they sent him out of the room to make tea and told me, 'Now you answer the question.'

The chairman of the panel said, 'You've said it would make a difference in that you could now hear confession and give absolution and bless dying people with the sacrament, and this seems as if it would be an advantage. If I give you a straight question, now, do you wish to be ordained priest – what is your answer?'

Richard came back at that moment and said, 'She was born a priest. I don't care if she says no. She's going to be a priest.'

So I said, rather weakly, 'It seems like it's the mind of the church.'

Elizabeth
My daughter couldn't come to my ordination, and anyway she wasn't awfully keen on the whole business. My son and his wife came, but didn't sit in family seats. They thought that might be a bit too near the front for them.

I was moved to tears mostly by the fact that being ordained just in front of me was Elizabeth Malloch. She was my mother in the church. I relied on her wisdom. I had no academic theology, so I would sound out Elizabeth and she would point me in the right direction.

Elizabeth – who then was eighty-four or eighty-five and failing in health, stood probably four foot eight high, and was spherical – came up on two sticks to the altar. A godly woman, she had had a lifetime of service in education, then a second lifetime as a powerful lay worker in the church, a theologian, a deaconess and a deacon.

Fortunately we had a bishop who had the vision to ordain a woman of eighty-five, not because of what she could give to the church in the future, but because of what she had given to the church all her life. Priest as she was years ago, it was not her fault that episcopal hands hadn't been laid on her.

I would have stopped there forever

I knew Elizabeth was preaching the next day, and I knew that many of the men who had served in the cathedral were going to come and concelebrate. I'd cottoned on to all of that. What I didn't know until the Sunday morning was the fact that only one person would say the eucharistic prayer – and that that person would be me.

We were going to have a rehearsal, but it all took a bit of time, and we never got to my bit. So the last thing that was said to me was by Graham, 'Don't worry, I'll work the microphone.'

I had no idea what I was going to be doing. Normally on a Sunday, there are three of us. One does the microphone, one does the book and the other reads the prayers. As a deacon, I'd learnt to do the mike and the book – although not often the book because I'm a bit unreliable with the pages.

What I remember most was – surprisingly – not being terrified. And when I elevated the host, at the end of the consecration prayer, the circumference of the priest's host almost exactly covered the rose window at the west end of the cathedral, and the sun was shining and it made an aura round it. I was transfixed. I was holding the host up, with this golden aura round it, and I remember thinking that if I could, I would have stopped there forever. It was so beautiful, I could hardly move.

Here's Father Mother coming

Some of my high church friends found it difficult when I was ordained priest. They could cope with deacon but they had a traditional view of a priest. I have one friend who would always stand up when I came into a room after I was ordained. It took me quite a long time to realise what was happening and then I said to her one day, 'What is this with you?'

And she said, 'I can't stop myself.'

Some people say, 'We call our priest "Father" – what do we call you?'
I tell them, 'My name is Jane.'

I'm sometimes called 'Mother' by Roman Catholic friends and
colleagues. The workers next door were all Irish Catholics when they
were renovating the house next to my office, and they always used to call
me 'Father Mother'. Here's Father Mother coming.

I will almost always say 'Yes' – but I positively will not sing

I've fought for my people with AIDS. I've learnt all sorts of skills. I've
started up projects, I've spoken at conferences, and I've done all sorts of
things that are enormously difficult for me because I believe in them. I
didn't hear a call within me to be ordained, but having assented to that,
I believe in the grace of orders. I believe that we have a duty and a joy to
fulfil responsibilities. If I'm asked to do something, I almost always will
say 'Yes'. But there are a few things I will not do and I don't like myself
for saying that. I will not sing in the cathedral. I positively will not sing.

I have a liturgical role to sing. I should, for instance, begin the Creed.
I should sing Evensong, because that is part of the Office, but I always
find a cantor. The choir practises day in and day out; they are wonderful
and professional and it seems so bizarre to have someone who has a voice
vaguely like a corncrake to start them off.

The provost of surprises

I've been in Scotland, in Edinburgh, for thirty-five years now and I've
always gone into the cathedral. I keep being re-invented there. I used to
go in as a congregation member, then as bishop's chaplain, then as a
priest and canon, and now as vice-provost.

At first, after I was priested, I was still non-stipendiary. Most of my
work continued to be with people with AIDS. I only came into the
cathedral about once a month. I'd come in, make a muddle, and go again.
I didn't really feel part of the team. I never even appeared on the clergy
list in the red book. I kept thinking – in a way, I don't exist.

Then the provost asked me if I'd come half-time, and I was really
surprised, but I said I would. Then when the provost asked me if I would
be vice-provost, I was completely shocked. I could see a particular kind
of role for vice-provost in the cathedral, which is a kind of wise senior
clergy person. But that didn't relate at all to how I see myself – which is
as a pooper-scooper.

So I gave the provost a real hard time about my being vice-provost. I
did not think it should be me. But he hung on, and in the same way as I
thought the church had called me to ordination, I went along with it,
because I don't think the provost is silly. In fact, he is usually spot on.
Annoying, isn't it?

It's Graham's vision and trust that constantly astonishes me. It is his willingness to take a risk that gives me the confidence to have a go. It is something I find very humbling.

The abiding thing

I love working in the cathedral. I moan about it incessantly, but I actually love it. I love the people. I love the wayfarers that come in and the tourists, the music. I love my colleagues. They're exciting to work with, they're challenging. I learn an enormous amount. When I was ordained deacon, I remember saying to Richard, 'Please keep a clause in to say I never have to preach.'

He said, 'Sorry, honey, it's a job lot.'

When I started to preach in the cathedral it made me so ill, I went to Graham and said, 'Please take me off the preaching rota.'

But he said, 'Certainly not. What can we do to keep you on there?'

I went to see one of our senior priests and said I didn't know how you do sermons. He made one or two suggestions, but I think I've still got it all to learn.

I suppose the abiding thing for me – the thing that nourishes me and completely overawes me – is the huge privilege of it all.

I was at Melrose for an institution, and we had to administer Communion to three people in wheelchairs. My custom is to kneel when administering to people in wheelchairs, so that you're at their eye level. I did this at Melrose, and someone said to me afterwards that it had changed their whole understanding of what priesthood was.

She said that it suddenly made sense of Maundy Thursday and the foot-washing. She had never quite understood that in relation to priesthood before. Seeing me kneeling had made a connection for her.

That moment refreshed to me the privilege of it all, and the gift. It's a costly thing. Other people have found it very costly. Some have lost everything because of it, and it's something that I hope I never take lightly.

I'm still very interested in my outside work as well. I think a healthy ministry is a third for yourself, a third for the church inside and a third for the church outside. So I still do some AIDS chaplaincy work. If that comes to an end, I will then be on the search for something else, my other third.

I know it will arrive because I wasn't good with illness, and I'm noisy and untidy, but I ended up with people who are dying and that has been the most enriching time, hopefully for them and for me. So if someone so unfit can make something really life-giving out of that, I know I can find other things and do them. I'll probably argue about going – not because I don't want to go but I want it to be a right thing.

But mainly, I shall continue to be the pooper-scooper lady.

REVD BERNICE BROGGIO

4

An Honest Woman

REVD BERNICE BROGGIO

Rural Dean, Tooting

I have been a common law priest for twenty-five years, and
I just want the church to make an honest woman of me.

Introduction

*LB: Some of the women priests we talked to were well battle-hardened by the
time the vote went through on 11 November 1992. Bernice Broggio was one of
them. She had been taking an active part in the struggle for twenty years when
the Act was finally passed.*

'*In some ways I found it a damp squib when it happened. As I said before
at General Synod, I had been a common law priest for twenty-five years,
and I just wanted the church to make an honest woman of me. That's what
ordination has been about. I don't celebrate the anniversaries – at all. I'm a
little bit angry that it happened by stealth, but there it is, this is the bit of
history that I've hit.*'

*In July 2000 the General Synod were debating a private member's motion
being proposed by Archdeacon Judith Rose that the theology of the consecration
of women as bishops be discussed over the next two years. Canon Bernice
Broggio stood up and proposed her own amendment that asked for the working
party to bring forward legislation (instead of theology, which she asserted
had already been done) for the consecration of women as bishops within two
years.*

The amendment was not accepted.

*A long-time campaigner for the Movement for the Ordination of Women
(MOW), Bernice says that ordination hasn't in the end made a lot of difference
to her because, as she says, she has been a 'common law' priest for years. Fierce for
justice, her early training was as a Franciscan.*

*These days there aren't many people who would open their doors to welcome
an ex-sex offender, but Bernice has taken one in as a lodger in her vicarage in*

Tooting Bec. Bernice's home always includes two or more lodgers. These are usually people, often young and from care homes, needing another chance to have a go at life. At the moment there are three lodgers, along with two well-adjusted Labrador dogs – Maggie, an athletic swimmer, nearly eight years old and Jessie, coming up for five years old – who both rush enthusiastically to greet any visitor to this haven of organised chaos.

As we balanced our recording equipment carefully on high piles of books, files, newspapers, photographs and parish paperwork, after enjoying a delicious supper prepared with her own fair hands in the vicarage kitchen, Bernice began telling us a story which concluded with the words, 'You can't do everything.'

As you will discover, she pretty well does.

Bernice

Quite a difficult childhood

My father's father, my grandfather, was French, brought up in a Paris orphanage, but the name 'Broggio' is Italian. I think it is a contraction of Ambrose, the saint of Milan, who was ordained deacon, priest and bishop in quick succession. You will find Italian churches dedicated to St Ambrogio and families called Broggio are common in Corsica, which historically has been owned alternately by Italy and France.

I hated my surname as a child, but it's quite good now, because I'm the only one – well, there aren't many. 'Bernice' is biblical. She was a horrid woman – the sister, wife and mistress of Herod Agrippa the Second, who Paul got dragged up before – so, a highly colourful character! (Acts 25)

There were actors in my mother's family. Her grandfather acted with Irving and had his own Shakespearean company. Her father was chief accountant for the Smith Beef Company and worked in the City. He played the church organ. He even played the St Paul's Cathedral organ – they used to let people come in and play.

Neither of my parents were churchgoers. They had a pretty unhappy marriage, and there was physical violence at home to my mother, and also to my brother, sister and me. In those days you did not know how to do anything about it. I remember an NSPCC person coming round at school one day to give a talk and ask us to have bluebird boxes. I remember thinking – golly, should I tell her? But I just couldn't. Partly because I knew by then that I wanted to go to university, and I did not want to put a hitch in that.

So I had quite a difficult childhood. There were always money worries at home – I can understand now how stressful that can be. At the time we thought that it was our fault that our parents were angry or unhappy. But really it was because they were living beyond their means. Bills didn't get paid and there were always money problems. It was partly because my parents were snobbish. My mother was slightly upwardly mobile and wanted us to be Somebody. We all went to private school. We didn't take books out of the public library, because you didn't know who had handled them.

Home was a frightening place, so school was our haven. My brother was at a local public school and my younger sister and I went to a small private school called Belle View, out in the wilds of Buckinghamshire. It had started out in London, and moved out into the country with all its pupils and staff, because of the war. I failed the eleven-plus, but I stayed on there until I was sixteen. It was brilliant and I did very well there. I loved games and singing in the choir as well as the academic stuff.

We were all encouraged to take an interest in all sorts of things apart from academic work, to develop as people. I didn't know anything about the gay scene in those days, but when I saw the film of *The Pride of Miss Jean Brodie* years later I recognised some of my own teachers. I thought, 'That's it!'

There was one teacher especially, Miss Roberts. She taught me geography and religious knowledge up to O level, and those are the two subjects I later got first degrees in. She was very important in my life. I met her again, years later, but I never really thanked her for what she did for me. I regret that. It's difficult sometimes.

I came to the faith slowly. I knew Miss Roberts went to church, so I started going occasionally. I went on my own as we weren't a churchgoing family, and I happened to turn up at church one Evensong when they announced confirmation classes. So I went along and at the age of sixteen I was confirmed.

I was happy at school, and Christianity was part of it. It didn't come from home at all. I have often preached that teachers don't always realise what important people they are. They can lead people away, or they can lead people into things.

I'm going to be 'in' with the church

When I left school, I got a grant and went to London University to read geography and geology. It was the mid-1950s. I hit it at the time when a new chaplain had just arrived, a very dynamic person. Gordon Philips was really Anglo-Catholic, but he said we were not going to be 'high' or 'low', we were just 'church'.

St George's, Bloomsbury, was the university church. It had sound doctrine and scholarly teaching. The ethos was: you are studying academic subjects at university level so your Christian knowledge should not be at Sunday-school level.

Ivor Smith Cameron was a young chaplain there. Humphrey Green, who is now a Mirfield Father, was a lecturer at King's. These were inspirational people. It was an exciting time, the 1950s, to be a young Christian at that place. People like Rose Macaulay came and addressed graduate groups. Crème de la crème!

As a child, I'd always felt on the edge of things, an outsider, because life was so difficult at home, and I'd never had 'the right equipment' and things because of money problems. I can remember walking across Gordon Square and thinking – I'm going to be 'in' with the church.

I had rather hoped, well, I had assumed that I would get married eventually but I was rather frightened of it. If you grow up as a child in an unhappy marriage, it leaves scars and leaves you damaged. Looking back now, with hindsight, I think I'm better off not having married.

Afterwards I just knew that I was called to ministry . . .
We had a tremendous mission in my third year, over eight weeks, through the week and on Sundays, led first of all by the Cowley Fathers, then by Mirfield, then by Kelham and then by the Franciscans. One day at a service – it was the Feast of the Conversion of St Paul, 25 January – I went along to a weekday service.

And afterwards I just knew that I was called to ministry.

I was twenty-one, still a student. I didn't know that there could be women in ministry. I didn't know about lay ministry or deaconesses. I knew there were monks and nuns, but I wasn't sure that I wanted to be either of those. I felt I was called, but I didn't know what to do about it, so I went into teaching.

'Have you heard of Sister Ursula, and the Franciscan Community up at Gateshead?'
After I left university, I taught geography and games at a Channing school, and continued going to the university church as a graduate. But I felt that there was something missing, and that I wanted some kind of rule to live by. I discovered that you could become a 'third order' Franciscan, a tertiary – a layperson working in the secular world, but living by the rule of St Francis of Assisi. I thought that might be the next step for me.

When Father Edward, one of the Franciscan friars who had led the original mission, came to St Michael's, Highgate, to preach at services for Lent and Holy Week, I went along to ask him about it. He said, 'Have you heard of Sister Ursula, and the Franciscan Community up at Gateshead?'

This was a little group of Franciscan tertiaries living together in community, running a retreat house and being the spearhead of the Anglican Franciscans in the north-east of England. He gave me the address and told me where to go. They took in all sorts of odd bods at Gateshead, and so in January 1960 at the age of twenty-five, I gave up teaching and went up to join the community. Possibly, had we taken life vows, I would still be there today.

The community was just getting its second wind. Originally it had built up to eight women, and after a time they had wanted to have some affirmation of their ministry from the church and to take life vows. The friars had said, 'You had better get in somebody from Malvern to see if you are "proper".'

But Sister Frances Ann, a nun who came over from the Anglican Community of the Holy Name at Malvern, decided that they *weren't* 'proper'. So they were only allowed to take vows for a year at a time, and virtually all the original tertiary sisters left. Some went off to join the Poor Clares, some went to the Holy Name at Malvern – to be 'proper' nuns I suppose.

It was a great pity. They weren't trying to be like the Holy Name. They were a new thing. Brother Bernard said that it was a great shame that they did not recognise that this was a new thing, because it could have been so exciting.

There were just three community members there, including Sister Ursula, when I joined them. I was the fourth. We got up to five. We did mission work with the friars; local parish work; we gave talks and led retreats; took in waifs and strays and helped out in the parishes in Durham and in Newcastle.

The Franciscans have always had a role in caring for the outcasts of society. Historically St Francis himself cared for lepers. Franciscans have always had a prison ministry, and worked with the mentally ill and people who have been on the wrong side of the law. We took in young pregnant girls, because those were the days when if you were pregnant and unmarried it wasn't seemly to be seen around in your village. And then the babies were either adopted or fostered. Tramps came to the door regularly because we were just off the A1 and it was on the route between Edinburgh, Leeds and London. People came from mental hospitals. There was a man called John, who was a burnt-out schizophrenic and who for a time lived in a caravan there and always came for a meal twice a week.

At Christmas time we invited people and families and individuals who would have been on their own and wouldn't have had much of a Christmas. I found I enjoyed that kind of work and ministry.

Michael Ramsay had been Bishop of Durham. He would occasionally turn up at the back door of the house. With his eyebrows. He liked our group. Sister Ursula was invited to his enthronement as Archbishop of Canterbury – and we went to someone's house and watched it on television.

But after I'd been there for three years it was decided that we should move out of the retreat house and into a parish. The two younger ones of us thought that if we were going into a parish, we ought to get some proper church work training. So we both left – and unfortunately I think there was a bit of feeling that we had let them down.

Star-spangled theology

It was only then that I sussed that within the Church of England there were licensed lay workers and deaconesses. In those days you had to become a lay worker before you could become a member of the Deaconess Order in England. The men, of course, could go straight to becoming a deacon.

I went along to a selection centre and they said, 'Oh, you're a graduate. Good. See if you can get into King's College, London and read theology.'

I grabbed at the chance. I had never thought that gift would come my way. I'd always wished that I'd read theology, but I thought that I'd had my chance at university. But I'm one of the few people who have had two grants, to do two first degrees. I also had a little bit of subbing from the Bishop of Newcastle, Hugh Ashdown, Chair of the then Board for Women's Work and a great advocate for women's ministry. He said that he'd like me to come back to the north-east when I'd finished. So he gave me £100 a term – quite a lot of money in those days.

I was at King's at the same time as Desmond Tutu. I was twenty-eight when I went, and he was a year or so older. Desmond Tutu was very humble. I remember him saying how it was amazing, coming off the aeroplane, when someone called him, 'Sir'. It was his mother being treated with respect by Bishop Trevor Huddlestone that had made him want to become a priest in the first place.

There were about ten of us mature students doing the course. It was an interesting time to be there. Christopher Evans was there, and Morna L. Hooker. I had Professor Nineham's last year. I did liturgy with Dr Jasper and special doctrine with Eric Maskell – star-spangled theology!

And John Robinson, of course. I went up in the year that John Robinson wrote *Honest to God*. Whenever he was mentioned, Eric Maskell would screw his eyes up and look down the river. He couldn't stand him. I suppose I would have to say that the chapel at King's kind of emptied in those three years. When I first went there, in 1963, you had a very large contingent at Matins every morning. By the end of the time, there were far fewer people there. But I think that that was as much to do with the spirit of the times as anything, the 'swinging sixties'.

I was at King's College reading theology for three years and it was wonderful. The only thing I did not enjoy was having to live at Gilmore House, the training house for women, for the first two years. I found it terrible. It was run like I assume a nineteenth-century ladies' seminary would have been. It was about petty officialdom in the hands of women who couldn't have power any other way. There were all sorts of petty rules. So I rebelled quite a bit. I was the bad girl. As a result, they did not want me to be licensed when I was leaving and a job came up in the Newcastle Diocese. I said to the bishop, 'I'm not coming if you're not licensing me.'

He just said, 'I will license you.'

Interestingly, I think I have stayed in ministry longer than anyone else in that group. The wastage of women was high in those days.

An ecumenical church without walls

I became the licensed lay worker in Killingworth New Town, in the north-east of England. The new town concept promoted by the doctor of development, Roy Gazzard, was whole-person health – physical, social and spiritual. He was an Anglican, his assistant a Presbyterian. It involved all the local services as well as the churches – housing, schools, jobs, the lot. This theory of new towns was spelled out by – I know this from my geography – Ebenezer Howard in the nineteenth century.

Our project was to provide facilities for people moving into the new town. My job was to help start an ecumenical church in a house where we had the doctor's surgery in the kitchen, the health visitor in the living-room, and a childcare officer visited regularly. A church without walls. And I lived there. The first services started in the same room that the health visitor used.

Then we moved 'the church' into the school, and we had the first ecumenical confirmation service in 1968 – Methodist, Presbyterian and Anglican. We prepared all the candidates together. The superintendent, the minister and the bishop all came – the bishop laid on hands and the others gave the right hand of fellowship. We were way ahead of our time.

Our ecumenical Methodist-Presbyterian-Anglican worship was a fortnightly Eucharist, which we all celebrated, because in those days the Church of England didn't give communion to non-Anglicans. By concelebrating we got round it. Theologically you could see holes in it – but it worked. Hugh Ashdown, the Bishop of Newcastle, had said to me, 'Do what you think is right. If you think I'll have to say "No" – don't ask me.' What a great man!

So in my early thirties, and single, I fostered a teenager

I fostered a teenager while I was there. In a way, it was to help me financially, because there was a fostering allowance if you took someone in. I was permanently short of money. I was earning £400 a year, which was the bottom of a curate's wage. We were six miles outside Newcastle. I could drive – the Franciscans had taught me – but I didn't have a car. The local childcare people had on their books a teenager who had already broken up two foster homes. She was an orphan and was desperate – well, to be honest she wanted a man – and the two foster fathers couldn't cope. If you start from scratch, kids ideally need two parents and preferably of both genders, but if you have kids who are exceedingly screwed up, you sometimes need to place them in a special fostering situation. So in my early thirties, and single, I became a foster parent.

I thought, 'Bloody hell! I am the priest here'

I was beginning to feel less than happy about my subordinate role in the church. I had a pit village, Burradon, to help look after as well as the Killingworth New Town project, and in the pit village, which was traditionally Anglican, I would sometimes take the whole of the first part of the service. Then Jeremy Sampson, the vicar, would come along, ready vested, in time to say the Absolution and do the Consecration; that was OK, he was the vicar.

I used to go on funeral visits with Jeremy, and take part in funerals, but I was never allowed to take a funeral. I remember Jeremy explaining, 'Well, we want to give people the best care at this time.' What he meant by 'best' was: not me.

That kind of thing was what women had to put up with in those days. I am sure that Jeremy would regret it now. It was just that people in those days didn't think that things would ever change.

The real turning-point for me was at one of those occasions at the pit village when Jeremy was away in the summer. I'd baptised, preached and suddenly a complete stranger turned up at the door, ready vested. And I thought, 'Bloody hell! *I* am the priest here.' Here was this bloke who nobody knew... (He's actually an archdeacon now, and against the ordination of women! Hurrumph!)

That was the turning-point. Up until then I had accepted being a parish worker and following humbly after the men, but that really was the last straw. This was the thing that first said to me that women ought to be priests, and that I ought to be one, and that I was one.

By the end of four years I was quite exhausted. The New Town community had grown – I lived in the 145th house built when I went there, and there were over 2,000 houses when I left, so the population had increased a lot. To cope with this, they were going to get a full-time priest and, quite frankly, I did not want to be Number Two to a new priest coming in.

The person they appointed was David Wood, who had founded the Brotherhood of Prayer and Action in the East Midlands. He'd been out of the church for five years after his marriage had broken down, but had then remarried and come back. He asked me to stay on with him. He was a good priest and I probably would have got on with him all right, but I just felt that I couldn't. Having been there as Number One, I couldn't suddenly be someone's shadow.

The 'camel line'

I'd been called out in the middle of the night for various things during my time at Killingworth, and seen a man with hysterical paralysis – which is quite frightening if you haven't seen it before. I'd been doing clinical theology, Frank Lake kind of stuff, understanding personality. I thought I would try and get a proper psychiatric social work training. I applied for courses and I got on the Glasgow social work course. So in 1970 I went to Glasgow.

My brother moved me up there with furniture, but after that I was on my own two feet. I call it the 'camel line', because I travelled with a dog and a cat in a basket, and my rucksack – that was all the luggage I could carry. It rained solidly for the first two months, and it took me nearly six months to learn the language. The first year I lived in a council house above an old lady on the south side in Moss Park.

I had wanted to go to Scotland because with the Kilbrandon Report they were way ahead of England in integrating their social work teams. They were bringing together childcare, probation, psychiatric social work and hospital social work. I had a DHSS grant – which was slightly more than my previous church salary. That had just gone up to £700 a year, with house, when I left and I think I got £1,200 for my grant from the DHSS. I wasn't flush, but I could manage.

I got to like Scotland – and learnt all about the arrogant English. I was influenced by a lot of people I met there. My course said, 'We are, as we are in relation to other people.' I learned later that that came from the Edinburgh school of theology; and on my Sabbatical recently I learned that it is also an African tribal saying.

The Gorbals group

I really liked the political ideas of the Iona Community – that you can't separate politics from theology if you are going to love your neighbour as yourself. It's integral. In Glasgow I came upon the Gorbals group. These were people for whom socialism and Christianity were all part of the same thing. My parents, especially my father, were Conservative with a big and a small c, and I think it was at university in the 1950s where I first discovered that for me socialism and the gospel went together. Now in Glasgow I found many like-minded people and became confirmed in my commitment to living life along socialist principles.

The Gorbals group had an open-house policy to everyone in the inner-city neighbourhood. Half of the Gorbals had been pulled down, but John and Molly Harvey were still living there and every month they had an open meeting, an integrated meal and Eucharist in their house for anyone in the neighbourhood to come to. It was very moving. Geoff Shaw, a Church of Scotland minister and radical politician who wanted an independent Scotland and would have been the Donald Dewar of his day, the First Minister, had Scotland succeeded in winning devolution in 1979, was part of the group. They had a café shop in Glasgow, which had prayers at lunchtime. Lillias Graham, who was an Anglican parish worker at my own Episcopalian church, St Margaret's, ran a second-hand shop called the Wee Red Shop, which recycled clothing for people. The curate of St Margaret's was also a member of the Gorbals group, but he had left to become vicar of Old St Paul's in Edinburgh just before I arrived. So I missed meeting Richard Holloway, later to become Bishop of Edinburgh and Primus of Scotland.

There was a good ecumenical chaplaincy in Glasgow, and the Catholic chaplain was Father Gerard Hughes. He used to say, 'I'm not allowed to invite you to receive communion, but I can assure you that nobody who comes will be refused.' He got into trouble for that. But all the chaplaincies, used by foreigners and ex-pat English students, intermingled – we were one Christian group.

Kay Carmichael, one of my teachers on the social work course, was important to me because she was a feminist. She was making people aware of the difficulties you had just in being a woman. In some ways I hadn't really been awake to that before. I had experienced anti-female prejudice myself, in the church, but I hadn't picked up the feminist movement's ideas academically.

Living in a tent with a cat and a dog and picking up fleas in Govan

During my second year in Glasgow I did a placement at a psychiatric hospital for five months, doing casework. And I did a spell with the alcoholic consultant at the Southern General Psychiatric Hospital. It's all been of much more use to my work in ministry than the church's so-called 'pastoral training' was.

I'm always quite poor and, to save money because I wasn't being paid while I was on a placement, I spent five weeks living in a tent with my dog and cat. The cat loved it. And the dog was all right; she used to come and sleep in the tent with me, so it was a bit of a squash. I visited Iona, but Iona didn't like me going to church with a dog and a cat. They complained. But I couldn't do anything else. So I do know what it feels like being a single parent!

I did social work for a month in Govan, where people were living in the very pits of tenements. I picked up fleas there. I'd had to go and look after eight children in their flat because their mother had been rushed into hospital to have her ninth child. Her husband, who had beaten her up while she was heavily pregnant, was in Barlinnie Jail and had to be bailed out to come home to look after the kids. I waited for him with the children in the flat. They didn't bring him home from prison, or even give him his bus fare to get home, so I was there all day until ten o'clock at night waiting for him. I was so tired when I got home that I just fell into bed, and took all the fleas I had picked up in their flat into the bed with me. It took me weeks to get rid of them.

'Oh . . . Just look around and see where you might go'

The psychiatric social work course ended in 1972, and I started to look around for jobs. I applied for one in Glasgow – surprise, surprise, I didn't get it. It went to a Scot. I applied for a job in Edinburgh – surprise, surprise, it went to another Scot. I applied for a job back in Newcastle – surprise, surprise, I got it!

I went to work in the Nuffield Child Psychiatry Unit. I found myself working with Stuart Morton, another Scot, who taught me more about child development than anyone. It was a specialist unit for child problems, and it took kids from all over the north of England. I was part of the Department of Psychiatry at Newcastle University. I was sitting in on all the case studies alongside the medical team, because that's how medics learned. I was on another huge new learning curve.

There was an interregnum of bishops in Newcastle. Bishop Hugh Ashdown, who had always supported me, had retired. I spoke to the archdeacon and I asked where I could be most useful as a licensed parish worker in Newcastle. After Killingworth, and having done my course at Glasgow, I thought I had some useful experience to offer.

He said, 'Oh . . . Just look around and see where you might go.' Which really wasn't all that helpful.

However, I did look around, and found the St Thomas's city-centre church in Newcastle, in the Haymarket. It was opposite the university, and opposite the University Theatre and it seemed lively enough, so I got myself attached to the team there.

Ronald Bowlby, later to be Bishop of Southwark, came to be the new Bishop of Newcastle, and he licensed me to St Thomas's on Ascension Day 1973. I guess I was the first person he licensed as new bishop. I already knew him, because he was a Franciscan tertiary and had taken family holidays at the community house in Gateshead when I was there with the Franciscans.

He said, 'Yes, well you'd better kneel down and I'll give you a blessing. I'm not allowed to lay hands on you yet!'

Then Ian Harker came to be the chaplain at St Thomas's. He'd been a housing worker in Notting Hill. He was not at all conventional, very political and he soon started stirring things up. Working with Ian I learned about liberation theology, and we were the Socialist Party at prayer in Newcastle.

It was the time of the Queen's Silver Jubilee, and people were organising street parties. We did an Alternative Jubilee service. We talked about Jubilee as a time of giving to the poor, not for celebrating someone's reign. It upset certain people. Ian was quite a radical priest, and many people would say that, like John Robinson in the 1960s, he emptied the churches in the 1970s.

A terrible hoo-ha

In 1972 Christian Howard produced the first report on the ordination of women. She was a tremendous person, a titled lady who had great influence and aplomb, who converted the bulk of the bishops to women's ordination. She came to Newcastle to talk about her report and I went along.

In 1977 I changed jobs to become deputy head of a Roman Catholic school run by the Good Shepherd Order, still in Newcastle, for difficult teenage girls in care. Funnily enough, none of the girls there were in favour of women's ordination. There was the Virgin Mary on a pedestal, and there were all the nuns doing good things, but – no, no, Priests were Men.

The first American women priests were ordained in 1976. Florence Tim Oi Li was the first woman ever to be ordained in the Anglican communion, in 1944. Women priests had been ordained in Hong Kong since 1971 and Joyce Bennett came over from Hong Kong in 1977 and celebrated communion in a United Reformed church. One day that year I had to go to Manchester, and there I called in on Phoebe and Alfred Willets, great pioneers of women's ministry. I told them, 'You know, it's such a shame that Joyce Bennett had to celebrate communion in a URC church, because we had actually offered her an altar at St Thomas's.'

Phoebe said, 'Oh! So did we.'

She looked at Alfred, and said, 'We'd better tell you what's happening.' They were in touch with Alison Palmer, an ordained diplomat from the United States, and she sometimes dropped in on the UK. She was coming to celebrate the Eucharist at their church that October.

I said I thought it would be a very good thing if she could celebrate more than once. So back in Newcastle, I asked Ian Hooker if we could invite Alison Palmer to celebrate at St Thomas's as well, and of course he was dead keen. She came to us on Sunday 16 October 1977, having celebrated in Manchester the previous Tuesday. She was the celebrant in the morning, and I preached.

That evening we had another service. Alison Palmer preached, and people from other churches turned up and heard her say that she had celebrated the Eucharist at our altar that morning. The Vicar of St John's rushed off and wrote ten sentences of condemnation, which he pinned to his door, and then telephoned the media.

There was a terrible hoo-ha. There was a lovely little cartoon in the *Guardian* of a bishop looking at a woman and saying, 'I shall have to unfrock you!' Ian Hooker and Alfred Willets both got rapped over the knuckles by the Archbishop of York. But we hadn't done anything illegal.

We had taken it through our PCC and we had even invited our bishop. (Ronald Bowlby had put his head in his hands and he said, 'I know why you're doing it. I sympathise with you. But I do wish you wouldn't.' But his parting shot as he went out of the door was, 'Ian won't lose his licence.' So we had gone ahead.)

Twelve years in ministry – but only the dog gets to wear the collar!

After the fuss, we wrote to all the bishops on General Synod and said, 'Here you are – if people are worried about what women priests will be like, here are the American women priests. Why don't you officially invite them so they can see?'

The response of the General Synod was to pass a resolution saying that women ordained abroad were *not* allowed to celebrate in Anglican churches.

Early in 1978 Jan Selby started the Newcastle Ordination of Women Group (NOW). We started witnessing outside cathedrals at ordinations – giving people cards saying that we rejoiced that these men were being ordained, but what about the women? We were very much aware that the bishops were all getting loads of letters on the 'anti' side, so they needed some on the 'pro' side. The PCC of St Thomas's wrote to our bishop saying, 'This PCC asks that Bernice be considered for ordination as a priest.'

In 1978 the General Synod clergy voted against the ordination of women. The House of Bishops and the House of Laity were for, but the clergy were against. I was there, in the gallery, sitting two away from Una Kroll and when the vote went down Una stood up and said, 'We asked for bread, and you gave us a stone.'

I had made a banner saying, 'Twelve years in the ministry, but only the dog gets the collar' and I took along my dog, Delilah, in a clerical dog-collar. The picture got into *The Times* and the *Church Times*.

All the time I was in the Newcastle area during the 1970s I was preaching and administering communion at St Thomas's. I was also doing extended communion – using the Reserved Sacrament that had been consecrated by the priest on Sunday – at weekday services. But I didn't see why people should be deprived of the words of consecration, which are biblical anyway, so I used to say the whole thing. On one occasion I lifted the lid of the ciborium and there was nothing inside, so I went outside and got some wafers and came back and went through it. A man came up afterwards, and I suspected he was a priest in mufti. I thought, 'Uh-uh, what's he going to say?'

He said, 'It's the first time I've been to a celebration by a woman – but you were quite right.'

But then there was a complaint. This must have been in 1980 and someone complained that I appeared to be actually celebrating. Ian and

I got hauled up in front of the bishop and the archdeacon. We said that I'd been doing it for so long that I didn't actually say every time now that this was the Reserved Sacrament. But it was an open, city-centre church, so all sorts of people came in, and we were told to make it clear.

By then I was coming up to nearly twenty years' association with the Newcastle Diocese, and I thought it was time for a move. Newcastle was less multicultural than the rest of England. Also my parents were getting older and needed me back south. So I landed a job in residential childcare management in Bristol.

I never got stopped by the police

At the end of 1980, I moved to Bristol. This was the year of disturbances in the multicultural, multiracial St Paul's district of Bristol. I obviously wanted to live in that area because of my political leanings, but you couldn't get a house for love nor money down in St Paul's. The Bristol agents weren't selling them. The racism was such that they didn't even want to look at houses in St Paul's. I bought one up the hill.

I went as assistant county organiser, covering the whole of children's residential establishments, which included Kingswood and secure accommodation for child murderers as well as normal children's homes.

I was there for eight years and I ended up as team manager of children in residential care for North Bristol. I was the peripatetic manager of the staff. So I was hiring and firing, but I was also chairing case conferences, and I did get to know the kids. There were occasions when we were dead short of staff through illness or whatever, when I went and did the odd night shift. That's usually the time when there are disturbances in some homes, and I can tell you, riots in children's homes are frightening. You are dealing with very screwed up children, and when you've got a whole gang, it's very difficult. There were more accidents to staff than there ever were to kids in my homes.

You are dealing with teenagers – and with teenagers whom you hadn't got to know, because kids come in and out of care homes – they've fallen out of their families and out of schools and they are very angry. Parents blow in and out of their lives, they pin their hopes on them and they get dashed, and they take it out on the person nearest to them.

There were some very good people working in these homes. It makes my blood boil when every care worker is labelled a paedophile or an abuser. Most of them gave their hearts and their homes to the kids in their care and did very valuable work. Out of staff of many hundreds, you could count on the fingers of one hand the ones who were abusers of some kind. It was part of my job to weed them out. We worked hard to do so. The police picked up anyone who we had suspicions about but no evidence. You had to be dead careful. What has changed now is that the evidence of children is taken into account, and they will suspend people on a child's say-so, whereas in my day we weren't able to. You had to have firm evidence, but that has shifted, as it needed to.

All these jobs ask more than the call of duty. You have to have faith that these kids can pull through. That's terribly important. You've got to have hope with some of these kids, because some of them are so terribly disturbed.

When I first arrived at Bristol, I went to see the bishop, John Tinsley, and said I was now working in senior management in social services – could I help as a lay worker in any of the parishes? I'd like to go to a place where there was great need. I got exactly the same reply as I'd had a decade earlier in Newcastle, 'Oh . . . just go and look around and see where you might go.'

So once again I looked around. A woman worker who had been in St Paul's moved out, and left a hole there. Keith Kimber, the Priest-in-Charge, said he'd be happy to have me. There were three churches in St Paul's. One was Anglo-Catholic, one was 'flat' evangelical but didn't want a woman worker, and the third was the evangelical 'wedding cake' church. St Paul's said they would prefer to have a woman than have nobody. Then a couple of years later the two evangelical churches, St Paul's and St Werburg's, were merged together with St Agnes', so I became part of the whole team whether the others liked it or not.

I went to Bristol in 1980 and was a non-stipendiary lay-worker there for eight years.

In 1985 I managed to move into a house in St Paul's. I had several tenants, including a black lad and an Ethiopian refugee, and they were always getting stopped by the police. But I never got stopped. Extraordinary! But if I stood waiting for a lift at my gate, I would be asked, 'Are you doing business, dear?'

In some ways the waiting time was good

We started our own MOW group in Bristol. We had regular meetings. We did witnessing at ordinations. John Tinsley, our bishop, was in favour of women priests. At St Paul's they were all strongly in favour, and they liked me because I lived there. We founded a group called 'Chloe's People', which was an acronym for Creative Happenings, Liturgy and Other Events. The 'other events' meant American women priests coming over and celebrating the Eucharist in houses and private gatherings. It spawned creative liturgy.

People nowadays go through their training and into parishes and get stuck in – whereas we had time to do some of this creative work. Time – which I don't have now. I can't do the sort of things we used to do then, because I'm caught up with all the work. When you're a parish priest, you don't have time. So yes, in some ways the waiting time was good. And having a goal and fighting for it is good fun.

I do not want to be made to feel angry when I start singing hymns

I'm very concerned about inclusive language, because I think that it depresses people if you use male language to include female people. In secular language, you do not hear a mixed-sex group of people talked about as 'men' on the radio and television. But in church you'll still hear it preached, and the church language has not caught up. And the hymns! There's a new version of *Ancient and Modern*, and in the introduction the revisers say, 'The Victorian ones we've left unchanged, because that's how they were written.' Well, of course they were written like that. But they shouldn't be like that now. *Hymns Old and New* has adapted the language and I use that where possible, because I do not want to be made to feel angry when I start singing hymns.

Since being priested I've said the Prayer Book service every week and it has grown on me. There's some good stuff there, and you can make it gender-inclusive without hurting the language. You don't have to say 'every man'; you can say 'everyone'.

So Bristol was a fertile area for me. There were a lot of supportive people.

I had been wondering for some time about becoming an ordained deaconess. Canon David Isitt led the School of Ministry that was ecumenical, and encouraged me to be ordained deaconess at an ecumenical ordination at which three URC people were ordained at the same time.

Not long after I was ordained the General Synod passed the vote in 1986 to allow women to become deacons – not priests, of course – and in 1987 we were ordained deacons. We had a change of bishop in Bristol, and Barry Rogers wanted to be quick off the mark, so our Ordination was 12 March 1987. He liked doing things first, although actually Canterbury did the first women deacons, and we were the third. But Bristol was to be first when it came to ordaining women priests.

Once the ordination of deacons went through, you could see that the ordination of priests was going to go forward. Eventually. I had found myself working with children because the first job I took was child psychiatry. I saw that as having a strong link with pastoral work, with priestly work. But it struck me now that if the ordination of women priests was going to be a reality, I ought to be in situ in stipendiary ministry. So I started looking for a paid church job.

Nice work!

I eventually landed one in Charlton, South London, which brought me to the Southwark Diocese in 1988 – where Ronnie Bowlby was bishop, who had been my bishop in Newcastle. Funnily enough, he wasn't very keen on my coming, because he thought that the Vicar of Charlton, Tony Crowe, and I were too similar. In fact it's probably one of the best team partnerships I've had, and good for a church to have clergy who are different but compatible. Tony had always had women working with him, and he always gives you equal status. We were a team. We shared everything and backed one another up. It was a lovely, old, working-class parish east of Greenwich, with St Luke's, a nice seventeenth-century, pre-Georgian church which was small and cosy, and had a friendly, supportive, politically aware community.

With Tony's backing I was put up for General Synod in 1990 and I got onto Bishop's Council immediately. We – MOW – were highly politicised by then. It was extremely important to get people of the right persuasion on, and the other side were busy getting their people on. Peter Selby said to me, 'Well, you come into the diocese in April, and get on the Bishop's Council in September . . . Nice work!'

I feel a bit robbed of the normal experience of jubilation

General Synod took the vote in November 1992. I didn't speak in the debate. I bobbed up and down, but wasn't called. When David Lunn, Bishop of Sheffield, spoke about his Celtic heritage in the north-east of England and people being deaf-adders to their history, I wanted to remind Synod that Celtic history had affirmed the position of women, that Hilda, the Abbess of Whitby, was head over men. The debate was run according to synodical practice with speakers carefully matched, and called alternately to speak for or against, so we heard proportionately more opposition speakers than the voting justified, but that meant they had a good run for their money.

I felt quite flat, when it happened. I just gave a sigh of relief. My head rejoiced in this historic decision of the church, but my heart could not celebrate. Outside it might have been different, because we could hear the great cheer and they were singing *Jubilate Deo*. But we were kept waiting for a long time, and then we were asked to receive the vote in silence. We didn't want to react jubilantly for the sake of the ones who didn't want it. Nobody reacted very strongly. I think everyone was a bit stunned. One or two people in the gallery wept. But I actually felt, 'So what?' It has happened. It ought to have happened anyway. I think in a way I feel a bit robbed of the experience of jubilation.

In voting to ordain women as priests, the Church of England had taken one more step forward on the road of faith that believes that all human beings are made by God to work for justice, harmony and peace. There are, of course, many more steps still to take.

I have a few people who are on the edge of life

Since then – well, the gilt has rather worn off the gingerbread, I have to say. After all these years of supporting men in their ministry, of being a team vicar in all but name, because of decreasing numbers, now, for the first time in my life I have had no clergy colleagues. I was ordained priest in Southwark in 1994. In 1995 I was made an honorary Canon of Southwark Cathedral, and Vicar of Holy Trinity, Tooting. In 1996 I was made Rural Dean of Tooting, and that's where I am now, in a better-off parish than I'm used to, but with plenty of problems of its own.

One of the things that I liked when I first came to Holy Trinity is that on principle we keep our doors open. We have a loo in the porch, for the use of the community. Although we have had a few members of the congregation complain that they make it dirty, the church is there and it's open, and it's an asylum and a resting-place.

When people come to the door, as they do at most vicarages, I don't actually give them money but I always aim to give people food if they need it. There is quite a motley group who come here. I have a few coming who are on the edge of life, and on the edge of legal life sometimes. At Christmas, I keep an open house, as I've done nearly every Christmas since my days with the Franciscans.

Once a Franciscan . . .

I share my home. I suppose it goes back to my Franciscan roots, because there we had people living with us with all sorts of conditions and problems. Fairly soon after I'd arrived in Bristol in 1980 the Lodgings Officer where I worked said, 'We've got a lad working with us who has had cerebral palsy and he needs somewhere to live.' So Barry came to live with me. He stayed with me for nearly three years, and got married from my house. In addition I took on several children out of care in my years at St Paul's.

A couple of years later, the same Lodgings Officer said they had someone who had spent five years in a mental hospital, then a year in a hostel. The law had recently changed on what hostels had to provide for the ex-mentally ill, which meant they had to have far more facilities than they did have. So she needed a new home. The only problem was she had a cat. I said that was all right providing her cat could get on with my cat and the dog. So Ann came in 1983 and is still with me, and the cat died only last year.

Supportive living

I realised that what I was doing was 'supportive living' – enabling people who wanted to live on their own, but may not have been quite ready. I was providing an interim place where they could learn the skills of living on their own. I don't cook for them, I don't clean their rooms, but we interact together. We share the kitchen, washing machine and fridge, and the television sometimes.

So Andy, who was a kid out of care, would sit and drum away at the table and we'd have lots of conversations while he was heating up his baked beans. Since Ann is disabled I have made her a kitchen on the landing upstairs. I got her a Baby Belling oven with two rings, a microwave and a fridge-freezer. She comes downstairs to use the dish-washer and washing machine, but because she's grown increasingly disabled it means she doesn't have to come up and down to cook and carry trays and things.

And it works on two levels. Kids out of care are institutionalised; it's company, for them and for me. Second, they observe how to live and how to manage. I might not be quite a normal housewife, but at least I can cook and I have a way of living that works for an individual. And they can quiz me and ask questions and so learn. Most of them will say that they did learn ways of coping and managing from watching me, talking to me, and discussing things. They also help me; one young man, who needed support for a time, was my computer consultant and also built me a conservatory.

It's very much a Franciscan vocation. And it's about living the gospel, I hope. The Franciscans have always been people who will look out for the outcasts of society. Today's social outcasts are the sex offenders. We've had a lot of trouble locally in Tooting, because of a hostel for ex-offenders that's coming here, and it's unfortunately now a political hot potato. The sentence really starts for ex-sex offenders when they come out of prison and have to face a hostile community.

In our diocese, we have produced a document on what churches should do when ex-sex offenders return to their community. A much higher proportion of ex-sex offenders than other ex-convicts seems to want to have some church connection. The Wolvercote Clinic runs a high-powered treatment programme for ex-sex offenders who chose to go on it.

The probation officer who runs that programme came to talk to us. He didn't mince matters and said that, of course, people can be devious and manipulative, but there's a wide range of sex offending from incest to single incidents of abuse to paedophilia. One problem is that anything with 'paed' in the name nowadays gets demonised . . . including paedia-trician! Thankfully there are far fewer real paedophiles around than the *News of the World* would have you believe.

You can't do everything

We were made aware that one of the hardest problems for people coming out of prison is accommodation. When the probation officer from Wolvercote Clinic came to talk to us, I spoke in the group about the way I've shared my house with different kinds of people. Then I wrote and said I'd be prepared to house an ex-sex offender – and I try to always use that term – an *ex-sex* offender. I said to them that it may sound funny but my only conditions were 1) a non-smoker, and 2) likes dogs. If they don't like dogs they won't be happy here, and none of us smoke in the house so we wouldn't be happy if they did.

So Tom (not his real name) has come to live in my vicarage. I think he had a horrible, dreadful experience in prison, and he just doesn't want to go back, so he wouldn't put himself at any risk.

I have three lodgers at the moment, but they each have quite different problems. One is disabled, one is an ex-offender and one an employed pensioner. We're not a family. I have a full-time job; they've got to learn to live on their own. We sometimes pass like ships in the night and we have to leave each other notes. But we're around for each other if needed. For instance, Tom is tall, so he's very good and helpful for putting things on top shelves and getting things down – but I don't impose.

I'm not good at organising space for myself. I take advantage if other people organise things. When I was going to India for a sabbatical, I talked to them about going away. Two of them agreed they would organise to give the dogs their breakfast and tea, while someone else walked them.

At church, they all know I share my house with all sorts and conditions. But I've got to be careful. I've got to walk this tightrope, because if I say too much about it, I wouldn't be able to do it. Some people would start to make objections. I worry and feel guilty sometimes that I'm not doing the spiritual things enough. But I've tried to stop that, stop feeling guilty, because I think trying to live the gospel is enough. I hope so. You can't do everything.

REVD VALERIE BONHAM

5

From 'WAOW' to 'MOW'

REVD VALERIE BONHAM

Curate, Holy Trinity, Cookham

The process by which I passed from being a vehement opposer of women's ordination to becoming a priest has been a mixture of devastation, liberation and homecoming.

Introduction

LB: Being met at Maidenhead railway station by Valerie, with her husband Fred at the wheel of their family car, was one of those comforting, reassuring receptions that only a couple from a long-standing and secure marriage can give. You couldn't possibly guess from Fred's calm, friendly manner, or even from Valerie's more animated, talkative welcome, the sheer amount of trauma and distress they have both experienced over the past decade. And yet, of all the people Andrew and I have met in the course of preparing this book, I believe that these two have suffered the most on the Church of England's journey to women's ordination.

This is the story of Valerie's change of heart, from vehemently opposing women's ordination, to hearing the call to priesthood herself. But it is also about Fred. When two people have known one another all their lives, and been of one mind for most of that time on something about which they care passionately, it can be heartbreaking when one of them has a radical change of view.

At the end of my visit, they took me to see the church where Valerie is presently curate. To walk through the graveyard of Holy Trinity Church in the Berkshire village of Cookham is vaguely unsettling, even in the company of such down-to-earth people as Valerie and Fred. It is to walk through the setting of what has been described as 'the most important picture painted by an English artist in the twentieth century', Stanley Spencer's 'Resurrection, Cookham.' Spencer himself was once a familiar sight, wheeling an old pram full of paint brushes and pots in this same churchyard, where he depicted friends and neighbours climbing cheerfully out as their graves burst open on the

Last Day. Older people in Cookham still remember very recognisable charac-
ters so vividly painted by the village's most famous but eccentric inhabitant,
who also included himself in the picture, and a loving Christ cradling two
babies.

Spencer wanted not only to depict the Last Day but the whole experience of
resurrection, of a moment of overwhelming love and contentment, which could
happen to anyone at anytime.

And this is a story of another resurrection. When in 1992 Valerie, like Fred a
lifelong Anglo-Catholic, changed from opposing to accepting the ordination of
women in the Church of England, she knew she was making a decision that
would not only turn her own life upside down but also profoundly disturb and
hurt Fred.

'Fred had said to me before I went off to Synod, "You must do whatever you
think is best. If that means you have got to go through the 'Yes' door then you
have got to do it. You have got to act according to your conscience." But knowing
how hurt he would be, I just couldn't do it . . . it was a risk too far.'

After the 1992 General Synod vote to ordain women, Valerie, who had
abstained – rather than vote 'No' against her own conscience, or 'Yes' that would
hurt and disenfranchise Fred – received hate mail from people she had once
thought of as her friends.

'Somebody came up to me and said, "Well, I hope you are pleased with
yourself now. You've just unchurched Fred. You have just undone all his
ministry." '

Valerie and Fred have managed to survive almost a decade of pain and crisis,
and have triumphantly coped with one of the most curious consequences of the Act
of Synod – the two 'integrities'.

As an Anglo-Catholic, Valerie is likely throughout her ministry to have
the challenge of working in parishes not altogether convinced of the rightness
of women's ordination. Archdeacon Judith Rose told us, 'If they have a good
experience of a woman priest, that will sway a lot of people. If they have a
bad experience, then it will re-entrench their conviction that women should
not be priests. The unfair thing is, if they have a bad experience with a man,
people say, "Well, we must get a good one next time." But if it's with a woman,
we're still at the stage when they will say, "Well, we don't ever want another
woman." '

If Stanley Spencer had lived to see women ordained as priests, I hope he would
have included the Curate of Holy Trinity and her husband Fred in his painting
expressing that resurrection, a harmonious end to a long and often painful journey
through life that they have shared so far.

Valerie

Wing

I was born in 1947, an only child, in a village called Wing – not far from Aylesbury, in Buckinghamshire – where my mother, Stella May, lived all her life except for the last eighteen months when she came to live with us after my father died. My father, Horace Dean, was in the Post Office all his working life. He started off as a messenger boy delivering telegrams at fourteen, and ended up as an Inspector at the age of sixty when he retired.

My father's family was Baptist and Salvation Army – and my first experience of Sunday school was at the Congregational chapel just across the road from our home. That wasn't a happy experience at all. In fact, it was boring and I hated it! We moved to another house in the same village when I was six, so I stopped going.

My parents at that time were not regular churchgoers. My mother had been brought up in the Church of England, but neither of my parents was confirmed until quite late in life. They both died firm church members, but during my formative years in childhood and adolescence, they weren't regular churchgoers. However, they didn't ever try to stop me from going to church, and in fact my father was quite upset when I didn't want to go to Sunday school any more.

Fred

Fred and I grew up in the same village. He is ten years older than me, and had just returned from doing his national service in the RAF when I was about twelve. He was a layman then, but was very involved with the parish church, and was the churchwarden. At that time I was having a brief sojourn with the Church of England Sunday school. This was because I had a friend who wanted to go, but she didn't want to go on her own. So I went along with her, and I liked it, but she soon stopped going. I liked it . . . and I will come absolutely clean and say that Fred became my Sunday-school teacher.

There were one or two other older ones at Sunday school as well as me. The average age of the children in Sunday schools then was older than today – it wasn't a Mums and Toddlers sort of thing that you have now during the service, and the children come in at the Communion for a blessing. This was Sunday school in the old-fashioned sense, at three o'clock in the afternoon. It was a completely separate thing from the rest of church worship, and that was how people slipped out of it all, because you'd leave Sunday school, but there was no incentive to go to the main church services. And this was what happened with me. I stopped going to Sunday school when I was about fourteen, because I was beginning to feel embarrassed that I was too old, but I didn't go to church. Then, about eighteen months later, I met Fred in the village one day and he said the thing that everyone says you should never say – but it worked in this case:'Haven't seen you in church recently!'

I said,'I'd like to come to church – but I'm a bit nervous about going in on my own.'

He said,'Well, I'm there and so is . . .' and he reeled off a list of names of people I knew in the village. He said,'We'll all be there tomorrow' or whenever it was.

So I said,'Well, all right then, perhaps I will.' So I did – and I've never stopped going since.

Vocations

I was confirmed aged sixteen on 4 December 1963. I remember going into church on my way home from school on my confirmation day, and being tremendously aware of a sense of 'calling', and of offering my life to God. Ordination, of course, was not on the agenda in 1963.

In1964 Fred left the village to test his vocation as a monk. For the next five years he was at Nashdom Abbey at Burnham. Quite a lot of people in the village couldn't understand it. They would say,'Why does he want to go shutting himself away in a monastery?' They had no idea about the life of prayer, that in fact it's not an escape from the world at all – the world is there in microcosm. My parents and I, along with other people from the church, kept in touch with him while he was there, and we used to go and visit him.

I am not the reason why Fred left the monastery. Some people thought that, but that was not at all the thing. He tried his vocation as a monk but didn't make his life vows, and discovered while he was there that he wasn't being called to the monastic life, but that he was being called to the priesthood. But this was later.

Walsingham – one of my anchor holds

Fred's mother came from the village next to Walsingham, in Norfolk, and he had become very attached to the Anglican Shrine of Our Lady of Walsingham. Before he left for Nashdom he wanted to get a group of people from Wing and a neighbouring parish to go to Walsingham on pilgrimage. He hoped at least a minibus full would go, but it just didn't happen. In the end just a few of us went by car. This was in May 1964.

I knew at the end of that weekend that I had to go back, but it was a year later, in June 1965, before I did go back. My parents took me up there in the car, and I think this was one of the things that helped them discover that they too wanted to start going to church. They took a great liking to Walsingham. Fred was at Nashdom by then, and I had written to him and said I was going back. He was very pleased about that.

I was new to the church then, and Walsingham was fascinating to me because it gave me a taste of a part of the church that I hadn't really experienced before. Wing Church was a bit higher than middle of the road. Our vicar had a daily Mass and sometimes he would have incense at the main parish Mass, but it was still all from the Book of Common Prayer at that time. Walsingham gave me a whole new insight into Anglo-Catholic worship. There's a wonderful atmosphere of prayer at Walsingham. It's one of my anchor holds.

Friendship turned into love

After school, I went to the College of Librarianship in Aberystwyth. It was supposed to be the best place, in the days before librarianship became a graduate profession. While I was still at college, aged twenty, I considered joining a religious community. Fred and I have this thing in common: a leaning towards religious communities. But somehow it didn't feel right, although at the time I was unsure why.

I remember sitting in the shrine church at Walsingham trying to make a decision, and thinking that if I had been a man, I would have been a priest. (I didn't then know anything about selection processes.) I don't think I wished I was male so that I could be a priest (although subconsciously I might have, I suppose), nor did I wish I could be an ordained woman, because one didn't think in that way at that time. I just accepted the fact that because I was a woman, God must have some other calling for me. I think now that that was the first stirring of what eventually became my vocation to ordained ministry, even though I did not recognise it as such at the time.

Fred came out of Nashdom in October 1969, having decided that he was not called to be a monk, but to the priesthood. I was in my final year at the college. I finished at Aberystwyth in December 1969, and went to work at Slough Library and moved into a flat in Windsor.

Fred and I had always remained friends and kept in touch. By the middle of 1970 he was working in a parish in north London. He was in the time of waiting for selection for ordination, and his bishop had sent him there to see how he would fit into parish work. It was a church that certainly would not approve of me being a priest now. He was there for a few months and he used to come out to see me at Windsor on his day off. And, well, friendship turned into love.

A person in my own right

Fred was ordained in September 1972, and we had married in April that year. Although we were both glad about one another's Christian commitment, Fred's priestly vocation was certainly not why I married him. I wasn't looking for surrogate ordination. I have always tried to support his ministry, while remaining a person in my own right. I evolved my own lay ministry within the parishes in which we served, and became a writer specialising in Victorian church history. Later, when we moved to Windsor in 1975, I wrote the history of our church there, and this led to writing a three-volume history for the Community of St John Baptist, Clewer.

Although I had not opted for the life of a religious, over the years religious communities have become part of the fabric of my life. I was received as an associate of the Society of St Margaret in May 1973, in the Sisters' chapel at Walsingham. This is an affiliation of prayer, and giving support in any way that one can. The society has several houses, notably St Saviour's Priory, Haggerston in East London, which has been another anchor hold for me.

Vehemently opposed to the ordination of women

When Fred was ordained, women's ordination was not an issue in this country, though it was in the United States, and we had hardly heard about it. Certainly no one told Fred during his training that this might be on the church's agenda within the next few years. The first serious discussion in my own personal experience was at a women's group meeting in the church where Fred was curate, around 1975, the year that General Synod declared that there were no *theological* objections to women being priests.

I became vehemently opposed to the idea, mainly because I believed it was part of the secular feminist movement being imported from America. In the late 1970s and early 1980s that was the image many of us had of it. But even then I can remember thinking, 'What if this is of God? Supposing the Holy Spirit has inspired this?' But it seemed too secular, too aggressive, and it seemed right to be cautious before accepting such a radical change to 2,000 years of tradition.

WAOW

In the early 1980s I began to write articles and letters to the press and to make strong campaigning speeches against women's ordination. It became a crusade. But one thing that angered me at that time was that the clergy who opposed women priests were saying that the women of the church did not want women to be ordained. I did not need the men to speak for me – I was perfectly capable of speaking for myself. Other women must have felt the same way, because Women Against the Ordination of Women (WAOW) got going in the mid-1980s, and I was soon at the forefront. I also joined the Church Union, and served on several committees at national and diocesan levels. (From 1990–2 I served on the Executive Committee of the Catholic Group in General Synod.)

'Never' is a big word – when you have to eat it

In the media representations (and that's all that there was to begin with because there weren't any women priests or deacons in this country), it all seemed to come across as quite militant, and as part of 'women's lib'. It was the militancy that jarred. But in turn, on the opposition, I got militant. And militancy does jar. There's a very narrow dividing line between passion and militancy – and you can cross it very easily without realising it. I think that's what happened with me.

It's not that I thought the women's liberation movement was wrong. I'm not saying that at all. But I believed that to change something in the church after 2,000 years should happen only if inspired by God, rather than for the sake of equal opportunities and justice – right though equal opportunities and justice might be!

In 1985 I was persuaded to stand for General Synod. I can remember standing up in the hustings and saying – and I'm afraid I may even have thumped the table when I said it – 'I will *never* accept the ministry of a woman priest!'

I have since learned never to say 'never'. 'Never' is a big word – when you have to eat it.

I do not like the memory of how I was then

I wasn't elected onto General Synod in 1985, but I continued in the front line of the opposition. I do not like the memory of how I was then, because I was so uncaring about the effect of what I said and wrote.

At first I was an 'impossible-ist'. Impossible-ists are those who say it is *impossible* for women to be priests – because of our biological, ontological and psychological make-up and for all sorts of other philosophical reasons. One of the leading proponents of that argument was Graham Leonard, at that time Bishop of London. He was the bishop who ordained Fred, and he was 'our' bishop for the first three years, because we lived in his episcopacy. For that reason we found ourselves giving him hospitality at different times, and we got to know him quite well. I was – and I remain – very fond of him.

But 'impossible' – that was his particular line – and it was a line that I followed for a time, but not blindly. The more I prayed about it and thought it through, the more I came to think that this was unacceptable.

After 1987 women were able to become deacons, and at first I opposed them. Then at a Church Union conference, I heard a lecture about deacons in the early church, and several of us who were present changed our minds. I wrote about it in our parish magazine, and was challenged by a parishioner. I was devastated by the things she said to me, and I realised then how hurtful my own articles and speeches must have been to MOW people. From then on I tried to moderate my approach.

1990 Reading

Fred and I were at Windsor for fifteen years from 1975 to 1990, when we moved to a parish in Reading. It was to be a significant move, and a significant year, for both of us.

One of the arguments that had always irritated me was that women felt second-class in the church. I had never felt second class, and during our fifteen happy years in Windsor I don't believe anyone in the team that Fred and I built up together felt undervalued because of their gender. But when we got to Reading, we were both absolutely shocked, because here was a male-dominated church where women were clearly despised – and that is not too strong a word.

This is not to say that women did not hold any offices there; there had been a woman churchwarden and there was a female presence on the PCC – but they were tolerated, not valued. Our time in Reading, which was not a happy one, was important because it played a part in the process of changing my position about the ordination of women. Not out of anger or bitterness, as some people later alleged, but because it was necessary for me to experience at first hand how the church has treated women. It was not a lesson I was going to learn at our church in Windsor. Reading made me take another look at the motives of some of the male opposers to the ordination of women, and to see that many of them were motivated by misogyny, not theology. I also came to see that many of them used women like myself to fight the battle for them. The awful thing was that we did not see how they were manipulating us.

The deanery debates

In March or April 1990, just before Fred and I arrived at Reading, the Oxford Diocese asked me to join one of two teams of speakers travelling around the diocese to examine the legislation for the ordination of women, and to brief the deaneries.

By then I was no longer an 'impossible-ist', and Fred and I had both accepted the principle of the ordination of women deacons, but I was still opposed to the principle of women priests, and in particular the wording of the proposed legislation that we were being asked to consider. I embarked on the programme of deanery debates as if it was a crusade.

But my position had actually moderated quite considerably by then. I have got scripts from those deanery debates. I always said, 'If the day comes when I begin to believe that God is in this, then I will have to accept it under obedience.' This was quite a change from the hustings for the 1985 General Synod when I was saying, 'I will *never* accept the ministry of a woman priest.'

Quite a mixed audience had come along – to hurl abuse at all of us

In the same way that I was not an 'impossible-ist', I could not go along with the Evangelicals, who take the headship line – Christ is the Head, then come the men, who are head over the women and children. I remember doing one deanery debate with a priest who is now a bishop in the Church of England, an Evangelical, and I had to consult with him as to what our line of opposition argument would be. I said to him, 'I'm sorry, but I can't go along with the headship line.'

He said, 'Well, that is my line.'

I said, 'Well, I'll take all the other things – and you do headship!'

There were four of us, two in favour, two against. By this time I was speaking outside Oxford Diocese as well as within it. This was in the Chelmsford Diocese and quite a mixed audience had come along to hurl abuse – at all of us! It was funny, looking back, because it ended up with the four of us joining ranks to defend each other against the audience!

General Synod 1990

I had decided to stand again for General Synod in 1990 and this time I was elected. I believed that the decision about women priests should be taken by the whole church – certainly the whole Western church – which meant waiting until the Roman Catholic Church felt ready to take this step. I was also very worried about the potential divisiveness of the legislation that was before the General Synod, because of the provisions for parishes to 'opt out' of having a woman priest.

At the Inaugural Eucharist in Westminster Abbey, I first met Susan Cole-King. Susan had been ordained to the priesthood in America, but was working as a deacon in the Oxford Diocese. Both of us had been interviewed on breakfast television after our election to Synod, and we had both been badly misrepresented. We had been filmed separately, and a voice-over commentary had distorted both of our viewpoints. I'm not trying to have a sideways swipe at the media, but Susan was quite upset about it and so was I.

The one redeeming feature about this episode was that my father, who was dying of cancer, saw it when he was in Stoke Mandeville Hospital. They had television on in the ward all day long. Usually it was blaring out, but this time the sound was down and he suddenly saw me, and he said to the nurses, 'Stop! Stop! There's my daughter! There's my daughter!' I went in to see him later that day and he told me how pleased he was. He died a few days later, in October 1990.

My father could never understand why I thought women couldn't be priests. He kept saying to me, 'Valerie, I can't see it. I can't understand it.' I'd go all through this great theological argument with him, and at the end of it he'd say, 'Well, that's all very well – but I still can't understand it!'

That first day of General Synod was the first time I had met Susan

Cole-King face-to-face. She approached me in the abbey cloister and, with hand extended, said, 'Valerie, we meet at last.' We exchanged small talk about the breakfast television programme. Then we processed into the abbey and were all told where to sit. She and I had to sit next to each other, and I was bristling with indignation, but as the Eucharist progressed I suddenly realised that I did not want to end up out of Communion with her because of our differing viewpoints. We became very great friends, and during the next eighteen months had many conversations, lifting the issue out of theory and onto a human level.

Women just like myself – wanting to serve God

The point of the deanery debates was to examine the legislation, but of course everyone went on to arguing about the principle. And when they started going all through the reasons why women should be ordained, our side had to give the arguments about why women should *not* be ordained.

These debates had a profound effect upon me, because for the first time I was actually meeting, on a one-to-one basis, my opposite numbers, rather than seeing television programmes or reading biased press reports. Often we met beforehand, shared a meal and prayed together and got to know one other. Some were women deacons, others were laity, and some were male clergy, but it was the women deacons who most impressed me. I found them to be women just like myself, seeking to love and serve God in whatever way God wanted. I found it increasingly difficult to deny the possibility that God was calling them to priesthood.

I think what I saw was holiness, the presence of Christ in these women. It was such a contrast with the absence of Christian love in many of the people at our church, and with whom I had been working on the opposition campaign. I became friends with most of the people with whom I was debating, in spite of the still vociferous nature of my opposition, and those friendships have lasted. In the end it was these friendships and the experience in the deaneries which influenced my change of heart more than any of the arguments I heard at General Synod.

The last thing I wanted to do was to oppose God

I began to have doubts about my own arguments, and as the months passed I felt increasingly challenged. Some of the doubts that assailed me at this time were: 'It is God's church, so who am I to say God cannot allow women to be priests? Am I denying the Holy Spirit's role of recreating and renewing the church? If a woman could carry Christ in her womb, why could she not preside at the Eucharist?'

I had begun to read the Gospels with an eye to Jesus' attitude towards women (although at first this was so that I could say he had had this very enlightened approach, yet still he did not choose a woman apostle). Yet I began to feel increasingly challenged by what I read there. Maybe having women apostles wasn't such a big deal after all! It was to a woman (at Jacob's Well in Samaria) that he revealed his Messiahship, and to another that he commissioned the news of the resurrection. In St John's Gospel the great declaration of Jesus' Messiahship is made not by Peter, but by Martha. Mary and other women were present at Pentecost and received the Holy Spirit, and in his letters, St Paul lists a whole host of women who clearly held leadership roles in the early church. So gradually I was beginning to feel that I could not oppose the principle of ordaining women. The last thing I wanted to do was to oppose God.

Damascus road

Even after I realised I had changed my mind, I was still struggling with the whole thing. Wrestling with it. On the one hand I had decided that I agreed in principle with ordaining women, but on the other hand, the legislation before us was so potentially divisive that I felt I still had to oppose it.

In July 1991 at General Synod, Susan and I were having coffee together when she suddenly said, 'Valerie, I cannot deny my priesthood any more than you can your baptism.' In that moment I knew that I wanted to affirm her priesthood, but I dared not because I had not worked through the implications. I had to walk away from her without saying anything, and that in itself felt like a denial.

I agonised about it all summer and then in September 1991, I went for a weekend retreat at St Saviour's Priory, Haggerston, East London. Sister Helen, who is now a great friend of mine, had just begun her ordination training as a deacon, and there was a tremendous atmosphere of excitement there that weekend. Even though I was on retreat, I picked up on the vibes.

I went into the chapel to pray for her. As I knelt there, picturing her in my mind in prayer, I became aware of two people in the picture, and realised that the other one . . . was me. After several minutes of arguing with God about it, I understood that God was calling me, too. It was a Damascus road experience.

I realised it would turn my whole life inside out

I had to make sure that I wasn't just being caught up in the euphoria of being at that community at that time of excitement. I thought, 'If this is real, then it is going to be there when I go home.' And it was.

I remember feeling quite calm and at peace about it, as though a lot of things had suddenly fallen into place. I decided against sharing it with anyone for the time being. If it were an illusion, it would go away. If it was real it would not. It did not go away, and became a strong, affirmed conviction as time passed.

After the initial period of calm, the devastating implications dawned. I realised it would turn my whole life inside out. As indeed it has. But always at the centre, even in the middle of the worst times, there was a sense of deep peace and inner calm, and it has never left me.

I kept it to myself for three months. Then I told Fred; it was something that I dreaded doing. Fred strongly opposed the ordination of women, although he had never been an active campaigner. I knew he would be hurt, but in fact he was very supportive and from the outset he said he could and would affirm me as a deacon, which is as far as I could envisage going then. I think, though, that Fred was more upset that he admitted to me.

I went to see Susan Cole-King, who counselled me to wait and pray until after the vote before taking any action.

A spiritual minefield

The whole of 1992 became a spiritual minefield for me as I wrestled with my position in the opposition front ranks and my growing conviction that God was calling the church to ordain women. The crunch came in February 1992. I was giving a talk at Jesus College, Oxford, to a lunch-time meeting of students, and I found myself looking at my notes and thinking, 'I don't believe a word I'm saying.' I just put my folder down and said, 'There is, on the one hand, this argument, and on the other, this argument.' I got through it like this, being completely even-handed. At the end I said, 'You've heard from me. Now you need to hear from someone from the Movement for the Ordination of Women, so that you will have heard the two sides of the argument.'

Then I went home and said, 'Right, I'm not going to do any more.'

I felt increasingly as if I was living a lie. At the same time the situation at our church in Reading had grown much worse, and there was now a campaign to oust us. We could not leave then, much as we wanted to, because our daughter was midway through her GCSEs. From May to July 1992 I was ill with stress, and developed sinus and glandular infections that would not go away, but I think may have saved me from a worse breakdown.

'Has Valerie gone soft on the issue?'

I managed to get to York for the July General Synod, where we were having the penultimate vote on the legislation. I was still feeling terrible. We voted by the three separate Houses – Bishops, Clergy and Laity – and needed only a simple majority in each, and this was obtained. But in the House of Laity, to which I belonged, it would not have achieved a two-thirds majority had it been required. This gave the opposition a great boost, because at the next vote, in November, the motion would need to get a two-thirds majority in all the houses to succeed. They weren't openly rejoicing, but there was a great sense of subdued joy. They believed that this was how it would be in November. As long as nobody changed their minds, it was in the bag for the 'No' vote.

In spite of everything, that July I, too, voted against the motion. I was still very unhappy about the wording of the legislation and apart from that, I was feeling too ill to cope with all the flack I would get if people saw me vote 'Yes'. I made sure they saw me go through the 'No' door. But while they were rejoicing, I became severely depressed after the result was declared, and the opposition people saw this and became suspicious about me. They were saying, 'Has Valerie gone soft on the issue?'

I know I acted as if I hadn't done all that deep soul-searching, but I think that I needed to go through the 'No' door that day, to realise that I couldn't do it again. The feeling of depression afterwards was terrible. I felt that I had betrayed what I now believed in, and yet so many people were expecting me to do what they had always seen me do, and I would soon be betraying them.

I was in the front line of the opposition. This was why people perceived my change of heart as such a betrayal. It was dreadful, because I knew I was letting those people down. This was the dilemma. I felt I was living a lie, and that's an awful thing to be doing. And, of course, there was Fred, a traditional Anglo-Catholic, who I knew would feel that he could not remain in a Church of England that ordained women priests. I would be supporting something that hurt him.

MOW had a vigil that day in July, and I so wanted to join them. The women were praying and singing Taizé chants on the other side of the lake at York University, where General Synod meets. So it would have been symbolic to have to 'walk across water' to join them, but I just hadn't quite got the courage. One of my MOW friends – Rosemary Tucker, whom I had met during the 1990 Synod hustings and the deanery debates – had come to the vigil, and she 'walked over the water' and found me. She didn't know about my dilemma, although I told her shortly before the November vote.

Going public
So we entered the final stage, and in September a few Synod members joined Susan Cole-King and myself for a three-day retreat to prepare for the vote. Susan and I felt very strongly that people from both sides of the argument should meet and pray together on retreat before the vote. Very few joined us, but it was a valuable time of prayer and quietness. Later, when I went public about my change of stance, people inevitably blamed

Susan, because they knew of our friendship, but she had never tried to manipulate me or influence my decision.

As October dawned, rumours were going round that I was changing sides, and I knew that I would have to make some sort of statement to my Church Union members before the vote. About three weeks before the vote, someone wrote and asked me to state my position. I then resigned from all my offices, but refused to be drawn on how I would vote. I said that I could no longer oppose the principle of ordaining women as priests, but that I was still in a great turmoil about the terms of the legislation, because it was so potentially divisive. I didn't know what I was going to do about the vote, and would they please pray for me. I think that at first I wrote that I would probably still vote against the motion. Later I said I really didn't know what I was going to do, but please pray for me.

The whole idea of abstention seemed cowardly

A male layman friend of mine wrote and asked if I would abstain. I replied, 'I really don't think that I can abstain because that to me seems so cowardly.'

I was now being torn in two. I felt that I could not vote against those women whose vocations I now believed in; but neither could I vote for something that would result in Fred having to leave the Church of England. I also had to consider my loyalty to those people who had put me onto Synod believing I would vote against the Measure. I didn't think about my own vocation at that time, because I hadn't discerned it as a call to the priesthood, only to the diaconate.

The day before the vote was a normal day of Synod business, but the press was everywhere – in the corridors, in the tea room, in the gallery – and it was a very fraught and stressful day. I was being named in the national press as a 'waverer'. All the opposition people who had been so jubilant in July were now very worried, because a number of us had changed viewpoints since then. If we all voted in favour, the vote would go through.

I was pretty sure I would abstain. My area bishop had advised me it would be an honourable thing to do, because of Fred. But the whole idea of abstention seemed cowardly. I loathed the idea. It wasn't what I was there for. That evening, 10 November, there was a vigil of prayer in Westminster Abbey, and a lot of people went, but the Catholic Group members were conspicuous by their absence.

Earlier in the day several Catholic Group people had cornered me, trying to persuade me to vote against. They said, 'You can still affirm the principle, and vote against the Measure.' It was deeply insulting stuff, but a sign of their desperation, I suppose. I felt more manipulated by that than by the 200 or so letters that I (as well as every Synod member) had received in the previous few weeks. Most of those letters were asking for a 'Yes' vote, many from parishes with a woman deacon.

I knew what I wanted to do – and could not

So 11 November dawned, cold and damp. I went to the Eucharist in the abbey. As I walked through Dean's Yard it was crowded with people, and I went past them as fast as I could.

Susan and I sat together for the debate. All day long we stood to speak, but neither of us were called.

Then came the call to close the debate, and everyone prepared to go through the doors. Next came the fatally prophetic word from the platform: 'Divide' which is said before every vote through the voting doors. That's what we did, we literally divided, and that was an awful thing. So everyone left to do what they had to do, and I was left alone. Some of those who had to walk away from me to vote against the Measure walked away from me for good. Others remain friends.

All through the opposition campaign I had been a powerful writer and speaker, and I know some people changed their minds through hearing me speak. And now, sitting in the assembly hall was an experience of complete powerlessness. I learned a lesson in those few minutes that I have taken into ordained ministry – that ministry is about service, not power. And that power is transitory and can be lost as easily as a two-thirds majority.

There were four lay abstentions, but the other three had the presence of mind to move back near the doors. I was too distressed to think about it, and consequently the television cameras showed me sitting there. I just sat there alone and wept, unaware of being filmed. I wanted to vote 'Yes' – and I felt powerless to do so. I knew what I wanted to do, but could not. I am not someone who cries easily but it just happened; and then five minutes later they were all coming back and the result was declared.

'My God – it's by one vote!'

There was a second bad moment when the vote was declared. A lot of people had done the maths, and they knew what was required. I am no good at that sort of thing, so when they gave out the figures I still didn't know if it had gone through or not. Then the person in front of me said, 'My God! It's by one vote!' Susan Cole-King, who was next to me, said, 'Don't say that, for goodness sake.' All this was going on when we were supposed to be receiving the result in silence! I was in a dreadful state of shock – one vote, and I had abstained. It turned out that it was actually a margin of two votes, which made an enormous psychological difference to me.

There was still more business, more voting to be done, about the legislation. There were five votes altogether, but the other four only required a simple majority, so I felt I could vote on those. I set off with the others through the doors, and then, of course, I came face-to-face with various people who began to spit venom at me. Somebody said, 'Well, I hope you are pleased with yourself now. You've just unchurched Fred.'

Fred

As soon as it was all over I went and telephoned Fred. He had been at church most of the day, praying for God's will to be done. But he'd seen the result. He said, 'Well, it's gone through. I don't blame you for it.'

I said, 'I did abstain.' I felt a bit better after that.

Then I went and had a cup of tea and there was a great party going on outside in Dean's Yard. Quite a number of people in favour felt they couldn't face going out there. They said, 'I can't go out there and join in that, when there are people in here who are devastated.' So some went out the back door, the Great Smith Street entrance.

I left by Dean's Yard. I went out with a woman deacon, who took her collar off and we pushed through the crowd, the raucous party, and we walked on back up to the hotel and talked about these things that had happened on the way. It was like the road to Emmaus.

Coming home

Fred had said to me before I went off to Synod, 'You must do whatever you think is best. If that means you have got to go through the "yes" door then you have got to do it. You have got to act according to your conscience.' So it gave me freedom, but knowing how hurt he would be, I just couldn't do it . . . it was a risk too far.

Coming home afterwards, I was feeling inwardly glad that the vote had gone through, but I also knew Fred would be absolutely devastated. I knew he would be very unhappy, as he was, and for the first couple of weeks it was awful to see the effect that it had on him. He was really in turmoil. He didn't know what to do. His natural reaction was to resign on the spot. He wanted to go. I don't mean he wanted to leave me, but he wanted to go from the Church of England.

But of course it meant livelihood, home, stipend and we still had our daughter at school, and my mother had moved in with us a couple of months previously, so it wasn't just a case of the two of us. We had two other people who very much needed us.

We were still at Reading. It was not an easy time for either of us immediately afterwards. I'd made decisions that were painful to Fred. I had always tried to support his ministry, but I couldn't live a lie. We both tried very hard to see the positive side and to respect each other's integrity, and in the end we came to realise that we could still work together.

The odd thing is, I think one thing that helped as a healing process between us was the hate mail that began to arrive.

Hate mail

I got quite a bit of hate mail when people realised what I had done, not only from people I knew, but from people Fred knew, as well as from people who read about me in the newspapers. There was also a lot of very supportive mail. Not every letter that came through was hate mail, but when it did it was always very nasty. The fact that people who purported to be Christians could write in terms like that Fred found very shocking.

I was shocked by it because I was the object of it, but Fred was very upset about it and I think that made him rally to me.

The time has come

Somehow we managed to hang on in Reading until 1993, when our daughter had taken her final school examinations. Then we moved to Speen, as part of the Newbury team ministry. I couldn't do anything about ordination in our time in Reading because I couldn't work in that parish. They would never have had me, nor would I have wanted to work there.

I needed to get myself together after the vote, and work things through with Fred. So I waited until we moved to Newbury in August 1993. Very soon after that I felt, in view of my age and the length of training, that if I didn't do something now, it would be too late. I said to Fred, 'I think the time has come.'

He said, 'Fine, go ahead.' His view was that he had no right to stand in my way or prevent me from doing something that the Church of England had decided any woman could do.

I saw our team rector, who was supportive. I also spoke to the Abbot of Elmore (formerly the Nashdom Community) because the monks at Elmore worship in Speen Church on Sundays. I knew there were some in the community who were in favour of women priests and some who were not, and I didn't want to upset them. If they had thrown their hands up in horror, I would have gone to one of the other parishes in the team. But in fact, they were very supportive. The abbot said, 'All of us can support you to the diaconate.'

Then we took it to the PCC, and their immediate reaction was, 'Oh, but the brethren at Elmore wouldn't like it.'

I said, 'No, that has all been sorted.'

They said, 'Well, yes, then we can support you to the diaconate.'

But by then I knew that I was being called to the priesthood. I had come to understand that quite soon after the vote. I had always known it, but hadn't been able to face that prospect at first.

I said, 'I feel sure my call is to the priesthood, but I am prepared to remain as a deacon while Fred and I are here.'

In the natural order of things his five years would have expired at the end of my deacon's year, but I was still hoping that he would stay on and ask for an extension on his licence.

Fred's deacon at Speen

My mother had come to live with us after my father died. She stayed with us until she died. She had ovarian cancer. She had a brief time in hospital in May 1994, and they decided nothing could be done, and so she came home. We nursed her at home for ten days, with tremendous support from the district nurses and the Macmillan nurse.

I was all set to go for my ABM selection conference for ordination at the end of May 1994. She kept saying, 'You must go. Fred and I will be all right!'

But she died on 20 May, just before I was due to go. I needed time to get over it, so I went later in the year, in August. I got through the conference, was recommended for training on the St Alban's and Oxford Ministry Course, and started the three-year course in September 1994. I felt my mother would have been tremendously pleased and proud.

I was ordained deacon at Christchurch Cathedral, Oxford, on 5 October 1997. Fred was present as my incumbent, and my two clerical supporters were Susan Cole-King and Sister Helen. My family and many friends and colleagues were there too.

Fred and I worked together in Speen, with me as his deacon. It was a wonderful year. We worked together very well, and affirmed one another's ministry. In some ways it's an odd sort of thing when you have a husband and wife working together, but this felt like a gift.

There was one odd thing. All the time we were at Speen, I was a women deacon in a church that then passed Resolutions A and B. The week after they affirmed me to go forward for training, they passed the resolutions at the PCC. Resolutions A and B in the Priests (Ordination of Women) Measure allow a parish to refuse to have a woman priest. Even so, the people at Speen were always very supportive of me.

Fred could not live a lie any more than I could

Fred had never been comfortable in the Church of England since the vote, and it was sad to see him so unhappy. He believed that the vote had fundamentally changed the nature of the Church of England. It could no longer call itself part of the Catholic Church. After much heart searching, he decided to go over to Rome. He could not live a lie any more than I could.

His five years in the Newbury team ministry were due to expire in September 1998, and he decided not to seek a renewal. I went to see my bishop, the Bishop of Reading, and subsequently became assistant curate at Holy Trinity, Cookham.

Curate of Holy Trinity, Cookham

My new post began on 1 October 1998, and on that day Fred was received into the Roman Catholic Church at Douai Abbey. I was present at the Mass and read a lesson. On 13 December 1998 I was ordained to the priesthood by Bishop Dominic Walker, Bishop of Reading, at Holy Trinity, Cookham and Fred and our family were present. Sister Helen preached a memorable sermon.

Later that day I celebrated my first Mass wearing the chasuble Fred had bought for me. Fred read a lesson, and Rosemary Tucker preached. My ordination and first Mass were both attended by friends from all over the country, including friends from Speen. The people at Cookham have been wonderfully welcoming, and I have been happy here. I shall be very sad when the time comes to move on.

The road ahead

Because I was soon going to be ordained, I did not seek re-election to General Synod in 1995. But when Susan Cole-King retired just two months after my ordination as deacon in 1997, I was persuaded to stand in her place, and was subsequently elected at the end of 2000 for a further five years. I think I am the only person to have served on General Synod in both the House of Laity and the House of Clergy.

Fred took the line that if you are called by God, then you have to do what you feel called to do. The last thing I wanted was for him to leave the Church of England, which was why I supported the Act of Synod. A lot of us spoke in favour of it in 1993 because we saw it as a means of retaining a valued part of the church who might not otherwise be able to stay. Now it is being used in a different way from the original vision and a lot of the people that we hoped would stay have not stayed, including Fred.

I would not be in favour of rescinding the Act of Synod at the moment, because there are still people who need it and we would be breaking our word to them. But as the years have gone by, it has become clearer that those who oppose us are becoming more vociferous once again, especially as the prospect of women bishops comes into focus. There is still a great deal of fear around, and while women priests have generally been accepted, there are still some people who find it difficult to do so. This is especially true of some middle-aged men who have always been in sole charge, and now suddenly find that they are not. They say 'Our congregation isn't ready for you.' What they actually mean is 'I cannot cope with you.'

None of us who went through for ordination did so just because it was something that we felt we would quite like to do. It was something we profoundly believed ourselves called to do. The church discussed it, prayed about it, debated it, prayed again at every level – parish, deanery, diocese, General Synod – and having taken the mind of the church, then we voted and we got the requisite majority – plus two votes for good measure. Then we got consent of Parliament and went through all the legal processes and women were duly ordained.

I have little time for the equal rights argument, because no one, irrespective of gender, has a right to ordination, but I do believe that when God calls, it should be possible for those whom he calls to respond.

Walsingham and Rome

One person wrote to me, 'You will, of course, no longer be welcome at Walsingham.'

I thought, 'But Our Lady of Walsingham, the biblical Mary, said "Yes" to God, and I've said "Yes" to God, and I'm not going to be driven away from the place I love.'

So we still go to Walsingham, but I wouldn't dream of wearing my clerical collar there. I've got long-standing friends in the village, and I wouldn't wish to offend them. I go there as a pilgrim, as we all are, and I go there to pray. Sometimes we take our caravan and stay on a farm in a neighbouring village. Walsingham is still a great source of spiritual strength for both of us.

Some of my fellow women priests probably would not be looking Rome-wards in terms of ecumenism, but that's where I naturally look. Not just because of Fred, but because that's the direction I feel the most comfortable with. I naturally gravitate that way, and my ecumenism is pointed in that direction, although my own two feet are firmly placed in the Church of England and I do not envisage leaving it.

Fred and I went together on pilgrimage to Rome in October 2000. It was wonderful and I was even allowed to receive Communion because I was part of a pilgrim group, and the Jubilee Year 2000 was all about our common baptism.

In some ways, it is far easier to be part of an ecumenical marriage than a 'two-integrities' one, but we have succeeded with both. Fred is happy in his new church and he is very involved with it. We have made friends in one another's churches. The fact that we managed to work our way through this whole thing has absolutely confounded some people. But we have.

Susan Cole-King 1934–2001

I would just like to add a footnote to this chapter. I have been devastated by the news of the death of Susan Cole-King in February 2001, a very sudden and untimely death while on holiday in Australia visiting her son.

Susan was one of the key people in my journey to the priesthood. Her example and the presence of Christ in her, showed me what women priests might be in the church. It has been a terrible loss but as I come to terms with it, I am encouraged by some words from St Paul's second letter to Timothy. I think it is a very good tribute to Susan and to the debt that not only I, but all ordained women, owe her. The greatest thing that we can do now is to carry out our ministry to the full, to bring Christ's reconciling love to the world, and to the church. One of the great strengths of my friendship with Susan was that it was forged at a time when we represented totally opposing viewpoints. Yet we saw Christ in each other, and our friendship was a sign of the reconciling power of Christ's love.

> As for you . . . carry out your ministry fully. As for me, I am already being poured out as a libation and the time of my departure has come. I have fought the good fight, I finished the race, I have kept the faith. From now on there is reserved for me the crown of righteousness which the Lord, the righteous judge, will give me on that day, and not only to me but also to all who have longed for his appearing.
>
> 2 Timothy 4:5–8, NRSV

REVD MAXINE MARSH

6

'One of Those Women'

Revd Maxine Marsh

Rural Dean, Polesworth

It was wonderful, we just couldn't believe it. The vote went through and I was in charge of getting the booze for the evening meal. We stopped at an off-licence and I went in and I said, 'I want half a dozen bottles of champagne, please.'

The guy serving looked at me and said, 'Oh my God, you are one of those women!'

Introduction

AB and LB: Maxine Marsh lives in the heart of England and physically very close to the actual centre of Britain, which means almost nowhere in the UK is further from the sea than the home of the Rural Dean of Polesworth.

Her modern vicarage is built next to the small medieval parish church of Kingsbury, an extended village with a population of about 8,000, built on ground that rises slightly from the flat countryside of North Warwickshire. With its tower built in 1300, the church is beautiful but unexceptional; one of hundreds you find in the English shires.

The casual visitor might easily miss a more extraordinary building on the opposite side of the old graveyard, but it is one that explains why this community is called Kingsbury. It is strange in an age of heritage conservation and historic theme parks to find an apparently untouched and unexploited ruin of historic significance, but this decrepit building housing rather elderly looking farm vehicles, which we glimpsed behind a high wall, is just that. It is a late-medieval fortified house, abandoned perhaps after a Civil War skirmish, with glassless mullioned windows, but built along with the church on the site of the palace of the Saxon kings of Mercia, the territory we now know as the Midlands. So the Revd Maxine Marsh is the latest in the long line of priests who have been leading the worship of God on this site for at least 1,000 years.

Kingsbury (or Cyne's Burg – meaning the place of the Anglo-Saxon kings' fort) is a place where history has been made again more recently. In September 2000, the huge oil depot just north of the village was one of the terminals picketed by farmers and lorry drivers protesting at the price of fuel. To read the tabloid press, it might have been thought that the very principles of British democracy were about to be overturned. While we all began to learn to live without cars, the horror headlines grew daily.

Maxine Marsh's experience of those few days points up the effective witness of the Church of England, with a church and a parish priest always based almost within walking distance of wherever the rest of us live.

'I hadn't realised all of this was happening, so of course I had almost run my car out of petrol before I did realise, and then couldn't get any. So I walked up to the oil terminal and as I got there, about three police vans had just arrived and all of these policemen were getting out and putting on their riot gear. I thought, "Blimey, there must be a huge amount of people here, there must be hundreds of them!" I went round to where they were actually protesting, and there were seventeen.

'I went through the other gate, and there were a few more down there, but it really was overkill. The local farmers were there. Most of them didn't know me from Adam. I wasn't wearing my collar because I rarely wear my collar unless I am doing services.

'They were really pleased to see me, and so were all the protestors. I heard an awful lot of sad stories, those couple of days, talking to the people who were there about their concerns and their fears and their failing businesses.

'They said to me – and I am sure it was true – it shouldn't have happened. It didn't need to have happened. All they wanted to know was that somebody was listening to them.'

Many of the priests we spoke to felt aware of a call to work for God from their early youth. Maxine was one for whom the call came later, and who struggled against it for a long time. Politically aware from her teens, Maxine had a successful and enjoyable professional career in special needs education and dealing with child abuse cases on a tough housing estate for eighteen years before she even thought of training for the priesthood. Anyone further from the image of Anglican clergy as effete idealists with no experience of the tough realities of life can scarcely be imagined.

'I have my most theological discussions in the pub. I have more theological discussions in the pub with people who don't go to church than I ever have with people who are churchgoers, and I love it.'

The sturdy ashtray at her side slowly filled as she told us her story.

Maxine

Brownies, Guides and Sunday school
I was born in Bristol in 1949, and as an only child my parents decided that they had to socialise me in every possible way, so I was sent off to a little private nursery school when I was three, and then to Brownies and Guides. They were very keen that I should get on in life. And I think it was probably just to get me out of their hair for half an hour or so on a Sunday afternoon that one of the Sunday-school teachers who lived down the road picked me up and took me to Sunday school each week. In those days, if you were part of Brownies or Guides, you had to go to church parade. There were Cubs, Scouts, Brownies and Guides, a scout-master who had obviously been in the Army during the war, and we had a band and we used to march around the streets and go to church . . . and I loved it.

It was quite a high, traditional, Anglo-Catholic church – St Anne's in Bristol – and there was so much going on. It was like drama really. There were colours, vestments, bells, incense, processions and everybody plummeting to their knees at certain parts of the service and standing up again. I really loved all this. I was confirmed when I was about thirteen, as you were in those days.

My parents would only come along occasionally; they would come to the nativity play. They never dissuaded me from going, but they themselves were very much weddings, funerals and christenings sort of people. (Of course they go now that I'm the vicar!)

Political awakening
When I was in my late teens I went to teacher training college at Bretton Hall, in Yorkshire, to do drama. That was the time, I suppose, of my first real political awakening. Soviet tanks had gone into Czechoslovakia earlier that year, I was beginning to realise what was happening in South Africa, and it was the early days of what was then popularly known as 'women's lib'.

I was very interested in all of this, but it seemed as if the church had never heard of it and wasn't at all interested in any of it . . . so I left the church. I am sure it didn't miss me! Well, it was a natural break; I was going off to Yorkshire so it was a very normal thing.

Oh good – nothing much has happened
When I was at college in the late-1960s, early-1970s, it was the hippy era, and like all students I was reading a lot about Buddhism and the Far Eastern stuff, and meditation has remained an important part of my spiritual life. I went to church at Christmas and Easter, because I still loved the drama, but I was always glad to walk away from it thinking, 'Oh

good, nothing much has happened' because it always felt vaguely dangerous to go back in some way. It was all right as long as it remained set in
amber. And this went on for years and years and years.

First of all I taught at a boys' school at Knowle West, a tough housing
estate on the outskirts of Bristol. I taught drama and English, but I hated
teaching drama. I loved the theatre, but for so many of the kids drama
class was an excuse to swing from the light shades and go absolutely
bananas. And like so many young teachers, I had very fragile control over
a class, so this was just not something that was ever going to work. On
the other hand, I loved the English classes I took, which were with the
slow learners.

It was obvious to the headmaster that I was never going to make the
grade as a drama teacher, so he contacted the girls' school in the area
where they had a post going to teach special needs classes. They took me
on, and I worked there mainly teaching English and maths to the girls
with special needs and learning difficulties, for the next eighteen years.

The 'named' person to deal with children who had abuse problems

At the end of the 1970s I went on a year's exchange to teach special
education in Des Moines, Iowa, in the United States. When their term
was over I travelled round for two and a half months with another teacher
from the school, in an old trailer that broke down all over America. I
came back and – it's strange, isn't it – but just because you have been to
the United States, people somehow think you must have learned an
awful lot. You suddenly become extra qualified in some way, and I started
to get promotion. I was made Head of Year 7, head of the first years.

When children first come to secondary school you have quite a lot to
do with their parents. It drops off quite rapidly, but in that first year you
get to know them quite well, so I got to know a lot of the parents and
the problems they were having. They all came from Knowle West, from
the same tough housing estate. I found I was having quite a lot of dealings
with abuse cases.

Then I became the 'named' person on the staff to work with children
who had abuse problems. So then, whichever year the child was in, if she
said she was being physically or sexually abused at home, I was the person
who dealt with police, court officials, social services and the family.

I was involved in the team discussions of what was going to happen to
the child. It depended on how their mothers reacted to a great extent,
because so often they would not believe the child and therefore it was
the child who would have to leave the home, and not the father or
partner. Very often they wouldn't take the case to court because they
didn't think it stood a chance of actually getting a conviction, and it
would be putting the child through a nightmare and getting no result.

It was terrible, but it was also good, in a way, to work with people with problems and try and find answers, and there are things you can do to help. The children can recover. I don't know how well they ever really recover from it, but they can recover.

Before you can sneeze, you're on the coffee rota

Meanwhile, I had gone to church one Easter Sunday, to my childhood church. There was a new vicar there, Mark Waters, a liberal catholic, very into social issues, who preached a sermon that made me sit up.

Previously I had always felt as though the church had no link into real life; it was just this wonderful sort of drama going on somewhere that had nothing to do with what we did the rest of the time during the week. But with this new young vicar, it had changed. He made me think.

I went away and I said to myself, 'I needn't go back.' But, of course, I had to, because I had to see if that was just a fluke. So I would creep in and he would be going great guns, and I would creep out again. I kept doing this, creeping in – timing it so I would be a few minutes late – and leaving during the final hymn, so I didn't have to talk to anybody.

But one day Mark was too quick for me. He didn't go round to the vestry to say his prayers. Instead he was waiting for me just as I was leaving. He said, 'I have seen you a few times. Do you want to talk?'

I said, 'Oh, no. No. Yes.'

I got more and more involved in the church after that. You know what it's like, when a new youngish person comes into the church. Before you can sneeze you are on the coffee rota and on the PCC, and I found I was churchwarden before I even knew anything about it.

I suppose I had something like six months when I would go and talk to Mark, and I would question everything. He helped me to re-examine things. To start with he was getting me to read books, things like *God of Surprises* and we quite rapidly went on to Don Cupitt, which I found absolutely fascinating.

One night in 1987 there was a small group of us having dinner at the other churchwarden's house, and I said to Mark, 'I sort of feel I would like to do a bit more. Do you think I should go on a lay reader's course?' Just as I said that, there was one of those sudden silences as there are at dinner parties and in it he said, 'No. You should be a priest.'

I said, 'No, no. Don't be silly.'

He said, 'Go on, you'll be good.'

'No, no. I would never do that.'

It's such a difficult thing to explain

I spent the next nearly two years not wanting to admit that he had actually struck a chord. I was very happy teaching. I was doing a job that satisfied me. I didn't want to leave. But I was feeling more and more discomfited, knowing I had to do something more.

So I tried all sorts of different things. First of all I thought I would change schools, but none of the jobs I looked at were quite right. Then I thought, 'Well, I have done so much counselling; I'll re-train as a counsellor.' But none of the courses seemed right. I even thought of having a loft conversion done, to keep myself busy.

In the end I had a long talk with Mark, and *very* reluctantly said, 'I'll let the church test this,' feeling quite sure that the church would say, 'Thank you very much, but no thank you'.

In May 1989 I went to see John Porch, the Diocesan Director of Ordinands (DDO). He asked about my church history and what I believed in and what I was reading. (Mark had warned me that I shouldn't mention Don Cupitt on my reading list!) John was a lovely, saintly man, who said after a couple of meetings that I ought to see the bishop's chaplains. So I saw the bishop's chaplains, and they all said I ought to go for a selection conference.

Everybody asks you, when you go to see all these examining chaplains, 'Why do you believe you have a vocation?' In the end, I used to get so tired of it all, I thought I'd say, 'I think I had one when I came in, but I must have put it down somewhere because I can't find it now.'

It is such a difficult thing to explain why. It sounds so presumptuous to say, 'I think God is calling me to do this.' It is awfully difficult to explain why you think that, because I mean you might be a lunatic, you could be completely mad.

Thanks, Bishop, those are two things I can really work on!

I thought it would be at least the following year before I had a selection conference, but in fact I had one that September. The whole process had gone through really fast and it all happened between May and September.

I saw Bishop Barry Rogerson, who said to me, 'As far as I can see there are only two problems. One is your gender, and the other is your age.'

I thought, 'Thanks, Bishop, those are two things I can really work on!'

The bishop was very insistent that I should look at Westcott House in Cambridge as a place to do my training. I said, 'I want to go to Salisbury or Cuddesdon. I don't want to go to Westcott House. It's too far away and it's too cold in the winter. There is nothing between Outer Mongolia and Cambridge, not an anthill.'

But I went to look at it, and just fell in love with it, and they offered me a training place there for the following September, 1990.

Forget everything you have ever learned

I went to Westcott House in 1990, and it was quite a difficult time, because I couldn't afford to keep up the mortgage payments on my house in Bristol. I had to give that up. Changing from living in my own house to two small rooms was hard. And I couldn't take my old dog – McGee, a red setter – with me. I don't care what you say about red setters, McGee was highly intelligent and could have done anything he wanted in life. He went to live with my parents. They loved him to bits, but it was hard to part.

My first impression of Westcott House was of a lot of petty rules, and that it was absolutely dreadful. It was a strange cross between a monastic life and a boarding-school. Then there is this awful thing in theological training, because when you arrive, especially if you are older and you have had a career, they will say, 'It's wonderful because you bring with you all your life experience . . .' But once you get there, they deny it all, and say, 'Now you have to learn to look at things this new way, and forget about everything you have ever learned before.'

They didn't notice it was all the men doing everything

One of the things I had been impressed about when I had visited Westcott was that there seemed to be a lot of mature students there. What they didn't tell me was they were virtually all leaving, so when I arrived there was an intake of a lot of very young men – and they were so pompous, some of them. I can remember one young man saying to me – we had had a few drinks in the bar, I must admit – 'I don't know, it's not only because you're a woman that we find you so difficult – but you're so old as well.'

At just forty, I suppose I wasn't much younger than his mum.

There were quite a few students who were not at all in favour of the ordination of women, and they made no bones about telling you. I must admit that all the staff were in favour, but sometimes they didn't make it well enough known. It was a rule that in chapel inclusive language should be used, but it got so bad some weeks when the men were just not using inclusive language – and we are talking here about inclusive language for humanity, not for God – that it made me mad. The staff didn't even seem to notice.

Then I'd say to the staff, if we were having big services – I wouldn't say it every single service, but when we were having a big, important festival – 'Mightn't it be nice to hear a woman's voice in it?' They didn't notice that it was all men doing everything. It wasn't malicious, it was just not noticing.

I didn't know men could be priests!

I had one wonderful experience at Westcott, in the sense that they did an exchange every year with Seabury Western Theological Seminary in Chicago. I applied and I got it, and went over to do my long summer work experience with a woman priest there. In fact, I ended up working with four women priests, one each week.

On the first Sunday I was working with a woman called Joy Rogers, the team rector at St Luke's, Eddiston, a suburb of Chicago. I went to their big Communion service. I had never seen a woman preside in her own church before. I can still see the choir and servers all lined up; they were all ready to go, and I suddenly thought, 'What if I don't like it?' It was a bit late now, but what if I didn't like it, with a woman presiding? But she was wonderful, and I found myself sobbing my way through the whole thing. Joy and I have kept in contact ever since and she came over both for my deaconing and my priesting.

I also worked with a woman priest who was working in a little mission church, with the woman who was Acting Provost at Eddiston Cathedral and with another woman who had a little rural parish. She told me how normally, when she went away on holiday, she got another woman priest friend to cover for her, but this year her friend hadn't been able to, so she'd asked a male priest to do the services. After his first service, one of the kids said to him, 'I didn't know *men* could be priests.'

The glass ceiling

What I found so fascinating over there was that women like Joy, and others who had been priests for a long time by then, still thought that there was a long way for women to go before they were on a level playing-field with the men. By contrast, a lot of the younger women in training, who hadn't been part of the long struggle for women's ordination, had this idea that it was all lovely; women had been priests for twenty years and there were no more problems. I think it is rather the same here now, and that we have to be very careful to monitor the situation and make sure that women are getting promoted, and are getting a chance at the good jobs.

My own first job was at King's Norton, in the Birmingham Diocese, because there was no job in Bristol when I left Westcott in the summer of 1992. You sort out your job in the summer before you leave college, because you can't be ordained unless you have a job. I went to see the bishop and he said, 'There is a job, it's liberal catholic, it would suit you. There's a good chap there. I want you to go and be the first person to be interviewed.'

So I went to see him, this vicar, who was slightly younger than I was, and we had a three-hour conversation. A few days later I went back, and the talk was full of things like – there is a special school in the parish, and you could be chaplain, and you could do this, and you could do that . . .

I thought, 'This is great.'

Then he suddenly said, 'I am sorry. It's not going to work.'

So I said, 'What isn't going to work?'

'You are too multi-talented for this parish.'

I thought, 'Oh, no. You are going to say it to me.'

So I went on and on, and finally he said, 'I am really sorry, but you seem like a strong woman and I just can't cope with strong women. Please don't tell the bishop.'

I did, though, because it was ridiculous. This was the one post for a woman in the entire diocese, being looked after by a man who couldn't work with women.

Because I had worked in a girls' school for so long, where the heads of department were women, the head was a woman, the deputies were women, I hadn't realised exactly how bad the situation was. Even in theological college, I didn't realise how powerful we were, or how frightened they were of us.

When I telephoned the bishop, he said, 'Well, I am really sorry, but there just isn't another job for a woman in the diocese. We will have to lose you.'

So I went to King's Norton and was ordained as deacon and priest in the Birmingham Diocese. I did three years' curacy there, and then came to Kingsbury, the first woman to come to the Polesworth Deanery.

Why is Maxine going to Kingsbury? That's a nice church!

When I came here as vicar, five and a half years ago, quite a few people had applied for it, because it's a really nice parish, and I think there were five or six of us on the shortlist. Much to my amazement I got it, because this was my first job after being a curate at King's Norton, so I hadn't thought I stood much of a chance.

Just before I came it was the bishop's conference that he calls every three years at Swanwick. I was in the bar one evening, as I often am in bars, and I could hear some men behind me talking. At that time, I think I was the third woman to go as vicar into a church in the diocese, and the other two women had gone into quite difficult parishes, inner-city and struggling churches. These men were saying, 'So-and-so will be good in such-and-such a church, and so-and-so will be so good in such-and-such a church . . . but why is Maxine going to Kingsbury? That's a nice church!'

So it's only OK to go to the places that men don't want.

The problems are more hidden in the country

There are nine of us in the deanery when we are all in post. It's the biggest deanery geographically, but the smallest population-wise. There are sixteen churches, and some of them are quite tiny and rural. The villages around here, although they started as agricultural settlements, became pit villages when there was the North Warwickshire coalfield. The pits have all closed now. It looks idyllic, but there are huge problems.

We are in a large village at Kingsbury. We've got shops; we have three schools: the infant, junior and secondary schools. We have got a youth centre. So we have quite good facilities. But there are lots of other villages where the only shop now is a post office. There are problems with young people because they can't get to anywhere at night. The buses stop quite early so they can't get into the nearest town, Tamworth, unless they have parents who have cars. Not just the teenagers, young couples or lone parents can't get out of the village for a night out. Then there are the usual problems for people who have been brought up in villages not being able to afford housing. There are debt problems. Problems here are hidden more than in the cities, I think. They aren't so obvious.

Folk religion is alive and well here

There is a very good feeling about the church in the village. They feel they own it; they feel they can use it. I do so many christenings you wouldn't believe it, but they don't come back. Folk religion is alive and well and living in Kingsbury. We have quite a few weddings, and lots of funerals.

My predecessor had a very, very strict baptism policy. The parents of the children he baptised had to come for four sessions and watch videos and give their lives to Jesus but he wouldn't baptise children if the parents were not married but living together. He wouldn't baptise parents if one or other had been divorced.

They wanted somebody who would make strong links with the village, and somebody who had a sense of humour, and they didn't care whether it was a man or a woman or how old, as long as they were young at heart.

You change things just by the way you are

I wasn't going to come in and make huge changes. I wanted to get to know people first. But you change things just by the way you are in many ways, and they were obviously taken aback that I should reverence the altar.

I come from a much higher tradition than they were used to. I have introduced different services. We now have a lot more Holy Week services; we have the washing of feet, we have the Good Friday liturgy, Holy Saturday and a Service of Light. And we have a few more saints days celebrated than before, but basically it's what I would consider to be normal in any church, so it is just bringing things back.

I always do a 1662 Book of Common Prayer service and it was wonderful to think I was doing this in a church which was old when the Book of Common Prayer was being written, and when I came it was the first time a woman's voice had done it.

I am very careful with my language when I am preaching. I try and call God 'God' as often as I can. Occasionally you have to say 'He', otherwise the sentence gets so complex, but I don't think of God as He or She.

The vicar is infectious

I always have been a bit of a workaholic. But this isn't just living over the shop; it's living in the shop. At the beginning, I couldn't believe people because I would just be eating and the telephone would go. I would answer the phone and someone would say, 'Are you eating?' and I would say, 'Yes.'

And they would say, 'Yes, we thought you would be in, so we would call you now. It's about next Sunday . . .'

I would be thinking, 'What!'

I find it very difficult to take time off. I do relax, obviously, but you never know when the phone is going to go, when the door is going to be knocked. Finally my secretary put a notice on the door for me, saying 'The vicar's day off is Monday. She would be grateful if she was only disturbed for emergencies.'

Most of the people in the church are very good about not bothering me on my day off, but if it is a nice day and somebody is walking the baby, they seem to think, 'I'm in this part of the village, I'll just nip in and see the vicar about the baptism. She won't mind.' So they ring the bell and then they read the notice, and then they are covered with confusion. So actually I have got to be even nicer than I would have had to be if there wasn't a notice.

I had shingles two years ago, and I had to be off work for a couple of weeks. I obviously didn't particularly want to see anybody so I stuck a notice on the door, saying, 'The vicar is ill.' People were still knocking on the door, so I put another notice up saying 'The vicar is infectious.' Nothing. Perfect peace. So that's obviously what I must do in the future. If I want the day off I must have a notice saying, 'The vicar is infectious.'

I do love what I do

I have my most theological discussions in the pub. I have more theological discussions in the pub with people who don't go to church than I ever have with people who are churchgoers, and I love it. What amazes me is how many people live such quietly courageous lives who have had huge problems. They have overcome them; they have dealt with sad times but with joy as well, and had really full lives.

I love being part of people's lives, of being there at the tremendous moments, when they are getting married, when they are having their babies christened, when they are dying. If you ask me which is the best bit of all, for me, it is saying the Eucharist. I am doing it on behalf of a group of people, so it is a bit of a two-way thing, but that's what sustains me.

I have had a really, really good experience. I won't say 'lucky', because I don't think people should be lucky. I think people should have good experiences in life as far as they possibly can, they should be helped towards having good experiences. I don't know how typical I am. I think there are a lot of women who probably haven't had such an easy and accepting time as I have.

11 November 1992 – the more we give, the more they take
I didn't think it was going to go through.

A group of us who had trained together – we called ourselves the Westcott Women when we were there – went down to London to hear the debate. We went down and had dinner together the night before.

In the morning we went along to Dean's Yard, and we stood outside and sang as people came through. We had tickets for the public gallery in the afternoon.

We had arranged to meet Rupert Hoare, who had been our principal, and have a meal with him afterwards. We also planned to have a Eucharist, at which he would preside, at a Franciscan House, because we all thought it wouldn't go through, and we wanted to experience our first Eucharist after the vote had gone against us not in our own parishes. We thought if we were going to shed tears, we wanted to do it then and together, rather than the following Sunday.

But of course it was wonderful. I mean, it went through and we couldn't believe it. For some reason I was in charge of getting the booze for the evening meal. We all set off and we stopped the taxi at an off-licence, and I went in and I said, 'I want half a dozen bottles of champagne.' The guy serving looked at me and said, 'Oh my God, you are one of those women!' He said, ' I have been watching it on the television', and I thought, 'This is a right image to give to the general public!'

But when we got back, the women of the diocese were told not to be too openly happy; try to be realistic about it. So we felt a bit flat. We had had this wonderful gift given to us, and we couldn't celebrate. It was like you had had a baby and you had to keep taking it upstairs in case it upset the visitors.

It was a most strange time and I feel that most people since then have fallen over backwards to try to appease a very, very small minority of people. They just seem to be getting stronger and stronger, and more and more entrenched. And the more we give, the more they take.

'You do read such funny things about women priests'
I knew that the first time I did the Eucharist would be, for the vast majority of people, the first time they had ever seen a woman doing it. I wanted to do it so that it was normal, it was natural and it wasn't awkward and I wasn't getting in people's way. I spent *months* practising.

I practised in the kitchen, because the units are just the right height, whereas tables aren't. So I had a chalice and a glass of wine on one side and my ashtray on the other and I would go through it. I did this every night for weeks beforehand.

I was a bit worried even then, because when I was practising, every now and then I had a swig of wine and a cigarette. I thought – if I'm not careful, I am going to invent new liturgy here.

But when the day came, it was fine. I had invited quite a few men, because I know quite a lot of the more catholic priests and some of them had had to work really hard to come to terms with it. A lot of them didn't, but some of them had to work really hard. A couple of them said to me afterwards, 'I really didn't know what I was going to feel – but it was just so normal!'

I don't know what they thought we were going to do.

In this parish, when I was appointed, there was just one person, one elderly man, on the PCC who had said he didn't agree with women priests and he could never receive Communion from one. I came over a few times for a few social events before I actually moved in. And when I had my first service, this gentleman was one of the first at the altar rail, because he had got to know me and had changed his mind.

I said to him later, 'How was it?'

He said, 'Oh, it's fine, Vicar. Now I know you, it's fine.'

I said, 'Well, what did you expect? Did you expect me to be prancing naked round the altar?'

He said, 'Well, you do read such funny things in the papers about women priests!'

REVD SHEILA MCLACHLAN

7

What You See Is What You Get

REVD SHEILA MCLACHLAN

Priest-in-Charge, Kingsnorth and Shadoxhurst, Ashford

I'm content to be Sheila, the parish priest, who's been allowed to be a priest, and has been allowed to be herself. That's a big change, because when I was a nurse I think I'd have said I wanted to be Sheila the Archbishop!

Introduction

AB: 'You've got to include Sheila,' said one of the bishops among the many people we talked to before starting this book. 'She's cutting swathes through the youth population on our Ashford housing estates. Her group put on a full-scale musical last Christmas that brought tears to my eyes. And she has the youngest PCC in the Diocese of Canterbury.'

'I'll kill him when I next see him,' said Sheila on the telephone, on hearing that Gavin Reid, now retired Bishop of Maidstone, had put her name forward. And as the Vicar of Kingsnorth with Stubbs Cross and Shadoxhurst told me when I went to meet her, 'I say to folk – with me, what you see is what you get.' What I saw from the moment I arrived at her front door was the warm and friendly face that complements a direct manner, a combination that exudes beguiling honesty. What I heard was a story that is both funny and faithful, told by a woman priest who is, whatever the difficulties she faces, a winner.

In fact, I realised as soon as I arrived that I had met Sheila before. When I was covering the 1988 Lambeth Conference for Channel 4, I was the television person with the ever-hovering film crew looking for any excitement generated by theological debate (which included the ordination of women) among hundreds of Anglican bishops from all around the world. Sheila, then a deaconess, stepping out of her role as Chaplain to the University of Kent, was the person in charge of the team ensuring that no one – but no one – got in to the debating hall without a pass.

It was a vital but unenviable task. With so many journalists eager for a story, any story, it was not surprising that news went around the world of Sheila's encounter at the door with Archbishop Desmond Tutu. He arrived, smiling broadly as ever, with no pass and no badge, and dressed in a wildly improbable T-shirt.

'It would have to be Desmond Tutu of all people . . . but I had a job to do, and I was going to do it. There had been real concern about security arrangements, and everyone in the hall was in my care. I've never forgotten it – having to say, "I'm terribly sorry, I can't let you in." And thinking – This is silly.'

In the end Sheila let the world's most famous church leader pass, but the media had their story. Later she was able to leave her post guarding the door to participate in a night-time prayer vigil led by the charismatic archbishop. 'It was deeply moving as almost everyone joined the bishops, the leadership of the whole Anglican Communion in the world, praying together as a candle was lit.'

Sheila arrived in Kingsnorth in February 1994, one of the first woman deacons in the Diocese of Canterbury to be appointed in charge of a parish. From her front garden she can see the busy primary school across the road and the old church, signs of stability in an area that has changed dramatically in the last few years. Kingsnorth is on the edge of Ashford, a population – not only of Kent but of the whole of the south-east of England – that is growing faster than anywhere else.

Where once there were acres of marshland south of Ashford's former railway works, there are now huge housing estates. Ring roads connect up new districts and lead to the brand-new international railway station where in and out glide the sleek Eurostar trains, en route for France and Belgium.

People are coming to Kingsnorth looking for a home and a place to start a family, while also hoping to earn their fortune. Hence the parish magazine advises parents to give plenty of notice if they want their children baptised. And in the edition for May 2001 I read, 'Couples wanting to marry in 2002 are asked to book early to avoid disappointment.' This is the sort of item most parishes would envy.

Sheila pointed out the view of fields from her window: 'It's in an interesting position, this rectory, because I've got the fields and the countryside this side, and on the other side I've got the new school buildings and all the hustle and bustle of Ashford. That's the busy side – and this is the sanity side.'

Earlier this year, I took part in a conference where church leaders, mission and youth workers were confronted with the sociologists' profile of the two youngest generations, Generations X and Y. Generation X have grown up since the 1960s without any religious inheritance, and Generation Y, born in the 1980s, will experience all their adult life in the new millennium. Graham Cray, newly consecrated Bishop of Maidstone and keynote speaker, urged us to help make sense of the gospel for generations whose lifestyle seems to be cynically exploited by consumer analysts and the ad-world. The successor to Bishop Gavin will find his challenge is being answered in his own diocese with some impressive work well underway in Kingsnorth and Shadoxhurst.

I had come chiefly hoping to hear about Ark Drama 2000, whose performance had so moved Bishop Gavin, but first I discovered than an extraordinarily dramatic actual incident in Sheila's own life, the sort that documentary television and Songs of Praise *producers yearn to film, had marked her card on the road to becoming a priest.*

Sheila

Moment of truth

It was in 1980. I was an SRN at the John Radcliffe Hospital in Oxford, but on sabbatical from the National Health Service. I had done a year of a basic course at Wycliffe Hall in Oxford, a theological college, because I had been beginning to feel that Christian ministry was something I should explore. I had some kind of romantic notion of becoming a missionary overseas, but I didn't want to be pushed into the church and certainly not as anything so boring as a deaconess. In fact, I was pretty sure I would go back to my career in the NHS when I had finished my course.

I went down to Lee Abbey, in North Devon, on a student working party from Oxford University, and two of us went off for a walk. A lovely March day – very windy. The sea was wonderfully rough and we were rather stupid and walked too far round the bay into the next one, and got cut off by the tide. It was impossible to swim back – the currents were too strong and we were under an overhang of the cliff, so we couldn't climb up anywhere. We were trapped.

The sea grew rougher and the wind grew stronger and the tide rose higher. We waved frantically at some people we could see on the other side of the headland, but they just waved back. We were getting very cold, very wet and very miserable and I thought, 'Well, this is it. We're not going to get out of this mess.'

We weren't praying the whole time as we waited to be rescued. That sounds a bit too holy for me. But we were singing a bit to keep our spirits up. I remember we had a disagreement about the words and the tune of the 'Gloria' and almost had a falling out over that.

There was a gale blowing around us by this time. First of all the coastguards tried to reach us. We knew there was some activity on the cliffs above us, but we couldn't see them because of the overhang. But they couldn't get down to us. The coastguards were part-time farmers, so – bless them – they'd left their lambs to come and see if they could save two idiotic girls stuck in the bay.

The lifeboat couldn't get in – the wind and waves and rocks made it impossible.

Eventually a helicopter came from RAF Chivenor. Apparently what had happened was the folk who we'd waved to on the other side of the headland had returned from their walk and had seen us still in the same place and thought – that's a bit odd – and had gone to the nearest cottage and raised the alarm.

It was utter relief when we heard the helicopter arrive, but then having to watch it try to get in, flying along the cliff, seemed like an eternity. I made a pact with God. I made all sorts of conditions, saying, 'If you get me out of this, *and* my friend out, and nobody else is injured and everything is absolutely fine and hunky-dory, then OK, I'll see if the church wants me. I'll go on a selection course for deaconess. I really don't want to, but I will.'

When the winch man came down, he said, 'Have you ever done this before?'

I don't think I should repeat what I said to him – it wasn't very churchlike.

Anyway, he just grinned and said, 'Some people do it all the time.'

This experience left a deep impression upon me that was to profoundly affect my life. It brought home the reality of Romans 5 where St Paul writes, 'Very rarely will anyone die for a righteous person, though for a good one someone might possibly dare to die. But God demonstrates his own love for us in this; while we were still sinners, Christ died for us.' We owe our lives to the courage of those men who didn't know us but who risked their own lives to come in and fly the helicopter under an overhanging cliff to rescue us. How much more do I owe to Christ?

Anyway, the end result of it was that I kept my promise. And so I went forward for selection and interestingly enough, the friend who was with me, Amiel Osmaston, is also now a priest. Neither of us knew it, but we had both made the same promise.

Changing direction

As soon as I got back to Oxford, to Wycliffe College, I knocked on the Principal's door and said, 'I think I ought to go forward for selection for ordination.'

Geoffrey Shaw, the Principal, and his wife sat in their sitting-room and they just smiled at me and said, 'We've been waiting for you to say that!'

I think it had to be like that, probably, to push me into leaving the NHS, something that was safe and with a secure salary, to go into an unknown world where you got paid a pittance. Women priests weren't even on the agenda at that point, certainly not in my life. And for somebody who was ambitious in the NHS to go into being something like a deaconess where ambition just didn't exist – it was a big turnaround for me.

Beginnings

I was born in Poole in Dorset, but I was adopted as a baby, and went to live with my new family in London. There was nothing happening church-wise in my childhood. We never even went at Christmas. We went for weddings and funerals and that was it.

There was one event that made a lifelong impression: the death of a playmate of mine, Henry, when he and I were about six or seven. He ran out behind an ice-cream van and was killed. We had been inseparable friends at school. Complete devastation. More so because at our school, he was the only child of ethnic origin. He was from the Caribbean and, like me, he'd been adopted. He had two white parents, and to my child's eyes, it appeared to be a wonderful family, all very close.

That was perhaps my first spiritual moment, wondering and asking about what had happened to Henry after his death. I didn't know anything about heaven then, but I couldn't believe that anything cruel could happen to him.

The Red Cross

One of the things I had loved when I was younger was belonging to the Red Cross; first the Junior Red Cross when I was ten, and then the Senior Red Cross. I had been removed from the Brownies because I refused to polish my Pixie badge – I thought it was a waste of time. They said I was a disruptive influence.

So I had joined the Junior Red Cross because there were no badges to polish. And I absolutely loved it. Tuesday nights were Red Cross nights but then, once you'd been in the group for six months and you'd earned your first aid badge, you could go off at weekends and be a first-aider at athletics meetings, sometimes at the theatre or cinema. I was even fortunate enough to be asked to represent the Red Cross at events abroad.

That side – the caring side and my nursing experience – is useful nearly every day of my life. It's much more holistic now. Then, I cared for the physical needs; now, as a priest, I see myself as caring for the whole person and sometimes that includes the physical as well. I have never regretted my nursing years, and the Red Cross sparked that off.

I didn't really like school. I scraped by, got my GCSEs. I was good at English, hopeless at maths. Later it was discovered that I have numeric dyslexia. I'm good at maths now – if I have a calculator that tells me the answers. I live with it quite happily, but there's no point in me being on a finance committee.

Many young girls seem to go through a phase of wanting to be a nun. Not me. I wanted to be a dentist. I don't know why on earth I ever thought that. I didn't like, and still don't like, going to the dentist. I probably just wanted to be different from everyone else – most of the girls at school were going to be teachers or secretaries. I knew what I didn't want to be. I did not want to be a secretary – the last thing in life. A lot of girls were going into computer programming – and I knew that I did not want to do that. I thought about being a teacher but I was told that to be that I would need to do a lot better in my examinations.

I did the first year of my A levels, but by that time I was bored with school and I left before I started my second year. I became a cadet nurse, somebody who was going forward for nursing training but was too young to start the training. And I did that for about nine months, and then I started my State Registered Nurse training.

In that case, no, you're not a Christian

When I was a student nurse, the first ward that I went on after I'd been in preliminary training school was a geriatric ward and I remember then – I was eighteen – being asked questions like, 'What's going to happen to me, nurse, when I die?'

My own question, when Henry had died.

And not having any answer and wanting to find an answer, I went to one of the hospital chaplains. For some reason, I asked him if I was a Christian. He started off by saying, 'What church do you belong to?'

I said 'Church of England. Everybody does, don't they?'

He said, 'That's fine. Have you been confirmed?'

I didn't know what confirmed meant, so he explained that and I said, 'No, I've not had that.'

'Have you been baptised?'

I said, 'No, I don't think I've had that either.'

'In that case, no, you're not a Christian.'

That is such a clear memory. 'In that case, no, you are not a Christian.' And I can remember feeling quite relieved.

I think I felt that gave me free rein to go off and try different things. I read books by Christmas Humphreys on Buddhism, books on Hinduism and Judaism. I started trying different sects and cults. Because I wasn't a Christian, I could do all this now. I was free. This went on for three years, dabbling here and there, but I wasn't a Christian, so it was all right.

There was a glorious point in my life when every night of the week I was having some sort of religious instruction from different groups, including Jehovah's Witnesses, but I finally ended up with the Seventh Day Adventists.

Full immersion baptism

I had qualified as a State Registered Nurse. I was fascinated by the emergency services – coronary care, accident and emergency, intensive therapy. I really enjoyed orthopaedics – bones. I became a staff nurse in an orthopaedic unit. I enjoyed it, and quite quickly, when I was still only twenty-two, I became a junior ward sister.

It was Christmas Eve 1974. I was staff nurse on the Orthopaedic Unit at Mount Vernon Hospital in Northwood, and we got notification that there'd been a really serious road traffic accident. Two people had already been killed. There were two that were very seriously injured and one that was so critical that they really didn't think she would survive the night.

It's never a popular time to have major accidents, Christmas Eve, particularly when there's a very good film on that you are expecting to get off to see. But I had to stay on – so I have never seen *The Graduate,* the film I missed that night.

They arrived – the two seriously injured ones. We sorted them out, and got them as comfortable as we could. And then the other person arrived on the ward and by any normal standards, she should not have been alive. I remember handing over to the night nurse saying, 'I won't see her in the morning.'

She was there on Christmas morning and the morning after that and the morning after that. She was a Swiss lady and so they flew her family in from Switzerland. They started praying round her bed and laying hands on her, and I got really rather uptight about that. I didn't think it was appropriate behaviour, laying on hands and praying for people. What good would it do?

I went in and said to them, 'Excuse me, but you can only have two visitors at the bed at any one time. Would one of you please leave?' I think that's probably when they started to think they ought to pray for me as well.

She continued to hold her own and then one day I just happened to be in there with her and her two daughters when she had a cardiac arrest. I did what one does, which was to press the emergency buzzer and thump her on the chest – which sounds really brutal, doesn't it? But her heart started beating again – and she came round. As far as the family were concerned, if I hadn't have been there, she would not have come back.

So I suspect that deepened their desire to pray for me. I have a memory of going into the cubicle one day and hearing my name as they were praying. I remember thinking – hmm. I don't know how you put 'hmm' in a book, but it was what I thought.

They were Seventh Day Adventists, and I became intrigued and, because she was in for nearly six months, I got to know the family very well. But I was not going to make a commitment. No way. Just because they were praying for me. I was trying to say, 'This is nothing to do with you. This is *me*, this is *my* decision.' But after they had gone home to

Switzerland, I went along, and eventually I was baptised in the Seventh Day Adventist Church by full immersion.

It felt like a momentous occasion. When you rise up out of the water you have to give your testimony, tell the story of what brought you to this point – very much more dramatic and outgoing than anything Anglican. Their worship pattern is different too, in that you worship on the Jewish Sabbath, on a Saturday.

So I was ticking along quite happily. I went to church in Watford every Saturday I could get off. But after a few months I changed jobs and moved to Oxford, where there wasn't a Seventh Day Adventist church within easy reach.

Motivation questionable

For a while I stopped going anywhere, but it seemed that about half the staff on the intensive care unit were active Christians. There was a very lively Christian fellowship in the hospital as well, which I joined. In the end I ended up going to the church that the majority of them seemed to go to, which just happened to be a Church of England church, St Ebbe's.

In many ways, except for worshipping on a Sunday instead of Saturday, it seemed very little different from what I had become used to in the Seventh Day Adventist church. Same hymns, same long sermons – 'long' being the operative word – reading the psalms. The whole ethos seemed very similar, and I was happy. There was a very energetic young professionals group there, and I was in that. After a couple of years, they asked me if I would be chairman of that group. But you had to be a confirmed Anglican to be a chairman, so I had a problem. Interestingly enough, I had to go and see Patrick Rodger, the then Bishop of Oxford, to be cleared, because they weren't convinced that I'd even had a proper baptism. But he was wonderful, and he said that of course it was fine.

In the end, I was – as far as I was concerned – confirmed as an Anglican in 1976 by the laying on of hands, simply to become chairman of the youth group. Motivation questionable.

The flower rota, the cleaning rota or cooking Sunday lunch

Now I'm fully fledged as chairman of the St Ebbe's' After Eight Group for young professionals and that's great and I love it, and as I have some position in the church as the young people's leader, I begin to think, 'I quite like this.' So when my term of office expires, I go to a very holy man, a wonderful man who I have great respect for. I wanted to explore what else I could do, as a professional woman, perhaps in some kind of leadership role.

I was offered either cooking the Sunday lunches for the students, going on the cleaning rota or going on the flower rota.

Well, if you'd seen my flower arrangements, you would know that's certainly not me. If you knew anything about me at all, going on the church cleaning rota is certainly not my thing and as for student cooking, I wasn't even going to consider doing that. But it seemed that it was one of those things or – nothing.

About this time, I met some folk from another Oxford church popular with students, St Aldate's. I was in any case beginning to feel that the conservative evangelical Anglicanism at St Ebbe's was just a little bit too conservative for me. So I thought I'd try St Aldate's. It was at that time under the leadership of Michael Green.

I blossomed there. There was a drama group and I joined that. Within the drama group, I became part of the mission team and began to evolve in my own faith. I moved in with some friends from St Aldate's and we formed a small community of four who were all very deeply involved in church work – in music, drama and pastoral work. I helped open up a drop-in/coffee centre for young people. Ironically, I often did the catering there – but because I'd chosen it, I didn't mind doing it.

I also did a teaching certificate in nursing. Instead of working shifts on the wards, as a clinical nurse teacher I was working from eight till five every day, which meant I had every evening off to do church things and I also had weekends off. So it was Saturday and Sunday – church; Monday, Tuesday, Wednesday, Thursday, Friday evenings – church; daytime Monday to Friday – nursing. It had got to the point where I was working almost full-time in the church as a volunteer, while I was also holding down a full-time NHS job at the John Radcliffe Hospital, and there just weren't enough hours in the day.

Speaking in tongues

I suppose the next significant point was when I went with a group of friends to a meeting at another church, to hear a bishop, David Pytches, who had recently returned from South America. He spoke about the Holy Spirit. Up till that point, the Holy Spirit had not been significant in my life. I had never before heard anyone speaking about the Spirit and about the gifts of the Spirit. At the end of his talk, he did something that I'd only ever heard of people like Billy Graham doing before, and that was he had an altar call.

Now, me, I'm not into altar calls. I'm not going up. No way.

I don't know what made me go. I think that God has had to kick me on a number of occasions in life, and this was probably another one of those kicks. I was one of the last to go up, reluctantly so, but I went up, and knelt down. David Pytches came along to me and said, 'What do you want us to pray for?'

I said, 'Just to know what God wants of me in my life.' And he prayed for me, in tongues, which I'd never heard before. I knew something incredible was going on, because I had the most amazing sense of warmth going through me and a tingling sensation, but I didn't know what any of this meant.

I went back to my seat and I remember speaking to somebody about how odd it felt, and they said, 'Oh don't worry, it's just the Holy Spirit.'

Have I ever spoken in tongues?

Honest answer? Oh dear, yes. But I'm not one of these people who goes round emphasising it, because I believe in all the gifts of the Spirit. Tongues is just one that may be given to people. When I've used it, it has been when I've not known how to pray or what to say. I've been in prayer and said, 'God, I just haven't got the words, I just don't know what to say here.'

There have also been times when I have felt that I was dealing with something dark, and I use tongues then when I don't know quite what it is I'm dealing with pastorally. I know I have the gift and I know I can use it or not use it. It's like a tap.

I've done it mainly as a private prayer. But singing in tongues – I have been party to that – now that is a most amazing experience. The first time I heard it was when I went along to Greenbelt in 1976, and suddenly this incredible singing started going on in the local church. It sounded absolutely extraordinary and beautiful, complete harmony to be with all these strangers, people who had never met, singing together in tongues. It felt a profoundly spiritual experience.

Nursing + Christian = Missionary

I was beginning to think – Nurse plus Christian equals missionary. God would send me out to some wonderful foreign place and I could be saving souls and bodies left, right and centre just like Mother Theresa. You can still see my ambitious side coming through at that point. I was going out into the world to do this great and important work. God was relegated to being a convenient way to get me there.

Then a group of people in St Aldate's Church said, 'We want to support you in this idea, because we think you're doing the right thing.' So that was how I ended up taking a sabbatical and going to Wycliffe College to study theology. They helped finance it. It was, to be frank, from my side, almost purely a financial motivation – a means to an end.

But then I went to Lee Abbey, and got stuck on the rocks – and we've come round full circle to where I began – how my decision to offer myself for full-time Christian ministry came about.

Spaghetti bolognese – is this a test?

I think I'm one of the few people who enjoyed ACCM – the selection process for deaconesses and ordinands. The first night when we were all there – it was all single gender – they sat us down for a meal of spaghetti bolognese. You know that you are going to be judged on absolutely everything, including your sociability. So you're sitting there and you think – Is this part of the test? How do you eat spaghetti bolognese anyway? Do you wrap it round your spoon? Do you cut it up?

So we all had a nervous laugh about that, and the next morning we turn up for breakfast and there is the egg cup with the boiled egg sitting next to it, and we're all looking at each other and wondering – Which way up do you put the egg in the cup? The fat end or the narrow end? Do we tap it on the top? Do we slice it? Do we cut round it? We were all convinced that this was part of the test – whether you got in to the church or not depended on how you ate your spaghetti bolognese and your boiled egg.

You look shattered

I was setting out into an unknown future, I suppose, having to trust in God for the future because for deaconesses – it was not good. When I began looking for jobs, I was very concerned with the motives of a parish for wanting a deaconess. In one place I went to look at, it seemed they just wanted a glorified caretaker of the church hall. Bishop Patrick had warned me when he accepted me for going forward for ACCM that he could not guarantee there would be a place for me in the diocese.

Then I was contacted by one of the ACCM selectors who had been on the panel, Ruth Wintle, who asked if I was aware of a chaplaincy position that was going at the University of Kent. I would never otherwise have thought of going for a university chaplaincy, never having been to university myself.

I had the most horrendous set of interviews for it, of which the only salvation was the Roman Catholic chaplain at the end of the day. By the time I got to him, it was about ten past five in the evening, and I'd been in interviews with different people since before ten o'clock in the morning. The worst part had been a sit-down lunch with about twenty people – all men, all university dignitaries – when I was petrified that I would eat my guinea fowl the wrong way or drink too much wine. Finally I got to this Catholic chaplain – this wonderful man – and he looked at me and he said 'You look shattered.'

He poured me out a lovely big sherry and sat me down and said, 'I'm not going to even bother interviewing you. You just sit here and drink this, and then catch the train home.' And that won me.

Much to my surprise I was offered the job, and chiefly because of him, I accepted.

The making of a deaconess

So I left Wycliffe College and came down to Kent, to Canterbury Diocese, to be made a deaconess. (By the way – I was the first ever woman president of the Junior Common Room at Wycliffe. That's my one claim to fame, such as it is.) As soon as I arrived in this new diocese, I had to go on pre-ordination retreat – and that was when Robert Runcie won my heart and my loyalty.

There were men on the retreat about to be made deacons and there were men about to be made priests, and we all gathered at the Old Palace. I came from a pretty relaxed, charismatic, evangelical background, hanging relatively loose to church pomp and circumstance. Now I found myself in a situation where all the men were wearing their black cassocks with the thirty-nine buttons, walking round looking holy and pious. Of course, once I got to know them they were lovely chaps, but there's me in my blue cassock with only four buttons, and I had to go into silence with these strangers.

I was really getting into a heck of a stew, and wanted out. I had a lovely room – a fantastic big room all to myself – but I was penned in, in silence, with all these strange men floating around looking holy in their thirty-nine-button cassocks. That was my impression. I know I wasn't fair on them.

Then they all started talking about when they were going to make their confessions and I was sitting there thinking – This just isn't me. This isn't what I got into this for. I'm not cut out for this. Above all, the times of silence really got to me.

Robert Runcie called me into his study and he sat me down on the sofa and he said, 'You're finding it really difficult, aren't you?'

And I said, 'Yes I am. I don't think this is for me.'

'What in particular are you finding difficult?'

I told him what I was feeling and that if this was the Church of England, I didn't want to be part of it, and that I'd made a big mistake.

He came and sat beside me and held my hand, and then he prayed. Then he said, 'What you need to do is leave this building. Just walk out of it. Take your cassock off, put your ordinary clothes on, go and get some fresh air, come and go as you please, walk round Canterbury, just do what you like. If you need to talk, talk. And there's only one other thing I'd like you to do, and that is go and talk to the diocesan adviser in women's ministry. Just go and talk to her.'

So I went back to my room. I threw my cassock off and I got out of the Old Palace and I wandered round Canterbury. Then I went to see the diocesan adviser of women's ministry who gave me a large drink. I've already said about the sherry at the university. This is obviously how the church moves things. She talked to me totally normally, I stroked the cat for a while, and we had a chat. Afterwards I felt so much better. I went back to the Old Palace and because I'd been given the freedom to get out, and to leave, and not to wear my cassock, I was absolutely fine after that.

I was probably within a hair's breadth of giving up. I've always said that Robert Runcie, on a one-to-one basis, was a great and holy man, someone very special, anointed by God. I think many other people might not have recognised what was going on inside me and wouldn't have given me the freedom to go and to come back. I think he knew I'd come back.

After that, it was all right, because he'd won my heart, and I walked into the cathedral with the chaps. It was absolutely jam-packed full – and as we walked in everybody was singing 'Paddy's breastplate' – 'I bind unto myself today'. It was mind-blowing.

So I was made a deaconess in Canterbury Cathedral. We deaconesses were done alongside the men who were being ordained, but we were 'made'. We were very clearly told this was not an ordination. It was a making. And we wore a different-coloured cassock, so we were identified as different as well. And we didn't get to wear a dog-collar. We got a big cross, which I've never really enjoyed wearing, because I'm not somebody who walks around with a huge cross hanging from their neck.

And then I started my work at the university as one of the chaplains. I had no expectations, because I'd never been in a university set-up, and so my ministry evolved while I was there. I was there for over eleven years, during which I surprised myself when I achieved a Master's Degree while still working full-time and I was also elected by my academic peers to be the deputy master of one of the university's colleges.

The deacon

I became very involved with MOW locally. I was in the committee and I was a representative on the National Council for the Ordination of Women. Of course, in Canterbury, we were the first to be ordained as deacons, in 1987, because that was the thing about Robert Runcie. He led from the front. I think all the women who were there respected him for that. It was not an easy place for him to be. In his own mind, I don't think he was totally at ease. He was always very supportive of women in ministry, but I think he also saw the larger picture, and the repercussions and problems that it would raise for him as head of the Church of England, particularly with the Roman Catholic and Orthodox Churches. But what was so great about him as an archbishop was that he led from the front.

In fact, we were so ahead of schedule that we were still waiting for the royal signature on the day we were to be ordained deacons, the day of the service in the cathedral. It had to be rushed down.

Once again I had gone on pre-ordination retreat. But this was very different from the last time. For one thing, we all knew each other. The women who were there were good friends and we knew each other's foibles. We knew we represented a complete breadth of churchmanship, but we were at ease with each other. On the ordination morning, we all gave cards and support to each other. We wanted to make sure that we were with each other in this.

Some of them had been deaconesses for years, since just after the Second World War. It made me sad for a couple of them who had waited for ordination for so long, that now they had finally got there, they were nearly at the end of their active lives. In some areas there was debate as to whether people who were nearly past being in active ministry should be ordained. I'm very glad they were, because they had been part and parcel of it all. They'd kept the faith. I was struck by their graciousness.

The next generation

Last year, I had a young female ordinand staying with me for six weeks as a placement. She'd never been involved in any of the battles to become women priests or women deacons. And what saddened me was her complete lack of knowledge about the issues that women – not just me – but many, many women fought for. She'd never even heard of Lee Tim Oi. I couldn't believe that somebody who was to be a woman priest had not heard of Florence Lee Tim Oi [see Introduction]. This younger generation, they have had no waiting, they've had no pain, no anguish, no being patronised or undervalued.

All over in a flash

History was being made. I had sense of tremendous awe. I had a feeling of great humility that I was part of all this. I think we all did.

Then it was all over in such a flash. The actual ordination is over in about ten or fifteen seconds, or it seems to be. I didn't like the television cameras being there. I certainly didn't like somebody who was wandering around with a flash camera taking photos of us during the service. But those were the only two niggles.

The rest of it was just the complete sense of – This is what I've been waiting for. I thought at the time – That was it. I really did. I thought – We're going to be deacons, fantastic. We are being recognised as having an authentic ministry.

The 1992 vote

I was at home at the University of Kent with a whole group of women, including the Bishop of Dover's wife, Jennifer Llewelyn. We were all crowded together in my sitting-room, watching the debate on television, listening to the people's comments, watching all the protestors outside when the news items flicked on. I had faced the possibility it wouldn't go through, and I had been seriously considering two options that had been offered to me. One was to move over to the Methodist Church and the other was to go to America where I had been offered a job.

I would have been deeply disappointed and hurt had the vote not gone through, but we weren't sure. We all sat there, watching the screen. We were a pretty tense bunch. When the voting figures were flashed up, we were all trying desperately to work out our sums on fingers and thumbs. Had we got the 66 per cent we needed? It was very close in one of the houses, the House of Laity.

We were all very silent for a bit. Then we all cheered and celebrated.

Kingsnorth and Shadoxhurst

Bishop Gavin and Bishop Richard suggested that, as I had done eleven years at the university, perhaps now I ought to be looking for another sort of job in the diocese. I was given a list of five parishes to consider and on one of my days off, I took the car and drove round Kent. I didn't even know where half these parishes were. I drove to one, stopped and looked at it and then said, 'No, thank you.' I drove to the next one and found that the house that was being offered was on an island with main roads all round it, so I never even bothered to stop there. I drove out to another and drove straight through that one too, and then I got to Shadoxhurst.

All I knew about Kingsnorth and Shadoxhurst was that the last parish priest had been anti women priests, that it was a church with a predominately senior-citizen membership, that it was entrenched in the Book of Common Prayer, and hadn't changed very much in recent years. I drove out here and strangely enough – anybody who knows this area will be quite amused by it – I couldn't find Kingsnorth. I found Shadoxhurst. Nobody ever knows where Shadoxhurst is, in the middle of nowhere.

It was a lovely, glorious August day, and I arrived at Shadoxhurst Church. I got out of the car and went up to the church, which was locked, but a notice told me where to get the key. I got it and walked back to the church. I opened the door, looked inside and at that moment, I knew that I was coming here. The church was bathed in white light.

Shadoxhurst is a lovely little church set in the middle of the countryside. Just a few old houses round about it. It seats only about forty-five or fifty people. Mostly clear glass, light-coloured pews, the most comfortable pews I've ever sat in.

The sunlight was just flooding in. The only stained glass window of any note there is one that is predominantly clear but with the crucifix on it. It caught the light and I sat there looking up at the crucified Lord bathed in sunlight. There was an incredible sense of coming into a church that was filled with the glory of God, that was warm, that didn't smell musty and dusty and unused. You knew it was loved.

I came out of the church, returned the key, got back in the car and finally managed to find Kingsnorth. The church was open and I walked in.

If I'd gone to Kingsnorth first, I'd never have gone to see Shadoxhurst. It was dark, it was dingy, and it was damp. That was my impression. It was such a contrast, having come out of a beautifully, brilliantly lit church. But the feeling was still with me – I was coming here.

You don't stand a chance

So I went back to Bishop Gavin and said, 'Kingsnorth and Shadoxhurst.'

He said, 'You don't stand a chance.'

'Why not?'

'Well, first and foremost because the previous incumbent was anti women priests and so the congregation will be, and second because there are two gentlemen who are interested in it.'

I thought – Fair enough. But I said, 'I'm still interested.'

I was carried along by this utter conviction. There are definite events in my life where I've been utterly convicted about things, and this was one of them.

I came and looked around the church again and met the four churchwardens. We sat in a house and one of them made it absolutely clear that he was not going to support my application under any circumstances. One of them smiled sweetly at me all the way through. Another one seemed quite positive in my favour. I subsequently learnt that these two had come into the meeting saying, 'No way a woman', but had gone out saying, 'Yes, please'. And the last one was a lovely lady who had been told by her husband not to have a woman priest under any circumstances. He was a very firm Catholic. She was very quiet throughout the whole interview.

With the first three I realised quite quickly where they stood, but she – I could not decide where she was. But it was she who carried the day. And two years later, when her husband died, he had left instructions that I was to conduct the service.

In the end, three of them said, 'We really would like to give her a go.' That was a very brave decision for them because they were looking at somebody young, from the university chaplaincy, untried in parish work, and a woman.

Because of the trickiness of the situation of being one of the first women to be appointed with incumbent status in the diocese, they decided that the whole PCC should have the opportunity of making a decision about me. At that point, in 1993, I was still not a priest; I was a deacon. So I had to come back again one night and meet the whole PCC, who were then allowed to vote on whether they would have me or not.

The archdeacon rang me up the next day with their answer. I'm here, so we know which way the vote went. I've always said to the church since then that they have to look back to that group of predominantly senior citizens who had the courage to say, 'We will have a woman minister.'

Three people – two women and a man – left the church as a result of me coming here, and my sadness is that of those three, only one of them now has any regular church affiliation. Two of them left the church completely; they didn't go anywhere else. That has been a real source of sadness for me. I do talk to them on a fairly amicable, pleasant basis. As long as I'm not wearing my collar, they treat me with courtesy.

Deacon-in-charge

There are two people from my life who I would have really, really liked to be at that service when I was licensed to serve in the parish – and both had died. One was my adopted father, who had died on 14 February 1992, and the other was an aunt who had been a mentor to me for many years, who died on 24 February 1993. I moved to the parish on 14 February 1994 – exactly two years after my father died. I was licensed on 24 February 1994 – exactly one year after my aunt had died. I had no control over these dates, because these things were not in my hands.

The following day, I was doing my first real tour of the church, with my own set of keys, and up in the clock room I discovered that the clock was made in 1868 – by the company that my father had worked for all his life.

There's a phrase in one of the new Common Worship services – liturgical prayers – that just sums up for me everything I feel, the sense of completion. It has the words, 'gather up into your loving arms'. I felt when I came here that God was gathering me up and setting me in this place to be his servant.

While I was a deacon, I was in a very tricky pastoral situation with somebody who needed to feel forgiven. In the end I had done something which at that time I thought was justifiable pastorally, but in terms of church law, wrong. I had absolved them. I felt that was essential for them. I had that sense of needing to be able to offer a whole ministry, not to cut off halfway.

I talked about it to a senior church member afterwards. He said to me, 'How did you feel afterwards?'

I said, 'I felt it was utterly right.'

'And how did the person feel afterwards?'

'Utterly relieved.'

'Then you did the right thing.'

Three months after coming here, I was priested on 8 May 1994.

Parish profile

Ashford is one of the biggest exploding areas in the UK in terms of population and industrial growth. We are caught up in that. When I

arrived, Kingsnorth and Shadoxhurst were two small villages connected
by the little hamlet of Stubbs Cross. We had a population of around
3,000. We're now up to somewhere round about the 8,000- or 9,000-
mark population, likely to go up to about 15,000 or 16,000, possibly
even more. It's a huge new estate and they're now talking in terms of
over 2,500 new houses. They have also started building three more estates.
So there has been a complete shift in the average age.

We've got a lot of young families moving in. A number have come
from south London because they can get a much bigger house here for
the same price as they had in south London. A lot of them have come
from inner Ashford, because they see this as the next step up the ladder.
Houses start at what is at the lower end of the market in this area,
£80,000, right up to ones on the new estates, where you could be looking
at up to £300,000.

The church at Kingsnorth has grown exponentially since the estate
has happened. In fact, the estate has brought much needed life to the
church. We've now got a dynamically different congregation, quadrupled
the numbers and halved the average age. We have managed to keep all
those surviving members from 1994 who are still resident in the area,
and it is really great that they have come along with us. Make no mistake,
they've not only had to put up with a woman priest, they've had to put
up with major changes in the church's direction – ethos, worship – almost
everything about this church has changed.

Though having said that, the worship does reflect the different patterns
in the church at large, from the traditional through Common Worship to
the informal. We have, and continue to work hard at providing a balanced
pattern of worship that can offer every member of the community
something they can identify and relate to.

We have now outgrown the building. We've got to a point where we
have a small, beautiful Norman church but – like most churches – it
needs an awful lot of work done on it. Dilemma. We want to preserve
our church, but equally it's totally impractical for our needs. We haven't
even got running water. As for putting in toilets or anything – it's just out
of the question. The pews were made for what I call 'little boys' bottoms'.
There used to be a boys' industrial school in the parish, and in order to
cram all the boys into the church, they ripped the box pews out in 1868
and replaced them with incredibly narrow pews. Fine for little boys'
bottoms but hopeless for anybody else. But what can we do?

Sometimes I wonder if I would have come if I'd known the challenge
I was going to face, but I thrive on it. It gives me a bit of a buzz. Equally,
I think – Oh, my goodness, how am I going to cope with all this? But
we're a young church. I think this must be the youngest PCC in the
diocese, both young in faith and young in age.

People come to church now because they want to come. I get really fed up when I hear about how church numbers are falling. Gone are the days when people went to church because they had to go to church. You look back at the church attendance roll here 100 years ago. Yes, it looks great, but that's because the servants went because the master told them to.

We have a policy – sometimes I have to keep reminding parishioners – that when people come along to the church, we don't bully them into doing things for six months. We let them find themselves, see if this is their spiritual home. We want people to feel that they belong to a family and even if you only come to church twice a year, you're still part of the family. You've got some members of any family who are always in and out of each other's houses, but you've also got other members who go off and come back every so often. The church is like that. We have a lot of folk who work at weekends. They have to. Therefore they only come to church once a month or so. They are still family members of this church no less than those who come every week are, and I want them to know that they're no less valued, no less wanted and appreciated.

The drama group

About two years ago, a couple in my congregation came to see me and asked me if I would support the idea of a youth drama group within the church. So, yes, of course I was very excited about it. They wanted to tie it in with the millennium, so they decided to call it Ark Drama 2000. We had absolutely no idea what the response would be other than that their own children would come along to it.

It just grew phenomenally. We advertised in the local paper, said it was happening; news travelled by word of mouth in the schools and currently we've got over fifty young people involved in it. It is a church-based group, but it's not pushy. There are still the teenagers bored stiff about coming to church. They love the drama group but they really don't do church. It's not cool to go to church. But I went backstage just before they began the show, and I overheard this. One of them said, 'Right, now we're going to pray.' And it was such a simple prayer. They just said something like, 'Please God, bless this show and be with us tonight.'

They are involved in singing, acting, dance, stage scenery making, and all the backstage activities. By giving them an aim and a challenge, they're responding, they're achieving and they're performing. So many kids on these big estates, even from good families, run wild because they are bored. These are too busy to run wild.

The first year they put on *Scrooge* and with great courage booked the local civic centre. Everyone was astounded because they filled it. And they put on a brilliant show. I've never seen a bishop cry before, but I saw Bishop Gavin cry that night.

A butterfly on my cassock

Bishop Gavin said to me once, 'What do you think you're really good at?'

And I said, 'I do a good funeral.'

I like the idea of the caterpillar that has to die in order to be born again as a butterfly. I talk about the caterpillar, the chrysalis and the butterfly as a symbol of resurrection. Like any analogy it isn't perfect, but children and many people can hold on to that image. We had a very moving occasion at a funeral where somebody much loved in the parish had died, and because nearly 500 people turned up at Shadoxhurst Church, we had to hold the service outside.

Now, there was a cause for prayer. Never have I prayed for a warm, dry day so much as on that day. We had the service at the graveside. The sun shone. And for nearly the whole service, I had a butterfly resting on my cassock.

The future Archbishop of Canterbury?

I couldn't do the job if I was married. I've come to know that. The person I am, the job I do, the way I do it, I could not be married. When I get back into the house, I don't want to have to start thinking about anybody else and worrying about them and their lives. My sanity is my space and the older I get, the more I appreciate it. I know I could not have done what I have done in the last eight years here if I'd had to worry about a home and family. But that's me. I would never say anybody else couldn't. I'm sure other people could. Whether single women priests are more vulnerable than male priests, only time will tell as statistics come out, but it is a lonely job. There is a price to be paid. Commitment is costly, but the job satisfaction is tremendous.

I think any priest – any pastoral priest – is somebody who needs to be needed and at the same time feels they've got something to give. I feel I have something to give because of my past experience and because of my faith. I'm content to remain Sheila, the parish priest, who's been allowed to be a priest, and has been allowed to be herself. That's a big change in my outlook, because when I was a nurse I'd have said I wanted to become Sheila the archbishop!

But I do believe that in my parish I may have the first woman Archbishop of Canterbury. She's only just five, but I have this feeling. Her father took her to see Canterbury Cathedral not so long ago. She was running around, looking at everything, exploring and asking questions. Then she went under the roped-off area and sat on the archbishop's throne. The verger was not amused by this and gave her a sound telling-off – which I think was a bit too strong – but she wasn't in the least bit intimidated. She said to him, 'When I'm in Reverend Sheila's church, I can sit in any chair like, and she wouldn't ever tell me off.'

Jeremiah in the Old Testament was worried that he was only a child when he was drawn to God – and look what happened to him!

REVD KATHARINE RUMENS

8

City Priest by Design

REVD KATHARINE RUMENS

Rector, St Giles, Cripplegate, in the Barbican

Many women of my generation have a tremendous sense of indebtedness. Reading the accounts of the early days of the campaign, and knowing the cost, what it is to be ostracised, to be laughed at, to make yourself unpopular because you believe in the ordained priesthood of all believers. We feel much is required of us.

Introduction

AB: 'Here is the little door', an anthem about which I can remember nothing except its title, came to my mind one minute after I had ended my visit to Revd Katharine Rumens. We had talked in her rectory, a still, quiet house looking out on to a paved area, in which stands the beautiful floodlit church of St Giles, Cripplegate, for which she is responsible. It was very tranquil and even the sound of rain could be heard falling in the small garden outside the window. Now we had said goodbye, and I left through a little door (not the way I had come in) and found myself suddenly in a busy, noisy, City street at the height of the London rush hour. Looking round in shock to adjust my bearings, I could no longer see the little door behind the scurrying masses pouring out under umbrellas from surrounding office buildings.

Made of slabbed concrete, these office blocks create sombre canyons along the city streets. Apart from the eye-catching dome of nearby St Paul's Cathedral, there is little to suggest that this was once one of the great medieval wards of the City of London, once itself divided into six parishes, with the parish of St Giles in 1775 containing almost 2,000 dwelling houses.

Katharine views it all with an appreciative but practical eye: 'It is beautiful here, especially in view of everything else around, which is 1960s architecture, and all the concrete looks grim in wet weather. So to have the church with its stone tracery and the brick tower, and then the exquisite cupola, to look out on is wonderful. I often sit here and think how lovely it is – but it gives me a worry because I think – someone's left a light on! I do get concerned if there are lights on that I can't account for.'

Katharine is the first female incumbent in the City of London. William Maitland's eighteenth-century history provides a contemporary account of her parish, founded in 1090. In Wood Street, not far from the 'little door', was a prison built in 1555. The area was packed with little courtyards and alleys. There was Three Dagger Court, Angel Alley 'long and good', and the Green-yard which in 1775 was 'made use of by the City as a Pound, for such cars and coaches, whose drivers commit any offence in the streets, contrary to rules and orders'. An eighteenth-century car pound, and the equivalent of today's traffic wardens no doubt patrolled 'Barbican, a good broad street well inhabitated (sic) by salesmen for apparel'.

A century earlier, the parish of St Giles benefited from the generosity of the Bishop of Winchester, who donated thirty-six shirts and twenty pairs of stockings each year; Henry VIII left funds for the Minister of Lamb's Chapel nearby to provide each year 'for twelve poor men and as many women, a good pair of winter shoes'. In the parish church is buried Edmund Harrison, embroiderer to three kings: James I, Charles I and Charles II.

Uncovering such a history, it seems extraordinarily appropriate to discover that Katharine Rumens has forsaken a career in fashion design to take holy orders. She is an artist, and her impressionist landscapes fill every wall of her home overlooking her church, which survived the 1666 Great Fire of London and later a huge nineteenth-century fire, only to be bombed in 1940.

Today the area is best known for the modern Barbican with its theatre and Arts Centre, whose huge blocks of flats make highly desirable homes for those who want to miss commuting out of their lives. The church, much restored since the Blitz, is home to the joint congregations of St Giles, Cripplegate, and St Bartholomew, Moor Lane, with St Alphage, London Wall, and St Luke, Old Street, with St Mary, Charterhouse, and St Paul, Clerkenwell.

The principal dedication to St Giles, the hermit of the Rhone and saint of cripples and lepers, may well have been influenced by the existence in medieval times of a well in the adjacent but now vanished Jewin Street. The water was described by Maitland as 'very good for sore eyes; and some say, it is very good for men in drink to take of this water, for it will allay the fumes and bring them to be sober'.

Jewin Street was laid out on the ancient burying place of the Jews of London, whose skill and artistry were, as Katharine Rumens told me, the foundation of the 'rag trade', the glamorous world that which the Rector of St Giles has elected to leave.

Canon Lucy Winkett, in nearby St Paul's, said that she understands only too well from her own experience Katharine's irritation and anger at many remarks and 'compliments' she receives, from people whose actual – if unconscious – intention is to diminish her authority.

Katharine

I do hope you say that to your male priest as well

I have never been so consistently patronised as I have since taking up this job. 'Are you the curate?' Or, 'Are you just helping out?' Or, 'You're too young and pretty to be the Rector!'

Somebody said, 'May I say, what a most attractive priest?'

I was feeling uppity, so I said, 'Of course, and I do hope you say that to your male priest as well.'

I wonder sometimes about losing my calm or getting lippy. I belong to a consultation group. We meet once a week on a Wednesday and there I can do what I call my 'spillage', and compare notes. It helps to hear of others in the same boat.

I am the first female incumbent in the City of London. The archdeacon led a morning on City churches, and three of us who were recently arrived were invited to speak. I was told that one church had absented itself because I was going to speak.

What I find even more disheartening is, I might take a large service for the community, a Christmas carol service, perhaps, for bankers or lawyers or something like this. After you have shown your authority and conducted the service, there's always somebody at the reception at the end of it who will tell you that they, of course, don't think women should be priests.

It can be very undermining. We are still in the days when you may have a big family group coming in for a baptism who may have never seen a woman conducting worship before. It takes a lot of stamina, it takes energy, to be on top of what is happening in the service, and then to keep going when you are meeting new people afterwards. There are 2,000 of us now, ordained women priests, but we nearly always work in isolation, so we have to deal single-handedly with the comments we get at the end, and it does seem hard to me when we get sniped at after a time of worship.

It is hard to live with a lack of generosity

I like to get as many people involved in leading worship as possible. Somebody who never thought she'd had it in her started to read the lessons, and she said to me afterwards, 'I just didn't realise how terrifying it was.'

I wanted to say, 'Told you so!'

The whole language of the Bible can seem very disempowering, if you think of things like, 'we are children of God' and 'sheep for shepherds'. So what happens if we say, 'Look, we are adults, partners with God in caring for the divine creation'?

All clergy – men and women – spend a lot of time feeling misunderstood. We slug our guts out trying to get a service together, then somebody's run off with the key, the sacristan's poorly and nobody can find anything, and all anybody at the end says is, 'The hymn boards weren't out.' It is the easiest thing in the world to criticise.

So there are all sorts of complications and levels of irritation and of interaction, and sometimes it's a question of who is pastoring whom. It doesn't help to lose one's calm. I am aware when we say, 'Go in peace, to love and serve the Lord' – that means us as well.

The last parish
I was previously at St John's, Waterloo, a mile and a half away, and not as different as it might at first appear. Part of my work there, as here, was initiating chaplaincy work in the arts and media. Worlds I know. I was chaplain for the Festival Hall and the Hayward Gallery, so here the Barbican Art Centre was familiar territory. I was chaplain to the Old Vic and to London Weekend Television, and here I am chaplain to the RSC.

There was a residential population of socioeconomic contrasts, just like here. Towards the Elephant and Castle it was council housing, while along the riverbank at County Hall, it was all pieds-à-terre. I used to walk the whole length of the parish in Waterloo, down Waterloo Road, through all its dimensions, at least twice a day on my way to and from the church for Morning Prayer. The difference here is that I live in the posh bit of the parish, next to the church. That's a real disadvantage in many ways.

I applied to come to St Giles because I was looking for a post of responsibility. The incoming curate was being ordained deacon at Michaelmas, so I felt I needed to be out of the way by early autumn.

It gave me a sense of panic when nothing happened. I was applying for jobs and sending out my CV to the London, Oxford, Guildford and St Alban's Dioceses. People were saying, 'Yes, we're putting you on our wish list.' But nothing really happened. Then I was short-listed for three jobs in quick succession. And this was the second one.

A dinner-party conversation – without the dinner
The interview here was unnerving. It was like a dinner-party conversation without the dinner. There was no structure to it at all. I had the just-after-lunch slot, so obviously my job was to keep everybody awake.

I was so thrown by the interview, I thought they couldn't possibly have enough information from it to be able to appoint me. It was time to try for the next one. So later that afternoon, I went for a walk round the next parish I'd applied for, to be up to speed for that interview, which was to be about three days later.

But then they said, 'Yes'. They did want to appoint me here, but first it would have to be ratified by the Bishop of London, Richard Chartres.

So I worked hard, preparing all my answers to what I thought would be his likely questions – what I thought about parochial ministry, what I was reading and what I felt about it, and how I would go about introducing Common Worship. Bishop Richard had known me a long time, of course, because I was a London ordinand when he was Diocesan Director of Ordinands.

I went to see him and all he said was, 'Do you want the job? When do you want to start and when shall we make it public?' So I did feel a bit over-prepared!

Famous antecedents

The dedication of the parish is St Giles, Cripplegate with St Luke's, Old Street. St Luke's covers the northern part of the parish and is very different in character from the Barbican, a modern complex, a place of great affluence, where people have come to live since the 1960s. As we go northwards, through the parish towards St Luke's, there's Whitecross Street, with Peabody Flats, and the Golden Lane Estate. I was talking to somebody from St Luke's just last week and he said, 'My family's lived here for 400 years.'

Milton is buried here, Cromwell was married here, and Shakespeare's nephews were baptised here. We have links with Daniel Defoe, and William Blake is buried in Bunhill Fields, the dissenters' cemetery, also in the parish.

We're very proud of our antecedents. The blocks of flats in the Barbican are all named after local people like John Speed the cartographer, and Martin Frobisher, explorer of the north-west passage; while Lancelot Andrews was not only the incumbent in St Giles, Cripplegate, but at the same time was also working on the translations of the Authorised Version of the Bible.

Outside the City walls

The church is central, middle-of-the-road, in terms of its thinking and tradition. There's an openness about our ministry here. Before I came there had been two women curates, which sets it apart from most other city churches, and my job was advertised, which again makes it seem more like part of the mainstream.

I rather like where the church is, outside the old Roman city walls, but inside today's City of London. We are idiosyncratic in that, unlike all the other city churches, there is a significant residential population. We have Sunday services and family services; there is a Youth Club and a junior choir. We don't have jumble sales but we do have a Christmas Fair, all the ritual of parish life in fact. Whereas St Lawrence Jewry, for example, or St Margaret's, Lothbury, are not necessarily open at the weekend, because there's no residential population.

But having said that, for the Barbican residents this too can be their Monday-to-Friday home, or they live here only when they're not in Suffolk or Norfolk or Arizona.

It's awfully solid, awfully male

Different places can become holy spaces at different times. I've started saying my prayers in different parts of the church. I'm always trying to find a nook or a cranny, a new area where I enjoy what I'm looking at. Because I trained as an art teacher and then I was in the fashion business, I have got a good eye.

I hope I'm not being neurotically extreme when I say about the building here that it's awfully solid, awfully male, because there's nothing rounded and gentle in it. There are the heavy pews and then the sanctuary has just four big blocks of square desks for those leading worship. Everything is colossal and solid. And then we've got all the uniformed organisations' flags, and the Master Barber Surgeon's Company insignia, and there are far too many coats of arms. I feel it needs to be more of a church and less of an overspill for the City.

Creating new focal points

The first artist puts her exhibition up here in a couple of weeks' time.

I'm interested in retrieving the space for worship and prayer. I think I can do that by working with artists, because they do see things in a different way and can help us create new focal points. You can make people move through the building in different ways, and learn to see nothing is permanent. We're all in a state of transition. We don't have to only say our prayers in the north-east corner. One day people may find the south side is sunny and think, 'Hey! This will be a nice place to say prayers.' Or if you've got an artist coming in with some sort of intimate sculpture, and you put them round the font, people might look at that bit of their church in a new way and see its potential. That's what I mean about working with artists.

Movement matters

I believe in liturgy being done well. It has got to be done clearly, distinctly and well, and I mind about that. I mind for members of the congregation, and I mind for the children who might not be able to see much or comprehend all that much. I mind for those who are visually impaired or for those who have hearing loss and might not catch everything that's going on.

Movement matters and ritual matters. It is interesting, coming to a new place. The crucifer charges off down the aisle in front of me, and I want to convey the sense that we're not trying to catch a bus. I suppose I am a performer in my sense of movement and space. These things that I learned through design and art very much affect how I lead worship.

I've always loved art and painting. My mother had a good eye, and my father can do line drawing. I find it interesting problem-solving, because you haven't got an immediate answer. You can't look it up at the back of a book and find it says, 'The answer is: 39.' You've got to work out when to stop painting because either it balances or it doesn't. By the time you put an idea down on paper, the two dimensions create their own discipline and you're not given the answer. It's to do with hunch and intuition and feeling your way through until you stop at a point where it feels right.

Like the Brontës

I was born in 1953, in Swanage, when my father was serving his title in Wareham. My father is ordained and served his entire ministry in the Salisbury Diocese, so I was brought up first in Dorset and then Wiltshire. It was a country childhood. My father comes to visit me and says, 'My daughter, my daughter, what are you doing in the City?'

After Wareham, we were in a village on the edge of the New Forest. But the church, the school and the vicarage were about a mile from the rest of the village, and my older sister Elizabeth and I, being the two eldest siblings, had a very isolated childhood. And then along came my younger brother, Jonathan, who wasn't allowed to play in the garden because there were adders, but my sister and I could put on our Wellington boots. We were very self-contained in what seemed to be a vast, very cold, Edwardian house with an enormous garden, and nobody came to play with us. It was the days when 'the village people' didn't mix with 'the vicarage'.

We didn't know we were lonely. We didn't know any other way. We became very self-sufficient and when I was about three my mother decided I was artistic so I had rolls of kitchen paper bought for me and powder colours. I really wanted those little hard blocks of bright turquoise. I wanted real colour rather than mixing it myself, which always turned brown anyway. But we always made everything we needed. I think the isolated childhood made us all very close. It sounds like the Brontës!

We went to the village school and that was quite dreadful. Susan – who was a sort of a matriarch at the age of six, from one of the big village families – tyrannised me. She set down the law. The front desks were kept for the gypsy children and Susan told me it was the village rule that we didn't speak to the gypsies because they didn't stay long enough. Elizabeth used to get it as well. We always had to have the window tight shut at night because a girl called Kathleen had told her that if you had the windows open, 'The owls will come in and peck your eyes out.'

There was just one big schoolroom, divided with screens and heated with a small tortoise stove at each end. Mrs Mortimer said, 'Hands up everyone who can't read.' I'd only just gone to school, so I couldn't read. She said, 'Right. Sit at that table and I'll teach you to read this afternoon.'

When I was seven, we moved from the huge, cold, brown, lino-floored house in the New Forest. We got very cosmopolitan and moved to Salisbury.

Katharine should be ashamed of her RE exam results

Religion and churchgoing was always in the background. My mother comes from clerical stock. Her grandfather was ordained. She had two brothers and they all went to church. My godparents all went to church. Godparents accumulated, from the congregation in Wareham. There was a big congregation in Salisbury and many of them became family friends.

Godliness might not ever have been voiced at home, but was there in kindness and friendliness and familiar things, like going for walks together. We always did things together as a family on a Saturday, which was my father's day off. I suppose it's to do with not having much money but we liked walking together on the beach or in the country. There wasn't much money for things like going to the cinema, but there were big open spaces for walking. So we always had a brisk family walk somewhere every Saturday. That was in the 1960s and the very early 1970s and lifestyles were more austere than today, especially in provincial towns.

I don't remember the village church, but I liked going to church in Salisbury, at St Edmund's. You could sit there and drift, and dream your dreams and listen to the music and watch what was happening at the front. I liked the movement and the colour of the vestments. The light was good and the space was good and the organ played and you sat on your chair and you just drifted for an hour. My father would preach, but it didn't really impinge.

But I hated RE lessons at school; they were tedious, it was awful. I came across my school report when I was thirteen. Miss Hatfield did religious instruction, and she wrote on my report, 'Katharine should be ashamed of her exam results.' My sister had the same teacher and did equally badly, so that wasn't a good summer for Miss Hatfield.

Learning about art

When I left the girls' grammar school in Salisbury, I wanted to do theatre design, because I liked the theatre and I was artistic. But the school gave us appallingly old-fashioned career guidance. All that they had lined up for us were careers in either nursing or teaching. Of those two options, teaching was going to be more my line.

I went off to train as an art teacher in Norfolk for three years. I wanted to experience living away from home. I went to Norwich because the art department there had a good reputation, and because it wasn't London.

There was excellent painting tuition, but I found the teaching practice part quite worrying. I was out of my element in secondary modern schools. It was a world I'd never come across. I'd never before met children who freely used obscenities. But I survived.

For the fourth year I was offered a place at Cambridge to do my BEd, but then I failed my art viva. I thought – Right. I'll show you. I said to my art teacher, 'I shall go and live abroad.' So having said it, I had to go and do it.

In 1974, I went to live in Madrid for a year and, to earn my keep, I taught English. Then I went back and I got my BEd in practical art at the University of East Anglia. I could paint it, rather than do a lot of academic theory and history of art, and that probably suited me better. Having done my BEd, I decided I still didn't want to live in England, so I went to live in Italy. Then I went off to Portugal, where I worked for eight academic hours a week, and in local terms I was incredibly well paid for doing next to nothing.

I felt a bit rootless. After a couple of years, I found that I didn't really like the expatriate world, because you are disadvantaged as a foreign woman living and working in relatively small towns. You have no family to support you, and you don't easily fit in with your contemporaries who are at home in their own culture and language, and are all living at home with their parents.

I wanted to establish myself back in my own culture and I decided to retrain. I investigated calligraphy, interior design and fashion design. It just happened that a fashion design course could be worked in with my job in Portugal, so that's what I did. It wasn't after any great deliberation or planning.

At the end of that course, which was just for a year, nobody would employ me and somebody said, 'Well, then, you had better start up by yourself.' So I did.

The fashion designer

I started up on my own as a fashion designer back in England, and quite early on I got coverage in *The Times*. I had made up a collection. A friend of a friend who had a little shop in Earls Court said I could come and use their window space. So I did and the people in the shop said, 'You must get this collection written about.' So I just went along to *The Times* with a suitcase of all this stuff, not realising you shouldn't really do it like that.

I had made absolutely everything myself, but I was economical with the truth, and implied that I was part of a far larger concern. When I got *The Times* coverage in 1981, I had to rope friends in to help make things like crazy, because we had all these telephone calls ordering things. In the end everything was made on just two sewing machines. It was quite hairy.

It's good to get the applause when the stuff's on the catwalk. It's a good feeling. After that I had virtually two collections a year over the next ten years. I started by doing individual customers, and then I moved into wholesale. I had a team, and we were selling through fifteen shops, with rather obscure monosyllabic names like Crème or Chic. Ambers was one of them. We were at the higher end of the price range, with no accommodation for reality whatsoever. It was clothes for the bride's mother, for whom no expense could be spared.

I've always found clothes interesting, the shape and colour and putting different textures together. I was brought up in vicarages, and therefore we never really did much shopping because there wasn't the money for it. I had always made my own clothes. I still do, in dribs and drabs, when I can find the time. I go to nearly-new shops and charity shops and modify things. It's more make do and mend these days than high fashion.

Clerical fashion

I even made some clerical robes when I was a freelance designer. For instance, when David Hope was made Bishop of Wakefield, I made his cope, and I see from the photographs that he's hung on to it.

I made my own chasuble for the first time I presided at the Eucharist, but in the main I wear whatever is there. What I wear to celebrate here is quite ghastly – viscose. But I wear what is here. I do make sure they're clean. At my last church, the vestments were so manky I said, 'Right, this lot has all got to be dry-cleaned.'

I was told they were old and precious. I said, 'Right. Well, if they don't survive dry-cleaning, we'll throw them away because I'm not wearing them like this.'

Something less stodgy

I hadn't been going to church much at all during the time I lived abroad. The embassy churches were rather stodgy. There was no interesting or radical thinking going on. After living in London for about a year, I started going to church because some friends said, 'You'll like this church, it's like your father's church in Salisbury. That was St James, Sussex Gardens. I was fairly soon on the PCC. Bits of it were very good, and I did like it there, but I was surprised by people there who made great decisions during the week, had positions of tremendous responsibility at work, but who didn't seem to have any sense of adventure in their faith. It became my church, and was important to me, but I thought it was still all rather stodgy.

It was about that time, the early 1980s, that my mother heard Margaret Webster speaking in Salisbury about the Movement for the Ordination of Women (MOW). My mother was just recounting to me how well Margaret had spoken when I realised I knew her name from Norwich. I'd lived for a year in the Cathedral close, and I'd met her. I decided to join MOW.

It was a breath of fresh air. It changed everything for me, because here at last were the prophets and the rebels and the people who said, 'We can bring about change.' I started going to gatherings and meetings. I found it exhilarating. I didn't see myself as a ground-breaker in MOW, because there were women there who were deaconesses, then deacons, and so they were the avant garde, who were already ordained, and I came into it late, with the groundswell. But I became very committed to MOW, and played an active part. It was the beginning of feeling that I could really belong to at least part of the church. And whichever church I belonged to after that, MOW gave me continuity.

St Hilda Community

I was still in the fashion business in the mid-1980s, still thriving. You don't stay in business if you're not good, because it's fast, competitive and cut-throat. But the buyers liked my stuff and I sold. But at this time my mother died. She had had a progressive illness, but her death still came suddenly.

I moved home again, still in London, and became based in Maida Vale, where I started to go to my local church. I think that's something you need to do, even if there are things you don't like about it, because it connects you into your home area. You get to know the person in the greengrocers or the man walking his dog every morning, because you also meet them at church.

Then I was told about the St Hilda Community, where the liturgy was different from anything I'd ever experienced. I don't know if this still happens when the St Hilda Community meets, but they would have the Gospel reading, and then people would all throw in their own observations about it. I remember one cleric saying, 'Oh, I do find John getting so tedious with all these "I am" statements!'

I thought, 'You're allowed to say that? Wow!'

I had often thought things like that, but I hadn't realised that anyone would ever actually say it, out loud, and in church. For me, it felt like coming alive.

And then – I suppose it would be about 1987 – the Revd Suzanne

Fageol was over from the States and celebrated communion at St Hilda.
It was the first time I saw a woman presiding. That really made me think.

'Too sophisticated'

It was then that I stopped going to my local church for a variety of
reasons. It certainly didn't help that it was entirely male-led. Spiritually, I
felt more and more as if I didn't belong there. I met my parish priest for
lunch one day and I heard myself saying, 'If I went to a selection
conference, at least the Church of England and I would know whether
we had a future together!'

I really don't know where I got that idea from. I suppose being in
MOW, meeting people in training, hearing different theological colleges
being discussed, and then seeing this great woman presiding at the
Eucharist, it was somewhere in my mind. But I surprised myself when I
said it out loud.

I went along to see the London Diocesan Director of Ordinands
(DDO) for women. I was going on to see the pattern cutter afterwards
and so I was dressed for the rag trade. I rather swept in, I suppose, dressed
to kill. The DDO talked to me, and I don't remember anything else she
said but this, that she couldn't envisage me at *any* theological college,
because I was 'too sophisticated'.

I thought, 'Well that's that. I made a mistake. Well good, that's solved
that.'

But in a way, this galvanised me into action. I went back to my parish
priest and I said, 'Look, why aren't lay people ever doing the prayers?
And why are we having more talks on the early fathers? Why don't we
do something on mothers in the church?'

So he said, 'OK. Do it.'

So then I found myself training people in the congregation to become
intercessors, and a school governor and on the PCC, on all these things.
I hadn't really planned or gone looking for them, but I found I was
getting involved in an increasingly demanding lay ministry. It
was becoming the most important part of my life. I became a daily
communicant.

I was running a visiting scheme, and I had to see my vicar about
something to do with it. Our conversation about it turned into one
about ordination. That was in July 1989. He said I should go to a selection
conference, and start training the following September, 1990.

I then had to wait for three months before I could see Graham
Leonard, the then Bishop of London, who believed in seeing all his
candidates, so he could agree to it.

Ceasing trading

There was a grim waiting time, before I got to see the bishop, when I wasn't sure if I was going to be accepted for training or not. Nobody would tell me anything for weeks on end. My letters weren't replied to, so I didn't know how things were progressing, and nobody was giving me any encouragement or telling me what to read or indeed telling me anything. I was still running my fashion business, and trying to cope with all this uncertainty from the church.

I didn't know where or whether I fitted in. I had stopped going to the main service on Sunday altogether at my own church, and I would go at eight o'clock, because I couldn't bear to speak to anybody. I didn't feel I belonged in the pew, because nobody else in the congregation seemed to share my feeling of displacement. There wasn't ever a woman in the sanctuary, and it was a church where young men received a lot of attention. I think they have now signed Resolution B, saying they don't want a woman priest there.

So I was waiting, and all the time I had this great sense of not belonging and not having a place. There was no one close I could talk to about it. At that time father did not really support the ordination of women, and had recently remarried so was naturally involved with his new wife. I couldn't talk to my friends in the rag trade, because it wouldn't mean anything to them and, of course, many of them were Jewish. Even my sample machinist, who was good and we'd worked together for a long time, a Polish Roman Catholic, when I finally was accepted to start training, said to me, 'When you come back, we'll start up again.' She thought I was going off to do some sort of secretarial course.

Just last year I ran into somebody from the rag trade, by the zips in John Lewis. I'd known him for years when I was in the fashion business, and he said, 'Are you still a nun?' So that was the sort of level of comprehension.

So even when I knew I was accepted, I didn't try to explain, I just told everyone that I was ceasing trading.

No surprise at all

I had three good friends in the local church congregation, who I had told, and they were not surprised. And I did tell my MOW friends what was happening, once I had a firm date for the beginning of training; coming through London Diocese with Graham Leonard as your sponsoring bishop was quite something!

You have to get people to write you a reference. I asked my sister's godmother, in Dorset, to be one of my referees. I found it took courage to voice this change of direction. So I was surprised when she said, 'We've thought this of you for some time.' I thought they would be amazed!

So what had been a deep, dark secret and appalling truth to me seemed to come as no surprise at all to other people. I felt rather slow on the uptake. I was the last person to realise how much I had changed. I had never seen myself as a religious woman, because I'm afraid I still rather had an image of them as being like my old maths teacher, who had been a deaconess and went about stoutly shod.

But then I thought of the people I'd come to know through MOW. I thought of Nerissa Jones, and I thought – If she can do it, so can I. And Anthea Williams, who is now in Canterbury Diocese. But I still wasn't altogether sure about what I'd taken on.

The family genes

On the one hand, I was changing my life completely, and on the other, it was no change at all. Here I was, just fulfilling the family genetic predilection. My great-grandfather, my great-uncle, my father, all were priests. My sister's first words are purported to have been, 'Daddy gone church.' My whole background was a gentle travelling in the Anglican tradition. It was a great disappointment to me to think I was being so unoriginal!

I said this to a friend, and he said, 'No, it's quite different. You're doing it as a woman. It's not a well-trodden path that you're following. You needn't think you aren't original!'

Westcott House, Cambridge and after

I always say I chose Westcott House because Sainsbury's was close to it. In fact, I did look at Cuddesdon as well as at Westcott. But Cuddesdon seemed too much of a rural idyll, miles out in the country, with ordinands' children coming in for tea and rock cakes at four o'clock. It was family-oriented. As a single person accustomed to central London, I thought this was not for me. So when Bishop Graham Leonard told me that he would sponsor me on condition that I went to Westcott House, in the middle of Cambridge, that suited me down to the ground.

After my first year at Westcott, I did my summer placement in Canada, because it was 1991, and there were still no women priests here you could shadow, and I wanted to learn from a woman with authority. Then I came back and served my title working as curate with a great guy, Richard Bentley, at East Ham, St Barts. It was part of a team ministry in a parish of 35,000. One of the churches in the team wanted to sign Resolutions A and B, which meant they wouldn't have to have a woman priest. So there was antipathy to me there, with people walking out even if I went just to preach. Or avoiding me and walking on the other side of the pavement.

But I had this brilliant brave, courageous man as the team rector, who was my training incumbent. Richard Bentley was a very exacting teacher, but that's what I wanted. For weeks before and after my ordination as deacon, we'd go through and through the eucharistic prayer. I would have to observe all the punctuation precisely and emphasise all the right words. But it is important to feel fully prepared, completely in control, when you have to celebrate for the first time for real, and that's what he did for me.

Richard had been actively involved with the London MOW, and had spoken out on behalf of women. He was also a member of POW, Priests for Women's Ordination. I asked him if he got a discount on his subscription because he was training a female curate!

Come and go quietly – remember the pain of others

After the vote, in November 1992, somebody wrote to all of us in the Chelmsford Diocese, telling us not to be triumphalist about it. Could we please rejoice quietly, remembering the pain of others.

I wrote back saying, 'Hey, you're not even allowing us to celebrate.' Nobody else questioned this pastoral letter that had come from Diocesan House, but I questioned how pastoral it really was.

I also organised all the women in the Barking episcopal area to see Roger Sainsbury the day after the vote, because he had said he would clear his diary and make himself available. So I booked a time with him for an hour for all the women to go and see him. But once again, we were told to come and go quietly, because there were people who were also seeing him that evening who were very upset.

I said, 'What are you going to do for *us* now pastorally, because this time the waiting might be difficult?'

It's an evangelical diocese, where there were a lot of women who had waited and waited so long that they were now an elder generation who had – I don't know – lost some of their fire? Wanted anything for a quiet life, I suppose. But there were a few of my generation and outspokenness, and we were always being accused of making trouble. It felt as if they just wanted us to keep quiet.

Priesthood

I was ordained in Chelmsford Cathedral at the end of April 1994. My father was there, and bursting with pride. I've got some photographs that show how thrilled he is. He had completely changed his thinking about the ordination of women. My sister Elizabeth came over from Canada, and Jonathan and his family were all there.

Celebrating the Eucharist for the first time is quite extraordinary. It suddenly all makes sense. Certain things make sense just physically. You stand with your arms out. And you've been there, in the church, all week, whether it's having custard creams with someone or looking for the stapler or worrying about a child or whatever you've been doing – and this standing there with arms outstretched is a gesture of tremendous incorporation.

This symbolism is important. Especially at East Ham and Waterloo and the grubby bits of this parish, where you have got real brokenness, people whose lives are broken. This is waiting at bus stops for the bus that doesn't come to get to the early shift, lives of costly living. The Eucharist symbolically connects with Christ's injunction to remember him in the broken bread and poured-out wine, and always with the mess and turmoil and slurry of it all. It is the sanctification of our daily being.

When you're doing the chalice, because there are usually two of you, you administer to every other one, but the bread comes to everyone, and you see the shape of people's hands. They may be hands that had washed up for you during the week or they may be hands that are having a hard time of it with money, or they may be hands that don't open easily.

So I always put the host in gently.

Making a difference

I often walk round this parish and think, 'God, how are we going to manage?' There are 11,000 people here. What was a two-stipendiary post is now a one-stipendiary. I am still finding my way. They've never had a woman in charge before and that change is manifesting itself in all sorts of ways.

Because I spend a lot of time listening to others, I too need to be listened to, so I see my spiritual director perhaps more frequently than some other people. We meet for a couple of hours once a month.

The thing is – women of my generation – we can carry a tremendous sense of indebtedness. Reading the accounts of the early days of the campaign for the ordination of women, and knowing the cost – to be ostracised, to be laughed at, to make yourself unpopular because you believe in the ordained priesthood of all believers, I feel now that much is required of us. We need to carry forward the hope that has been given to women – and to the men who have been marginalised because of their belief that women should be ordained priests. I feel a responsibility to do all that is in us to do, because of what has been done for us in the past.

We're in positions of leadership now. We're in a position to make a difference. So if we're asked, if we're invited, we should not say, 'I'm so sorry, I've got my new oxen to prove.' And I haven't got a partner saying, 'What about the children's education?' I've got nothing to get in the way of anything I might be required to do. So I won't rule out anything that might happen in future. I shall do what I am able to do, and do what I can.

'Hey, work is over for today'

Dr Helen Thorn, in her report 'Journey to Priesthood', commissioned by the University of Bristol in 2000, says that she was surprised at the number of women she interviewed who were single. And it *has* taken a single-mindedness and it is terribly exacting in terms of everything else you might want in life.

Having run my own business, there is a similar pressure and discipline needed in that too, when other people's livelihoods depend upon you. And because the studio was within my own front door, I often had to make myself say, 'Hey, work's over for today.'

My study is here. So I still have to say to myself 'Hey, work's over for today.' Then I have a Scotch. I sit in the bath with a glass of Scotch!

REVD ALISON WHITE

9

The Art of Surprise

REVD ALISON WHITE

Member of Archbishops' Springboard

Part of the difficulty is that the church so often represents a place of safety, and people are very frightened of those places changing. But one of the things that lots of people have discovered is that ordaining women to the priesthood doesn't necessarily make the place less safe. It may do for some. But the things that matter to them are still true.

Introduction

LB: Andrew and I often cross the county of Durham on our journey to and from Scotland. John Betjeman, H. V Morton and J. B. Priestley all waxed lyrical about this strange, barren and wildly beautiful landscape. We too know the countryside that J. B. Priestley describes in his English Journey: *'Some of us, wise or lucky, know West Durham, especially Weardale and Teesdale, which are very beautiful: rocks and heather, glens and streams flashing through golden woods . . . But who knows East Durham?'*

Travelling through East Durham today it is hard to imagine that until less than thirty years ago these green fields, these tree-topped hillsides, these wide roads and modern suburban housing estates, were unvisited by tourists, and known as 'the industrial north-east'. There had been mining here since Roman times. This was a land of coal pits, steelworks, shipyards, factories, and hard-working, often cruelly exploited, underpaid communities struggled to live off them and grew up round them, perhaps in conditions of extreme poverty, but with great pride. There was a degree of hardship and poverty for the people who lived here at the beginning of the century about which J. B. Priestley wrote an almost personal protest:

> *I met some of their wives, sitting round a fire in a sewing circle. They were worn but neat and smiling women, mostly on the small side. Their frank*

talk about their men's wages was not pleasant to listen to. They were glad to see me and were neither resentful nor whining, but nevertheless they made me feel like a fat rich man. And I object to feeling like a fat rich man. That is yet another reason why we must clean up this horrible, dingy, muddle of life.

Women were already playing their part in trying to clean up the muddle of life in Priestley's day. He writes of a Miss Jowitt, who ran settlements, community houses, places which weren't merely 'good to the poor' – they went to war with poverty, ignorance, hopelessness and misery. Women like Miss Jowitt received very little money, living frugally in the ugliest and most depressing surroundings and worked at least twelve hours a day.

Well, in a way you could say it has been cleaned up. There are no working coal pits in the Durham coalfield today, no steel works at Consett, no railway carriages being made at Shildon, and almost no Tyneside shipbuilding. It started in the 1960s, and the 1970s saw a rapid decline that has led to an almost total disappearance of what was once the chief characteristic of north-east England – its heavy industry. Whatever the human misery that life in the pits might have caused, the loss of the old communities has brought its own suffering. Boldon Colliery closed in August 1982. The last pit in the Durham Coalfield closed in 1994. Harsh employment has been replaced by unemployment. Women like Bernice Broggio, then a social worker now a priest, were hard at work up here during the 1960s, helping people to cope with the area's changing way of life.

These were the thoughts and images in my mind as I drove from Edinburgh to East Boldon, to meet Revd Alison White, a member of the Archbishops' Springboard Initiative, who has lived and worked in and around this area since she first came up from London to read English at Durham University in 1975. The call to begin working for God seems to have begun almost as soon as she arrived in the north-east.

Alison told me that she thought that one of the most positive effects of women's ordained ministry had been the broadening out of ministry to include the gifts of many people, not just ordained priests and deacons, but of lay people and formerly more passive members of the congregations. The life of a church is not solely dependent on the strengths of its priest. Alison herself struck me as having the most important gift of all for ministry, a very rare grace, that even though she is a busy person with limited time, for all the time that she is with you she gives you her full attention.

Alison

The doctors' daughters

I was born in 1956 in Liverpool, or near enough, and began my growing up there until I was seven and my younger sister Jan was three and a half.

Then we moved to London when my father's job moved to St Mary's Hospital, Paddington. My father is a professor of viriology. Both my parents were doctors, although my mother stopped practising when her children were born.

We were always greatly encouraged to think for ourselves at home; we had lots of debate, questions, exploring ideas, all that kind of thing. My father is very much someone who likes to have a good, energetic discussion and so do I. I remember my mother as someone with a strong faith, a strong personality, but not in good health through most of those growing years.

We lived in Ealing and attended an Anglo-Catholic church, St Barnabas, and the priest, Father Hetherington, was just wonderful. He was a significant figure, very supportive to us as a family. I don't remember how regular we were as churchgoers, but I know that I got a sense of the reality of God, the beauty of God from that church. I couldn't tell you exactly what that meant to me then, but it remains a strong impression from that period of my life.

The church had a beautiful painted mural in the apse. My memory of it is full of angels and saints and halos, a very beautiful space for me. And in the best sense, I think, I felt that God was a presence, a reality.

Then, when I was fourteen my mother died.

What kind of God were we up against?

We had talked about it. We had been prepared for it to happen, if such a thing can be done. We had been expecting something one day, but you can't know when. And there's a world of difference between having a piece of information, knowing that someone is ill . . . but if you see them every day and they're alive, death is very difficult to imagine. The real absence of somebody is impossible to imagine. I don't think you can, until it happens. I've always had quite a vivid imagination, and you think you have envisaged how it will be, but the reality when it comes is much bleaker and harsher. And also more mundane. Reflecting on it now, I think it's the ordinary things, the laying more places at the table than are needed, those little things that catch you. Not the huge questions.

It brought my sister Jan and me very close together, and we have remained so ever since. A lot of responsibility for care for her had always come to me because of my mother's illness, and did so even more now. It made us very close and that's been one of those good things.

My response to God was disillusioned, angry, alienated and bewildered. That period of time was very complicated for me. It was a very difficult time. It naturally colours my memories.

I think Father Hetherington was a very wise man. We delayed my confirmation until I was sixteen, and then he prepared me for it on my own so that I could ask what I wanted to ask and talk freely. We would meet in his study, after school, and he'd have those peculiar Roneo-ed sheets in purple ink with what we were going to talk about. He would give me one for the next week, so I'd have a chance to chew over things before going to see him. That was a great kindness on his part, and also wise. It didn't resolve this state of almost a stand-off with God that I was having, but it gave me the space I needed.

I don't think I've ever thought God didn't exist, but I did really wonder what kind of God we were up against. It was a very real question for me. At the time, especially if you are a teenager, you feel you are the only person in the world who has ever wrestled with this kind of darkness.

But I don't regret that time. That harshness, that darkness, and having to face all those sorts of questions are immensely important experiences. They have been for me, and it isn't that Father Hetherington made me stop doubting and questioning. I don't think I've ever stopped doing that in some ways, but what made such a huge difference was being able to do it in the company of a priest who wasn't put off by any of that.

Durham

My father remarried fairly soon after my mother died, and the first of my half-brothers was born when I was in the sixth form, Paul. He was a great joy and still is. I went to school at one of the Girls' Public Day School Trusts, Notting Hill and Ealing High School, which was excellent for me. I loved it. We had all the same kind of stimulus to think, to explore new ideas that we always had at home.

When I left school in 1975, at eighteen, I had no idea that there were any bars to a woman doing or being whatever she wanted to do, not the first thought that there could be any difficulty. It wasn't until I went up to Durham University to read English that it struck me for the first time.

But before then, I travelled up by train to be interviewed, and as we rounded the corner into Durham Station there was this extraordinary cathedral and castle on a mound. I was met at the station by somebody who had been at my school. We walked through Durham and by the time I got to the college where I was to stay overnight, I just knew that was where I wanted to be.

I find it very interesting that that instinct was so strong – this is really where I want to be. And in fact, I've never left, which wasn't at all my intention. It's very cold up in the north-east. I thought I would come to the end of the three years and go back south. But that's not how it worked out, and now I would find it very difficult to live in the south. I think the north gets into your bloodstream.

A degree of mischief-making

I went up to university in 1975, and that was when I began to think again about where I was with my own faith. I think it was being away from home, and in a very different environment, finding my own feet. That's perhaps a clichéd way of putting it, but I think that was important for me at university. It was time for myself. Not having to be so responsible. It was a time of being able to play as well as to study.

I had been very argumentative about religion when I was at school. There was a group of people there who must have been a Christian Union or a Christian study group, I don't remember – but I went along to their meetings occasionally and was really quite a wrecker. I enjoy arguing and I'm sure there was a degree of mischief-making and a good deal of arrogance in all of it. But also, I didn't like people saying things were simple or easy when I knew from experience that they were difficult and complicated. I know that the sort of questions that I asked were not acceptable questions for this group. It caused quite a bit of tension.

But when I went to university, it was much more possible to engage in argument and discussion. There wasn't that sort of restriction on what you could or could not say. So I did reconnect. The faith question arose for me again. I started going to church again. I chose the kind of church I was familiar with, a Catholic church, St Margaret's, very much caught up in the charismatic renewal of the 1970s, but in a Catholic way. I had another very good priest – Father Stephen Davis, who was another great influence on me.

A place with real geography and weather and buildings

I was also meeting and debating with evangelical students within the university set-up, while worshipping in a place where the eucharistic life was very familiar and where I felt at home. The vestments were the same and the sense of sacrament was alive. That was a very powerful mixture for me, that developing, expanding sense of, 'Ah, so Christian faith comes in myriad forms and people may have many different expressions and connections'.

For the first time at university, I was meeting Christians who talked about Jesus. That was a new dimension for me. God – that's who I remember thinking about up till then. Clearly, that can't be entirely accurate, but in terms of my affective faith, Jesus was a new idea. That whole understanding of incarnation, of God being flesh and blood, was quite revolutionary for me.

It also connected in my mind with a visit that we had made as a family to Israel. This would have been about the time I got confirmed, and for me the really disturbing thing had been discovering that the Holy Land was a real place. It wasn't just an intellectual idea. This was a real place, with real people in it and real geography and weather and buildings. I found it very disturbing, but in a good way.

That linked up with what I was discovering at university because I was now meeting people who had this very vibrant life experience of connection with, of contact with God, in Jesus Christ. I don't think that's just looking back on it and making it neat theologically. I think that is what happened to me. So those were heady days for me, engaging with faith on so many more levels and feeling challenged by it.

I remember it as a very rich time.

How do we communicate?

I come from a family of scientists so it was atypical of me to have an arts interest. But my A levels were English, French and medieval history, and those were the subjects that I loved. People always say to you, 'What are you going to do when you graduate?' I had no clear idea, except that I had an interest either in teaching people who were deaf or in working with children with autism. One of my grandmothers had been very deaf since early childhood and had really had a tough time of it. And over our back wall at home, there was a school for children with autism. I think those two things must have influenced me.

It was really the desire to communicate and to work with people who didn't find communication easy. The mystery of it has always interested me. How do we communicate together? In a variety of forms this question has gone on fascinating me all my life. So those were the directions I was looking in. That was what I thought I was going to follow as my career, but it is not what actually happened.

The King's Men

The other thing I really loved and enjoyed, first at school and then continued at university, was the theatre. At university I joined a drama group called 'The King's Men'. Terribly sexist title, but nonetheless that's what it was called, and it was a Christian group. It suited me well because here was yet another approach to exploring faith, through the arts. It was liberating because it brought together these different parts of my own living and experience.

What we did was new at that time, writing and performing short, sketch-like material. It was a form of community theatre. We were very much into humour. It had a message, but it was not heavy stuff, and I got involved with both writing and performing.

So that was a very creative time, with a lot of energy. I loved this pushing out of boundaries. It was about people not having to go to church to make a connection with faith, because this kind of performance theatre, small-scale, could be anywhere. It was infinitely portable. There are always lots of people on the edges and outside circles of the church who nevertheless want to come and see and learn what it is all about.

It is such an intriguing story, the first days of Christianity. The Gospels themselves were really the material that I was most interested in, in terms of theatre. They are endlessly fascinating because they're about who we are as human beings. They are about things happening, about encounters, about people finding their lives changing, not in a church, not in any ritual context, but in the middle of living.

A vicar called George Carey

One of the people I worked quite closely with in this university drama group was a man called Mark Townson. I don't know how it happened exactly, but we were taken by the idea that this business of writing and performing portable dramatic material was something we could perhaps continue to do after we graduated. We mused and we pondered. We thought we ought to go and talk to someone about it, as you do when you're that sort of age and you've had a bright idea.

We said, 'We're about to graduate. We really think this is worth a go. We've an idea maybe to do something like get some part-time work, write and perform, what do you think? Do you think this is a goer or not? Have we lost our marbles, or what's your own view on it?' The person we had gone to see was the vicar of the church where Mark was a member, St Nicholas in Durham, a vicar called George Carey, whose name I daresay you'll have heard in other contexts.

George was extremely supportive. He listened very carefully. And to cut a long story short, when we graduated in 1978 – Mark was a theology graduate – we went and worked for the next three years in association with St Nicholas Church.

They took us in, into the heart of their congregational life. We worked as a two-person team. We'd always thought there would be a third, but no one ever materialised. The church didn't pay us, but people gave money towards the project. We never wanted for anything, and not having money is fine when you're twenty-one. Members of the congregation gave us homes. We were part of the staff team and our work was to write and perform drama, in this community-theatre style. We did do a bit in the church, as part of the liturgy, but the greater focus of it was in schools, prisons and a lot of street theatre. We could work in somebody's front room or we could work in the Fairfield Halls in Croydon or on the Edinburgh Fringe, all of which we did.

Towards the end of our time, Mark met and married Sue, his wife, and in 1980 there came onto the staff the new curate of the church, called Frank White.

Enter Frank – a wise and holy man!

It wasn't love at first sight. I thought he was absolutely wonderful, but I'd been very fortunate in the previous curate and his wife, Peter and Sarah Broadbent, who had been very good to me. They were good, close friends, and I enjoyed their company, and it seemed to me a great shame that a single curate had been appointed. I thought I would have to observe propriety and it would not be so much fun at all.

When he arrived he was good fun, very supportive, a delightful person. He is eight years older than I am and I thought he was terribly wise and immensely holy, and so did not immediately fall in love with him. Frank didn't have any illusions about holiness, his own or mine, so he succumbed sooner than I did.

He arrived in 1980, and we were married in 1982. Mark and I finished working together in the summer of 1981. We felt it had run its natural course, and either something big and new would have to happen to recharge our batteries, or it was time to finish. I wouldn't have missed it for anything. We certainly had some adventures.

Involved with God big-time

By this time, over the three years, I had been struck by this dreadful feeling – and it really was not just an anxiety but a dread – that being involved with God, big-time, for my whole life, was seriously on the cards. I don't think I would say it was a call at that stage, but it was all the time a growing, worrying feeling.

By doing this job which I loved – this crazy job, writing and performing community and street theatre – I think I hoped that I'd bought God off. I was thinking, 'I'll do this for a few years, and by the time I get to the end, I'll have settled my account and then I can get on with doing something more sensible.' But this dread just would not go away. I couldn't shake it off, and I did try because I really believed that I was profoundly unsuitable.

I had not at that stage seen other women operating in a ministerial role in church. I met all manner of wonderful women doing all sorts of good things, but not the equivalent of being a vicar or in a leadership capacity. I think that's been a real problem for women of my generation, that there were no role models, or very few. If you weren't really in the heart of church land, as it were, you didn't meet them. I don't remember seeing any.

Eventually, I found I did have a very dear friend who was training to be a deaconess – that was all you could do at that stage, at the beginning of the 1980s. She was somebody in whom I could not exactly see myself, but I could imagine myself in that kind of role. I can't remember the details of the order of events after that, but I was in due course sent to see the appropriate person in the diocese to talk to, the adviser in women's –

or in lay – ministry, Margaret Parker. She has since retired as an honorary canon of Durham Cathedral.

I went to see her on a number of occasions for about a year, or even longer. She was immensely patient with me, gave me endless amounts of tea and let me talk. My recollection is that each time we met she would say to me, 'Now, do you think you are being called to be a deaconess or an accredited lay worker?' Those were the two options.

The Deaconess Order was a lifetime vow, almost like a religious order in a way, and accredited lay working wasn't. So she would quite rightly ask me the question and I would quite rightly – for me at that time – say, 'I just don't know. No idea. There is no writing in the sky.'

So she would say, ' I'll see you again in another six months.' Quite rightly.

I don't know how long that process went on for. But I think it was something like a year. When I met Frank and it became clear that that relationship was serious, I had come to the point where I was finally giving in to this massive wrestling match and saying, 'OK, I will offer myself. I can't do anything else. I cannot shake this off. I cannot walk away from it.' I would offer, but with the real, genuine hope that they would say 'No'.

The advice I received at that time, which I think was very shrewd advice, was that I should wait a year. Frank and I got married in January 1982. Our vicar, George Carey, left in the summer of 1982 to be Principal of Trinity College in Bristol. Frank was responsible for the interregnum, and it felt like a lot was happening all in one year. So their advice was – Wait, see how you go, settle into being married, cope with everything that's happening, and then we'll arrange a selection conference. I would find myself giving people the same advice in later years.

Being really listened to

I did wait, and then went off to a selection conference in the summer of 1983. The selection conference itself was an immensely positive experience. A good team of people interviewed me, and asked very good questions. I had filled in my form with exhausting, painstaking care but I also came away feeling that I had been really listened to. I had bent over backwards to tell them everything that I thought they ought to know and that might put them off. I was suspicious that if you were reasonably well-educated, reasonably articulate, young, fairly presentable – you might somehow, by accident, be recommended. Well, I'm now a selector myself, and I know that that is not the case, but that's what I was afraid of.

I wanted them to know I was a free spirit, a free thinker. I talked about my doubts, my views on things, my personal history. I kept thinking – They can't possibly want somebody like me. But I came away from it feeling wholly positive, very peaceful, and that I trusted them. I could abide by their judgment with complete peace of mind.

And in due course the letter came from Michael Ball, the Bishop of Jarrow, saying that they had recommended me for training. In those days, that was what you had, a charming, brief letter from the bishop telling you that it was all right. I was on my own at home when it came, and I burst into tears. I remember howling, absolutely howling, and then going off to find Frank, who was up at the church. But I think it was almost a relief that it was settled.

A ragbag of ideas

Training started soon afterwards, in October 1983, at Cranmer Hall because we were in Durham and it seemed crazy to go anywhere else, so I didn't even look. I loved the training. I arrived with my ragbag of ideas, experiences, all sorts of bits and pieces gathered from three years working with the drama group in churches all round the country, meeting all manner of people. I had done no theological study, apart from what you pick up, and I've always been a voracious reader, so it really was a ragbag, and I couldn't believe that the church would pay for me to go and study for three years. But that's the system.

I offered myself as a deaconess, because I felt that if I was going to go for this, I was going to go for it body and soul, and the deaconess route felt to me to be the whole-life commitment. Nothing held back. But by the time I finished my training, in the summer of 1986, there was a huge question about when the legislation for women to be ordained as deacons would go through.

For a while there was a question about whether our year of deaconess candidates should delay ordination and hope that by Advent it would have happened, because we had Petertide ordinations. In the end it didn't look as though it was going to go through in time, so we were advised to go ahead. Then in March 1987 those of us who wanted to be were ordained as deacons. Some wanted to stay as deaconesses, and had a clear sense that this was their whole-life lay calling and they didn't want to be made clerks in holy orders.

Chester-le-Street

For me, being a deaconess may not have been long in terms of length of time, but it was enormous in terms of life experience.

I had been both brought up and educated with a very strong sense that women are on the same footing as men. It never even occurred to me then that it could ever be otherwise. So it was mysterious to find myself in an institution that did not think in the same way. It wasn't exactly a shock, because obviously I'd been part of it for a while by now, but I still did think it was mighty peculiar and I couldn't find any theological argument as to why this was thought of as a tenable position.

I had joined the local Movement for the Ordination of Women group. Once I was made a deaconess, I became more actively part of the MOW scene in the diocese. We used to meet together as a group, and there was always a vigil before the ordinations in Durham – distributing prayer cards and that sort of thing. I went to work as a non-stipendiary minister in Chester-le-Street, really as a supernumerary, but in fact working full-time, in pastoral charge of one of the worship centres. Worship centres had been planted all over this big market town. There were two women on the staff, and two ordained men – one of whom for the first six months was Frank – and we all had pastoral charge of one or more of these centres. The men could celebrate Communion, but the women couldn't, so we decided that, as a sign of unity, none of the junior staff, men or women, would celebrate. Only the rector, Ian Bunting, would celebrate. We were bringing to light the reality of the situation, that neither Amiel Osmaston nor myself, even when we were made deacons, could preside at the Eucharist.

The little brown envelope

So there I was, happily working in the parish at Chester-le-Street. I thought I would be there indefinitely. As a non-stipendiary, there wasn't any pressure to move on. Probably somebody ought to have asked me at some point, 'What are you going to do next?' But I think there was an element of, 'Married, ordained woman? Very difficult to know what to do with them, really. So unless they're creating a noise about it, let's leave well alone.'

I wasn't creating a noise. I had three happy years, first as a deaconess and then as a deacon. I was working with a wonderful group of people in a very interesting parish. We made a good team. It suited me down to the ground, because basically I had started in at the deep end in a very big, busy parish with pastoral charge of a congregation, but also in a team. It was both shared responsibility and also flying solo – it felt like solo flight. Perfect for me.

I came home after one holiday. At the bottom of the pile of mail, there was a little brown envelope, with details of a new post working one-third in another parish and two-thirds as diocesan adviser in local mission. And a little note from the person who had sent them, saying, 'Thought you'd like to see these.'

I was very surprised and I couldn't understand why they had been sent to me or why it was thought that I would like to see them. I rang the secretary to the Board of Mission and Unity to say, 'I'm just wondering whether there's been some mistake and these have got into the wrong envelope – and something you were meaning to send me, you haven't sent to me? I'll pop these in the post and you can have them back again.'

He said, 'Oh no, no, no. We're absolutely serious. We think you'd be great.'

I said, 'How very surprising. And interesting. However, utterly impossible, because I can't possibly go to . . .' whatever parish it was.

It was in the Durham Diocese, but it wouldn't have been possible for me, because Frank and I couldn't envisage parish work being done commuting.

The secretary got back to me and said, 'That's fine. We're happy with that. If you would apply just for the Adviser in the Local Mission part of the job, we would like to consider you.'

I went down to Bishop Auckland, to Auckland Castle, to be interviewed by Bishop David Jenkins and three or four other very respectable men from the diocese. I think there was probably an archdeacon and a chair of the board, all sitting round in big leather chairs. I was put to sit in a small chair.

We had a great time. I quite liked being interviewed. I can't remember what we talked about, but the questions were challenging. I remember Bishop David getting enormously excited at one point and exclaiming, 'Yes, yes, yes!' and leaping across the room towards me, shooting up the ladder in his library to get a book off the top shelf and coming down reading out a passage from it.

Then they asked me if I would be kind enough to wait outside, which I did, and then they invited me to come back in and offered me the job.

I didn't think I knew anything about missions at all, but I was helped to see that in fact I knew quite a lot. This has been the story of my life. I've been taken by surprise every time. Every single time.

I was appointed at the end of 1988, and started in February 1989, and in the summer of 1989, Frank went to be Vicar of Birtley, about five miles north from where we were. We haven't gone in for moving big distances, despite our best intentions.

Diocesan Adviser in Local Mission

I had this wonderful freedom, to make a job of Adviser in Local Mission. It was an enabling job. It was teaching, running study days and parish weekends, working alongside churches who wanted to ask, 'What does it mean to be the church in this place? How do we reach the people who live here?' They could ask me to come and work alongside them.

Bishop David had said to me after the interview, 'I don't think there'll be very much for the first six months to a year, until people get the idea of what you can do, so don't worry about it.'

I had thought, 'Hmmm, well, we'll see about that.' And within the first couple of months, there was almost more work than I could handle. It was just huge. It really took off.

I'd always meant to be proactive, but there was so much need. Felt need. In fact it was perfectly possible to create a useful strategy entirely out of what people were saying and asking. I kept a very close eye with the mission committee on where I was working in the diocese, just to make sure that I wasn't only in one sort of church or area. I was working right across the board.

It was great, working with clergy, PCCs and lay groups. Pioneering, developmental work, with a blank sheet of paper and endless variety. Real possibilities in creating new material, new ways of doing things all the time. Nobody had ever taught me to teach, so that too was a learning experience for me.

I was being paid – for the first time – for the two-thirds time job, but in fact I worked full-time. Once again, that was by my own choice, because it was exciting. I also worked in a kind of honorary capacity in Birtley, in Sunday ministry, so I kept my roots in the parish, and had a place to belong.

I did it for nearly five years. I was still in that job in 1992 when the vote went through.

11 November 1992
I spent the day with the television on, and with radios on in every room, so that nothing should be missed. The vote was so close that you couldn't judge. I think there was both a huge optimism but also a kind of victim fear around. People were thinking, 'This is bound to happen again, we will not be given the opportunity this time.' Meaning not just 'we women', but 'we the church' will not be brave enough to do this.

We had arranged a gathering that evening, of ordained women. Whatever happened, we were going to meet that evening, so that there would be solidarity together. Frank was on the General Synod, so he was actually there at the debate, in London. We all met in somebody's house down in Darlington. Although I know the way perfectly well from home, this time I got completely and utterly lost, trying to get there. The whole world seemed to be turned upside-down.

We experienced everything that evening. Shock. Relief, disbelief, joy, jubilation, as each new person arrived, having to tell the story again and again. Friends and neighbours from nearby calling in and the telephone ringing.

The things that mattered are still true
I think we all felt quite exposed then. Because it had been such a long haul, you are the object of people's curiosity. Endlessly, with the very best of intentions, people would come up to you – whatever you were doing – to say, 'I'm in favour, I'm in favour'. You could be in the middle of doing something perfectly ordinary and people would want to talk about it or have your angle on it. Or there were people needing to say, 'I really

don't know how you can do this. This is rocking the boat beyond what we can tolerate.'

Part of the difficulty is that the church so often represents a place of safety, and people are very frightened of those places changing. But one of the things that lots of people have discovered is that ordaining women to the priesthood doesn't necessarily make the place less safe. It may do for some. But the things that matter to them are still true.

It has been a huge journey of self-discovery for the whole church. My hope is that we can discover that God is much more creative than we are, and infinitely more inclusive.

We are all compromised

I had had quite a struggle with the idea of priesting for myself. But by the time the vote happened, I did have a sense that it was right for me to be a priest. I'd been to see Bishop David to talk it through with him, because I had felt I would be compromised in some way if I went ahead. Talking to David, I told him exactly what I was feeling, my confusion and almost this feeling of, 'Should I just get out of the church altogether?' It wasn't only the issue of being a priest; it was a question of how much I wanted to belong inside the institution at all.

Bishop David was wonderful, because in his very direct way, he basically said to me – and speaking out of his own story which is what made it so powerful – 'We are all already compromised. Don't fool yourself.'

He meant that we are compromised because we are already committed to, employed by, servants of a highly problematic institution. I found that realism enormously liberating. I could then – with a feeling of real liberty – welcome the thought of becoming a priest. I could see how good it was that women should be priests.

I think I was one of those people, among many women, who had a sense that somehow this priestly life, this priestly calling, was something that had already been given to us long ago. It wasn't by fiat of the church solely, but by what God had asked, invited and given to us as ministry, and that we were getting on with. Even though you weren't an ordained priest, you were somehow an unordained priest.

Only one thing has been so sad for all of us is that sense that we have missed out on the particular gifts and contributions of some very remarkable women, who would have offered themselves for priesthood if they'd been given the chance.

Director of Mission and Pastoral Studies

In 1993 I was invited to apply for another new job, as Director of Mission and Pastoral Studies at Cranmer Hall, the college where I had trained. Another unsolicited brown envelope.

Once again I was caught by surprise. But I could see that in a way it could be a logical next step, so I applied, and was short-listed. I looked up the other two candidates in *Crockfords*, decided I knew very clearly who was going to get the job and it wouldn't be me. But I went through the two-day interview process, which was gruelling but fair.

I've never been interviewed for any job thinking, 'I really, really want this. I've got to get it.' I've always gone in thinking, 'Well, this is a bit startling! Fancy that.' It's very liberating. It means I can offer them who I am. If that's what they need and want, great. And if it isn't, that's fine by me too.

I got back home at the end of the two days, got into the shower; the telephone rang and they offered me the job.

The post had originally been Director of Pastoral Studies, but the college had rethought its philosophy, and advertised for a Director of Mission and Pastoral Studies. They wanted to find a proper place for mission in the curriculum, not just as an optional extra.

So the job was to develop a curriculum, and to reconceive pastoral studies in the light of mission. I loved it. By now I was also doing a Masters Degree in political theology in Leeds, which I'd started in the last year of the previous job, on day release one day a week. I don't think I'm an academic, I just like thinking about things.

I went into the new job thinking I should need enormous grace to go to the same office every day. I had not, at this stage in my life, ever worked regular hours in one building before. I am quite a free-spirited person and being able to rove had always suited me very well. So now I had a timetable, terms, an office, a building – it was going to be stretching.

It was a big department – I was responsible for all the practical placements as well as the curriculum in the pastoral and mission studies areas, so there was a lot to manage. I learnt a huge amount: to work with a secretary, and to work in a very close-knit team. I even had a brief-case, which got so battered it had to be thrown out when I left.

I was ordained priest in 1994, while I was on the staff there. Thirty-eight of us, all women, were ordained over two days. We did it chronologically. Those who had waited longest were ordained first. It was a lovely way to do it. I was on the cusp. Those of us who were ordained on the Sunday, went on the Saturday, so all of us were present on the Saturday. Not everyone could come on the Sunday, but most did.

I stayed at the college for exactly five years. I said when I was appointed that I would do five years, but not a day longer. I think with teaching that sort of very dynamic subject, it's not good for anybody to do it for too long. I was still serving in Frank's parish at Birtley when I was home at the weekends, but it's easy to get out of touch with the realities of life in a college. You hear yourself telling stories that belong to a while ago.

Diocesan Director of Ordinands

But the question was – What to do next? By this time, Frank had gone from being the vicar of Birtley to be the Archdeacon of Sunderland, and we had moved house.

I talked things over with Bishop Michael Turnbull, who had come to Durham by then. He asked whether I would be interested in applying for the Diocesan Director of Ordinands (DDO) job, which was about to be advertised.

The policy of the diocese is that all people exploring vocation, from whatever position, must come through the diocesan system. There is only one system. It meant that I did all the first interviewing, so I met everybody, whatever their views about the ordination of women.

Being DDO was a very good experience. I learnt a lot. I think there were things that I could contribute to the job at that stage in its development. I don't think it would have been very good for me long-term, because it wasn't very susceptible to new ideas. There was some room for developing how we went about discerning vocations in the diocese, but there isn't room for thinking it out on a major scale because that's taken care of by the Ministry Division. So I think if I had been in it for long, which as it turned out I wasn't, it might have been frustrating for me.

Better together

I have had some abuse over the years. Yes, it has often troubled me, but it's never been sustained and I've always thought it better to engage with it rather than walk away from it. It isn't just for the sake of arguing, but trying to listen and understand, so that you also may be listened to and understood. This business of entrenched positions and caricaturing one another and in the end demonising one another is wholly inappropriate to the gospel, and wholly inappropriate to human living. It just won't do. Even though I may profoundly disagree with somebody and they may profoundly disagree with me, we still are human beings trying to make sense of what it means to be alive and loving God. We've got to make something of that.

I think one of the great gifts of ordained women is their innate sense of 'We can do things better together'. Obviously it's not universal. One can easily get into sweeping generalisations, but I think that this is a contribution that the ordained women are offering, by making space for more people from the congregations to take active roles in the pastoral and liturgical sides of church life. It is partly because they don't have a long history, so they don't feel so much need to defend the territory. Maybe it is easier for them to say, 'Come on, this would be done so much better together.'

To me, we are now in a good phase in church life. It is opening ministry up much more widely and comprehensively, recognising the need to work collaboratively with people who are not part of a church and ordained people and members of congregations. So my hope is that now there need not be any barrier to anybody offering the gift that they have.

What people are doing out and about in life is part of it all. I think we need to make the connection more and more strongly that the life of faith is not about people doing things in church. It is about how we live our lives, and if it isn't about that, then I think we've simply missed the point.

Springboard

Although I'm against tokenism, I'm sure I've benefited from it. It's been possible to be part of groups or involved in different kinds of engagements of one sort or another because they want a woman to come and contribute. All through my life, I've been given freedom and opportunity beyond measure. It can be a huge plus, being an ordained woman, because there aren't that many of us yet, and I've been invited to do all sorts of things that maybe I wouldn't have been asked to do if I had been a man.

After I'd been DDO for only eighteen months, the Archbishops' Springboard team took it into their heads that I was the person they wanted to come and join them. So they set about being persuasive that this was what I wanted to do.

The two Archbishops, York and Canterbury, through the Lambeth Partnership, fund a small resource team. The team is available to any diocese to encourage, renew, teach and mobilise, in mission and evangelism. It was a great opportunity being asked to join, very much in the stream of what I've always been about, what I've enjoyed most – teaching mission, space to think, communicating. Only this time, instead of being in the diocese, it's anywhere in the country. And sometimes even further afield than that – there's some work in other countries as well. It's a high-pressure, very public role.

I joined the Springboard team in May 2000. They offered me a full-time post but I only wanted to work part-time. This is partly because I don't want to be itinerant all the time, and partly because over the years, other dimensions of ministry have developed for me that I didn't want to abandon.

I have had a variety of involvements, leading retreats, giving spiritual direction to individuals. I do some theological consultancy work. I am a Bishops' selector. And recently I've been part of the formal conversations between the Anglican Church and the Methodist Church. I really value the freedom to accept these kind of initiatives.

The biggest adventure

But I think for me, always, my deepest sense of call is to explore the life of prayer, although it has taken time to accept that. What does it mean to pray in this world we live in? How do we do it? Not just how do we think about it or how do we talk about it, but how do we engage with it?

You only have yourself to offer, in what is the biggest adventure of all – praying. I believe that personal prayer and corporate prayer are inextricably linked. We are never praying alone. I don't think there is such a thing as private prayer, because we are not private. We always belong. We always belong in the body of Christ. We always belong in the communion of saints. So even if we are physically praying on our own, we're not, because we're praying with the whole church of God and surrounded by this extraordinary company of people who have given their lives in loving God. I just don't think there's anything more exciting than this invitation to contemplate God.

It becomes irresistible. I think that's the thing. It becomes irresistible. Like this whole journey. So I'm happy to go for it and see what happens, and because that's a very hidden part of life, who knows? For me at the moment, the real challenge comes in holding together this very public, high-pressure life with Springboard with an inner, private, contemplative life.

But every time I've ever thought that I might have an idea about how the future is going to go, it has done something else. I'm always being surprised by the way things turn out. I would have thought that I was one of the most unlikely people you could imagine to get caught up in a serious pursuit of praying. It makes me laugh. I think God's got a huge sense of humour.

REVD ROSE HUDSON-WILKIN

10

Beautifully and Wonderfully Made

REVD ROSE HUDSON-WILKIN

Vicar of Haggerston with Dalston

On the day when the General Synod were going to vote for or against the ordination of women, I travelled down to Dean's Yard by train, carrying a notice which said: 'Women beautifully and wonderfully made in the image of God'.

Introduction

AB: The way into Rose's patch from Shoreditch tube station takes the visitor through the up-market surroundings of Hoxton, with its arts cinema, galleries and pavement cafés. Turning up into Kingsland Road, in the middle of a more nondescript inner-city scene, you find a gem of eighteenth-century architecture, the famous Geffrye Museum. Further along, on the same side of the road, in eye-catching contrast, stands a huge new mosque, just one symbol of the multiethnic face of London's East End today.

I always thought of Haggerston and Dalston, where Rose Hudson-Wilkin is parish priest, as classic Dixon of Dock Green *territory – a series I once worked on many years ago. I can't remember any vicar figuring in Jack Warner's Saturday-night morality tales, but maybe that's because in those innocent days of the distant past, it was 'just an ordinary copper down Dock Green' who proclaimed by his honest lifestyle the essentials of Christian living.*

Turning into Rose's Haggerston parish, the 'yuppy' parking-warden territory of Hoxton has been left behind in another world. In the street cars are being mended – or stripped of spare parts; others are clearly abandoned and there are many signs that life is harder here. Teenage youths moving around in noisy groups suddenly breaking into a run, dodging through the traffic. Across a little patch of green is a low Victorian church, well cared for, its brickwork the colour of dark putty. Today's Sergeant Dixon is a big, friendly face in a police van parked outside the church, who points me to the vicarage.

Rose Hudson-Wilkin makes an instant impact. She is small and incredibly lively, smiling readily, bursting with energy. By mid-afternoon she has already had a hectic day, writing a script, going to several meetings to do with her own parish family, sitting down and listening to the troubles of someone who called at her door, and arbitrating a problem for an adjacent parish.

She is often busy further afield, chairing the Church's Committee for Minority Ethnic Anglican Concerns, the SPCK Worldwide Committee, and is currently a member of the Broadcasting Standards Commission. She has appeared as herself in a television docu-soap; and recently hosted an action-packed BBC Songs of Praise special. Holy Trinity, Dalston, is known as the clowns' church, where every year the clown Grimaldi is remembered at a big gathering of Christian clowns – who are not averse to throwing the odd make-believe custard pie in the middle of the service.

Life in Haggerston and Dalston is not all fun. New properties are well beyond the reach of most local people, whose lives are stressed by lack of money and work, as well as poor health and drug-related crime. Murder is not uncommon.

I soon discovered that Rose had had plenty of experience of poverty and hardship of her own during her childhood in the Caribbean, where she was born in 1961. She knows what it's like, which may explain why today she is unafraid to go out and bang heads together when some of her wilder parishioners start to get out of hand.

Rose

A Jamaican childhood

Childhood was difficult – not only because we were poor, but mainly because my mother left Jamaica to come to England when I was an infant. Shirley, my older sister by two years, and I were left behind with our father, a labourer. We went to live with my father's sister and her family in Montego Bay, and my father lived locally so the idea was that he should have looked after us. But men are no good at that.

There were ten people, four adults and six children, living in a two-bedroom house. Daily life was quite hard. For the children, bed was a pile of clothes on the floor. There was no mains water, no flushing loo. As Shirley and I were the older children, we had to go and fetch water to fill up the oil-drum near the house for the family to use. Cooking was done outdoors in a little coal pot, but the coal had to be reserved for special occasions, so we children had to go and fetch firewood every day after school. It was just the daily grind, and lots of kids around were doing it, so it was normal. I tell my own children about this all the time!

When my mother left to come to England, I think the idea was that my father and us children would eventually follow her. But unfortunately, when she got here she met someone else and married him and started a new family. Eventually she did come back to Jamaica to live in Kingston, at the other end of Jamaica, with her new family, when I was about nine years old and Shirley was eleven.

I have a memory of her sitting in a rocking-chair, and I am standing beside her feeling a sense of pride, knowing that this woman is my mother. She was quite pretty, I thought, but there was no emotion there. There was no attachment. I have no recollection at all of her up until that point. I had seen photographs, but had no recollection. I don't think I was quite two years old when she left.

So when my mother came back, Shirley and I went to live with her and her totally new family. I think my sister and I both felt a bit like Cinderella. And it didn't really work out. There was a lot of tension. We felt she loved her younger children but not us, and I hated her for it, and hated them. My mother decided that I should go back to Montego Bay. So my sister and I, who had bonded for all these years, were suddenly separated. We were not asked, we were just told. That was very painful.

Years later Shirley and I talked about it. I used to go and visit her in California, where she works as a nurse and has a family. We've always been very close, and whenever I was leaving, she would not just cry, she would bawl. And I used to think, 'What is happening?' I didn't understand it. I mean, I was sad to be leaving, but . . . It wasn't until the last time I was there, we were talking and she said, 'You know, Rose, when Mama sent you away, I used to cry myself to sleep every night.' And it clicked. It made sense. That is what it is all about. Every time we are parting, it's as if she relives the whole episode.

I was sent back to live in my uncle and auntie's house. Life was still hard. We had electricity by then, and a television, but I still had to do all the chores like carry water, and there was still only an outside loo. There was very little money around. It was just pretty dire. I remember feeling very low.

Then when I started high school, there was a young lass there, a year ahead of me, and we used to go to the Student Christian Fellowship together. The songs we were singing there were just lovely, not old-fashioned like in *Ancient and Modern*. This girl talked about her faith in such a real way. It was much more real than I had ever heard it spoken of in church – although I loved my church.

I was baptised as an infant in the St James' Parish Church, the main parish church in Montego Bay, run by an English expatriate priest, who we all called Archdeacon Price. A lovely man. He had bushy eyebrows – there was something about his bushy eyebrows that I found attractive!

The system in Jamaica is that you have your main parish church, and from that you have several daughter churches on the outskirts, in the surrounding villages. I used to go to one of those, called St Francis. It was wonderful. We had fun, a good time and made lots of friends. Nothing to do with the sermons, it was a great social place to be. I really grew up there, and it was through the church that I met two people who I still call 'Mum and Dad'. They didn't legally adopt me; I used to stay with them but I didn't live with them because they are two separate people. They were just wonderful models of parenthood. They were the people who helped me grow up. My biological parents were Mother and Father, but Mum and Dad loved me and are proud of me, and I love them.

So from an early age I was caught up and involved in our youth fellowship, which is very strong in the Caribbean, and I took part in the life of the church. But when I started high school and going to the Student Christian Fellowship with this girl who talked with such ease about God, I wanted to know much more. She talked about her faith in this real way, because God was alive to her.

I think I was feeling very unloved. Our mother had gone away and left us. Then later I had been sent to live with her and had not been loved, and been sent back; and my father didn't really care. And so when I was given the idea of a God of love, I was overwhelmed by a sense of wanting to serve him.

I remember an experience of sitting at school, listening to her talking about how God loves us, and what it says in the Bible, all in a very simple way, nothing theologically up there over my head. It was just a simple message: God so loved the world that he gave his only begotten Son . . .

I remember thinking 'God, if you loved me so much that you were willing to send your son to die for me, then I must be worth loving. I am going to serve you.' And I never looked back.

Back from the brink
But then there was a stage, around that same time when I was a teenager, when I felt I had had enough of life. There was such a feeling of desolation and loss. Life was tough, life was hard. My uncle was an alcoholic. There was no space in the house. There was a lot of tension – I think it was just to do with the fact that there was no money – but I felt that there was nothing to hope for. I suppose it was partly a teenage thing; my parents didn't understand me or love me and I thought I wanted to die. I really did want to die.

But a voice inside my head said, 'If you try to commit suicide, and if you don't die and are just injured, then you will never be able to serve me in the way you want to.'

That was the thing that brought me back from the brink, and reminded me that life was worth living, and that I was worth loving, because there was a goal, there was something I could do. I came back from that low point and, yes, since that day I have never wanted to do anything else but to serve God, be his minister.

The Church Army

I knew I wanted to serve God, but I had no model of how, because at the time all we had in the church were male ministers. I had heard that there were deaconesses, but there were none in our area. Then I heard of the Church Army, that it was a lay ministry for evangelism, and that there were women involved with that ministry, because a Church Army sister came to visit us.

I did quite well at school and left with seven O levels, including English literature and English language. I worked for a year as a pre-trained teacher and while I was doing that, I applied for the Church Army and I was accepted and sent here, to London. All our officers in Jamaica were trained at the Church Army College in Blackheath at the time, so at the age of eighteen, I came to England.

All thrown out the window

I was excited about going. I was going to fulfil this dream I had. And it wasn't until I was leaving on the plane that I cried, because I suddenly realised I was leaving behind everyone and everything I knew and going to a strange place. I was going to train here for three years, and then I was going back to Jamaica. Three years — but it seemed like a long time.

You come in to theological college with a very simple faith — you had read it in the Bible, that's what it meant, that's what it said — and then you go into a theological establishment where this is all thrown out the window. They chuck it out by saying of a lot of the things you believe, 'Oh, that's nonsense. That never happened.' You think, 'What? It says in the Bible it did!' Everything that you have learned and brought with you, everything you have grown up on and fed on is taken away from you and you have to start working out what is essential.

One day recently, I went into a home to do a short service, and there was a man there who had obviously grown up in a Pentecostal tradition. He was upset that my hair was cut, that I hadn't covered my head, and also that I was a woman preaching, and so he went off in a huff. At the end I went to see him, and the first thing he said to me was, 'What was the name of the road that Jesus travelled on to go to crucifixion?'

I said, 'Is this really important? Do I really need to know the name of the road? Or that he died for me — which is more important? It is important that he died for me, not that I don't know the name of the road he walked on.' It was a little bit like that at Church Army College.

I had to learn the fact, for example, that the Gospels were written some seventy-, eighty-, ninety-odd years after Jesus died and that Mark was the first one that was written and the others came later. Things like that were new to me. So you thought, 'OK . . . Yeah.'

But then you must learn from that, and I don't think theological colleges are very good at helping you do that. You have to do it for yourself, and you do it for yourself out of the depth of your own spirituality. They don't sit you down and help you to work out what is essential and what isn't necessary, or anything like that. They are there to lecture – and they lecture.

I think what saw me through that was my relationship with God. That was not an academic relationship, it was personal. Those long nights of prayer, mornings of prayer, daytimes of prayer, the reading of Scriptures, spending time with God – that's what got me through.

'Do not go where the path leads, rather go where there is no path and leave a trail'

We were very short of clergy in the Caribbean, so there was a real need for lay people to be trained and equipped to help in churches that had no minister. That's what I wanted to do, and so I spent my last six months at college focusing on lay training, because I felt that that was what God wanted me to do.

There was very little vision in the Church Army in those days about placing people, and so each officer who came back to the Caribbean tended to end up in a post where they had always had Church Army ministry. Back in Montego Bay they had always had a Church Army officer in hospital chaplaincy ministry. So their attitude was, 'We have had that in the past, so that is what you are going to be doing.' I was really upset because I didn't think that was what God wanted me to do.

My tutor at the college had given me a poster that said, 'Do not go where the path leads, rather go where there is no path and leave a trail.'

I thought, 'Yes! I shall listen to this.'

I sent word back to my bishop and said, 'I am definitely not going to be doing hospital chaplaincy. I am very interested in that area, but it's not for me now. Now it's lay ministry.' I thought – Why did I spend all this time focusing on Christian education, learning about teaching and equipping the laity, if not to use it?

I completed my training in London, and went back home to Jamaica in 1982, where they eventually found me a post doing pioneering work in Christian education, but rather grudgingly, and it was quite difficult. The church in the Caribbean is very clergy-dominated, and you are expected to do what they say. I think they thought I was being obstinate, certainly the go-between for the bishop and myself thought I was being very obstinate.

Why do we have to wait for people with male genitalia before we can bring the sacrament to people?

At least I was working in ministry. I felt a longing, though, and I often argued at deanery meetings with the clergy and with just about anyone who would listen to me. I kept on asking, 'Why do we have to wait for someone with male genitalia before we can bring the sacrament to people, although we say the sacrament is so special and so important?'

I didn't get much response. I think people just had the attitude, 'Oh, here we go again.' They thought they would never go down that road, never be ordaining women. I suspect that even people who perhaps did want to see women ordained were very docile about it, not wanting to rock the boat, not wanting be troublemakers. I guess I thought I could afford to be a troublemaker.

While I was at the Church Army Training College at Blackheath I had met Ken Wilkin, a Geordie from the north-east of England. Ken followed me to the Caribbean, and we got married over there a year later, on 23 April 1983, in St Augustine, the church I was confirmed in. Dad gave me away. We stayed on in Jamaica for the next three years, both working for the Church Army.

Then Ken started to think that he wanted to be ordained. He felt it wouldn't be right to ask the Jamaican church to spend that amount of money preparing him for ordination because he knew he would eventually want to come back to work in England. So we thought, 'OK', and we all came back to London.

Astounded, angry and bewildered

I was happy and excited for Ken, but by the time we were leaving to come back to England, I was really feeling that I too should be ordained. Although women still weren't being ordained to the priesthood, they could be deacons. I thought there was something quite wonderful about preparing someone for baptism and gathering them in and baptising their child, all the work of a deacon.

Our first child, our daughter Amanda who is fifteen now, was born not long after we arrived in London. I offered myself for ordination almost as soon as we got here. But the DDO for the Southwark Diocese and the examining chaplain who I went to see – both of them elderly, middle-class, white women – basically took the view, 'You have a child, you have a husband, why do you want to be ordained? You ought not to think of it.'

I was astounded, angry, bewildered.

'No. You're a mother, you're a wife'

Things went to a lull. Nothing happened. There was nobody saying, 'Here we have got a woman from a minority ethnic background – we have very few of these – her qualifications are good, she has a faith, she is lively, why not ordain her?' There was none of that, it was always, 'No. You're a mother, you're a wife.'

I became pregnant with my second child, Hannah, and this coincided with the time when I went to them again and said, 'Come on, I want to know what is happening.' I decided not to tell them I was pregnant, because that was just going to be even worse. 'Two children? Stay home and look after them.' But they took quite a long time to move, so by the time I actually went to see another examining chaplain, Professor Leslie Houlden at King's College, I was literally two weeks away from giving birth.

I walked in and said to him, 'I hope your midwifery skills are brilliant, just in case!'

But he was wonderful. He respected my judgment that if I was offering myself, I had got my domestic situation sorted. He never said to me, 'You're pregnant, you have got another child, you have got a husband, why do you want to be ordained?' I found it very interesting that a man didn't come to me with that, and yet that was the angle of the two women. They were the ones who had said, 'A husband, a child? No way.' Deeply worrying.

I saw one of them again recently. I went to a friend's induction and she was there and I took great delight in going across to her and saying, 'Do you remember me? I came to see you. I think you would be interested to learn that I now have two churches; that I am the mother of three children, still the wife of one husband; that I chair SPCK Worldwide Committee, and the National Committee for Minority Anglican Concerns; that I am on the Broadcasting Standards Commission and I'm governor at my children's school . . .'

She just stood there.

Lichfield Diocese
Meanwhile, Ken had done his training and was to be ordained into a parish in the Lichfield Diocese, and so we moved to Lichfield. But that meant another delay in the whole process of my getting ordained. Once we got to Lichfield Diocese and we were in the parish I started work in a non-stipendiary capacity for the Church Army.

I got in touch with their DDO at Lichfield, a man, and he did not say to me, 'Woman, mother, wife . . .' Once again I really appreciated that, because I felt respected. But it was all being frustratingly slow and I think there were moments along the way when I was saying, 'God, what is happening? Is this not what you want? I thought this was what you wanted.' But I never gave up hope.

I never gave up hope, and eventually I was accepted and trained at Queens with the West Midlands course. I was ordained a deacon in 1991.

On the road
I saw my deaconing as just being on the road. I was still on that journey to priesthood, that the church had said 'No' to, but people had said 'Yes' to. It was like a long period of gestation, waiting to give birth.

Ken was at St Peter's Church in Wolverhampton, serving his curacy. My new parish was also in Wolverhampton. It was an evangelical parish. They struggled with having me, because of the evangelical position about women, and at first they had said, 'Why don't we have her husband instead of her?'

They didn't say it to me. They said it to the vicar, but he insisted that he was going to have me. It was at enormous cost to himself, because the whole PCC then resigned.

I went there knowing that they were not happy with me coming but I was determined that I wasn't going to discuss with them or argue with them about it, I was just going to minister, which was what I did.

I made mistakes that I wouldn't make now. Like when I had an operation on my knee. I insisted that my husband should drive me over to the parish each day, and I hobbled around with my walking stick. I remember thinking, 'I am not going to let this prevent me from going in, I am not going to let them say, "Oh, it's because she is a woman or because she is black, she can't hack the job." I just had to keep going. I wouldn't do it now.'

But of the number of people who had disagreed strongly about having me as their curate, gradually, slowly, one by one they came round. Just before I was ordained to the priesthood the final person said to me, 'I was one of those who had resigned when you were coming here, but I now believe that God has called you and women to be priests.'

So I believe that I did nurture that congregation and helped it to grow.

'Women beautifully and wonderfully made in the image of God'
Oh, the vote day, that was something else! There was such a buzz in Dean's Yard, such a buzz. We sang, we prayed, we listened to the debate on radios. There were obviously those who were opposed who came as well, so we argued.

There were some sad moments to it, actually. Sad, because you had to contemplate the fact that it might not happen in your lifetime, all that you had lived for and longed for might not become a reality. How do you then deal with that, having believed deep in your heart, the very soul of your being, that this is what God is calling you to be and do?

I had worn my cassock and with it I was carrying a poster. It was all done in secret, and it had cost me twenty pounds. I didn't want my husband to know about it, because he would not approve of me spending so much money on something he would think frivolous.

I had gone to the man who made signs for our church to ask him if he would make it for me. He asked me what I wanted on it. I said, 'I don't really know, but I want something that will underline and emphasise the fact that as women we are important, equally important as men, made in God's image.' Then I thought of Psalm 139: 'I am fearfully and wonderfully made' and I thought, 'Yes. That's it. Women are beautifully and wonderfully made.' So I asked him to put 'Women beautifully and wonderfully made in the image of God'. People on the train stared at me, the press took photographs, but it was all worth it when the vote finally went through.

It was tense, it was joyful, it was everything. You were on tenterhooks, really. You really didn't know. You experienced all sorts of emotions because you were thinking, 'Will it happen? Will it not? Will they grasp the opportunity? Will we be turned down again?' When the vote came through, there was a sense of disbelief and relief. The crowd had grown as the evening drew on. There was a sense of expectancy all around us. Inside the chamber, members of the General Synod were asked to receive the results of the vote in silence. We, the crowd outside in Dean's Yard, on the other hand, were not about to be silent. We burst into spontaneous singing, hugging and crying.

Ordination
I was ordained priest in Lichfield Cathedral on 23 April 1994, on our eleventh wedding anniversary. They were doing it over two days and I actually should have been done on the twenty-fourth, but I asked Bishop Keith if I could be moved around. The children were exceptionally excited for me. After the ordination I overhead them in the back of the car as we drove to church discussing which of them would read the bit that says 'priest' in the service book. They were very proud.

For me the moment of ordination to the priesthood was absolutely an out-of-this-world experience, like giving birth. There is this gestation period, which feels like forever. You are waiting and longing and hoping that it's all going to happen, that it is all going to be all right. But also there's the pain that comes with it, an amazing amount of pain. Then at the end of the day you have this beautiful thing, and I think for me giving birth is the only other out-of-the-world experience that I have experienced and can compare it with.

The pain was also enormous. I think it was not really a personal pain, but it was a corporate pain. It was thinking of the sadness and the longing of all the women who had waited and hoped but never had the opportunity to have their dream realised. People who were now at retirement age, having worked in the church for a lifetime. Deaconesses for years who had a dream and goal to have been priests – and it came too late.

Yes, we talked about it, we cried about it. It was the feeling that you had got the torch and you have got to carry that torch for the next generation of women priests.

The Vicar of Dalston
I am now, since April 1998, Vicar of Holy Trinity, Dalston, with St Philip and All Saints in Haggerston, two separate churches, one united benefice.

Actually it was Ken, my husband, who was looking for a new job. We were still in the Midlands and I was visiting Bishop John Sentamu in Stepney, nothing to do with the church, just socially because he's been a family friend since we came over in 1985 when he was vicar in Tulse Hill. I happened to mention to him that Ken was looking for another post. He said, 'Tell him to come and have a look at this parish here.'

So we both came down, but Ken took one look and thought, 'No, this is not for me.'

I accompanied him, just as a wife, but I looked at it and thought, 'Wow! What a challenge!'

The challenge was one church in particular, All Saints, Haggerston. It was looking absolutely dishevelled and almost ruined. The outside was overgrown and it was quite shocking inside. It was a mess and what I also noticed was that the area was extremely multiethnic.

Nothing much at all was happening at Holy Trinity, Dalston. There were about half a dozen, young, black people who were being prepared for confirmation, and I think maybe twelve or fifteen people at the most were worshipping here. A few of them would have been original East-enders; the rest would have been in-comers like me, from the Caribbean islands, or Nigeria, just a sprinkling. There was the sad feeling of it being on its last legs, so there was a real challenge to see if anything could rise from the dust.

I am a glutton for punishment, so I dropped a note to Bishop John saying that Ken wasn't interested, but that I was – if they would be interested in having me. Ken eventually found himself another job in London, in prison ministry, and I came back for an interview. It took them a while, because there was a struggle going on about having me. There are two churches and some folks from All Saints were very anti me, they didn't want to have me at all. But the other church, Holy Trinity, was adamant that they did want me. It was the local, indigenous, white people who were in charge at All Saints. There was a core of six people who were really against my coming. They were the wardens, the treasurer and three others, and they found it very difficult to accept the fact that I was a black woman coming.

I am very happy with myself both as a woman and as a black person
They wrote me a letter in which they said that they had changed their mind about having a woman. They didn't add the black bit to it, but I already knew that that was being said.

The living alternated between being in the gift of the bishop, and in the gift of the Lord Chancellor's Department. This time it was the turn of the Lord Chancellor, and so I was also interviewed by his representative. He was very happy with me, and when he knew about the letter, he wanted me to go straight back to the parish for another interview.

I said, 'No, I am sorry, I won't go back for another interview. They have interviewed me already. They can accept me or they can reject me, that's OK, but I won't subject myself to them again for another interview.'

So in the end, I came, whether they wanted me or not. We had the induction, and then we had the first service here and the whole church was full.

I had a meeting with the wardens about a fortnight later. They said many people were not happy about having a woman priest, and that there had only been so many people at my induction because they thought they were having a male priest. I said to them, 'While you are putting your cards on the table, why don't you put all your cards on the table. Has it got anything to do with the fact that I am black?'

One of the women said, 'Well, frankly, yes.'

So I said, 'You and anyone else who is unhappy with me either because I am black or because I am a woman, you are free to go. I have just arrived here, I have no intention of leaving immediately, and I am very happy with myself both as a woman and as a black person.'

Anglican racism

We practise racism in the Anglican Church in a way that is unchristian. The bishop had originally said that there would be two priests in the parish, a vicar and an associate priest. But because of the way they behaved towards me when I came, I said, 'Bishop, there is no way you are going to bring in another colleague here, especially not a white male, because I know what will happen; they are just going to ignore me.'

I will not be ignored in my church.

I think the Anglican Church is struggling with listening. I met a young, black male, whose father is actually an archdeacon in Nigeria, who said he had offered to do something in the church, and he thought they would say, 'Yes. Join the reading rota or the prayer rota . . .' or something. Instead they said, 'It's all right. We don't need any help. If you want to do something, you can go and cut the grass in the churchyard.' That's what they said to him. But when I shared this with my deanery chapter, there were fellow clergy who said, 'Well, if somebody asked me to cut the churchyard, I would happily do it.' They just didn't understand. People genuinely do not know what it feels like. And in the inner city, where you have so many black people, it sometimes fills me with doubt as to whether the church is really listening. How are we to encourage and nurture lay ministry?

We still have indigenous white people here, but they are in a minority now, and it is my responsibility to ensure that they are not marginalised. We are not going to turn the tables round on them. They are going to be fully a part of what is happening, participating equally as everyone else.

And sometimes people's attitudes do change

A man came to see me. I was to do his mother's funeral service. I hadn't met him. We discussed it over the telephone because although his mother had lived in my parish, he himself lived some miles away. So I did the funeral. But then a bit later, very tragically, his wife also died. She was only forty and she literally dropped dead at a barbecue they were having. He got in touch and insisted that I had to do her funeral. The funeral directors said, 'Oh no, she can't do it because you don't live in her parish.' But he insisted, and so they rang me up and asked if I would be happy to. I said, 'Yes, of course'.

So he turned up at the church to see me to talk about it. He's a big guy and he was sobbing his heart out. I just held him. We didn't talk about the funeral that day, because he was too distraught. A few days later I drove out to the farm where he lived, and he said to me, 'When you did my mother's funeral, I didn't know you were West Indian. My mother hated women priests and black people, and when we drove to the crematorium and we saw you there I went, "Oh . . ." and my relations in the car said, "Your mother is going to turn in her grave!" '

He said, 'But it was so beautiful. So that's why I have to have you for my wife's funeral. And when I came to see you the other day, and you held me, I needed that. If a man had done that I would have thumped him.'

You have got to come and see our new vicar!

Some people want to give you a whole string of Bible verses that say a woman should be silent in the church and all of that stuff. There was one man who said to me, 'Prove to me that God has called you to be a priest.'

I said, 'I am sorry. You can either accept me or you can reject me, the choice is yours, but I have no intention of proving anything to you.' I didn't battle with him. I just said, 'Here I am. Accept me or not, it's your choice.' I think he came to respect me for that. I don't have to prove anything to anybody. God has called me, that is the most important thing.

The congregation here has now grown from ten or twelve to around fifty regular worshippers. I enjoy preaching. I have an interactive style, where I talk to people and get them to ask questions and I ask them questions. I think it is growing because people enjoy themselves. There's a good crowd here now and they are telling other people about it, 'You have got to come and see our new vicar!'

The one thing that I think we haven't got right in the parishes is our music but although I enjoy singing, I am not musical. I think that is a great failure of the parish, and I feel part of that failure, because I haven't been able to find somebody to lead us musically.

It's tough – but you stand your ground

I have been in my car going along here and suddenly there are two young lads fighting, one with a hammer in his hand. I don't think. I jump out the car, leaving the engine running, and I get in there between them to separate them. 'You can't do this,' I say to them. 'You are going to end up in hospital, you are going to end up in prison for GBH.'

I am not afraid. Interestingly enough, I have never felt as if they would turn on me. I go, and I hope my very presence calms the situation down. It's tough, but you stand your ground.

You see a lot of abuse, and you see a lot of people who are on drugs. There is a real political agenda locally, with regards to the haves and the have-nots. There are a lot of so-called powerless people, high levels of unemployment, a lot of people who lack confidence, with very low self-esteem. There is some regeneration, new houses going up, but local people can't afford them. They are moving people out. It causes anguish and anxiety. Where are they moving them to? What are they doing with them?

But darling, I am the vicar

People are still facing crises. My phone rings in the middle of the night, 'Please can you come – Daddy is beating up Mum.' The police aren't called, keeping to the family's wishes, because they don't want the children to be separated or taken into care. So I go.

I work quite late into the night, and most times Ken goes to bed before me. When the door bell goes, which it does very often, I don't even think, I just go straight and open the door to deal with whatever the crisis is. We do have a panic alarm down by the door and I have got another one upstairs by the bed. Ken says, 'You should not have opened the door, you should have come and got me.' But that is him being protective, in his husband role.

I say, 'But, darling, I am the vicar. You are not the vicar.'

Me checking drainpipes? No, thank you

I am content with being a priest, very content. I am very happy. I am very much a one-to-one person. I am not a bureaucrat. I don't like pushing papers around. I enjoy preaching.

I heard that somebody had asked for me to become an archdeacon. I laughed at the thought – me checking drainpipes? No, thank you. I don't have any great aspiration. I don't think I have any ambition to be a bishop. I am very content serving God as a priest.

REVD BRIDGET MACAULAY
WITH HER JOB-SHARE HUSBAND, KENNY

11

Job-Sharing the Priesthood

REVD BRIDGET MACAULAY

Curate of Old St Paul's, Edinburgh

I was studying theology until summer 1992, just before the vote to ordain women in the Church of England was passed. I was aware of the issues from those around me, and thought it just had to happen. There were a lot of women at the college that it had a very serious, significant impact on. But not me. I didn't want to be a priest.

Introduction

LB: The curate at Old St Paul's Episcopal Church in Edinburgh is not one person but two. Bridget and Kenny Macaulay are a young married couple, both priests, who are job-sharing. They have two little daughters, Kayna and Chirstin, and they are 'job-sharing' parenthood as well as priesthood.

Their Cox and Box approach can be a little disconcerting. One day you may see Kenny fully robed in a golden cope, solemn and splendid, leading the procession down the aisle, while Bridget turns up at the end of the service in jeans, holding a toddler with one hand and wheeling a push-chair with the other. The following week it will be Bridget in the finery and the procession, and Kenny with the kids.

Una Kroll told us how, just before the Lambeth Conference in 1968, there was a lot of condemnatory language floating about in the church, saying, for instance, how disgusting it would be if a pregnant woman was at the altar. As a mother of four herself, Una was made very angry by this. So I know she would have loved to have been present at Old St Paul's one Pentecost when Bridget was celebrating, eight and a half months pregnant with her second child, and preaching cheerfully about the church 'groaning in labour pains'.

Another odd thing, in a famously liberal Anglo-Catholic church in Edinburgh, is that the 'curate' is Bridget, daughter of a Baptist minister and Kenny, who comes from a strict Brethren background in Glasgow.

Kenny: The Brethren experience of worship is in very plain halls with no crucifixes, no icons, absolutely no clerics – and an all-male leadership run by elders. They take the Scriptures, and the teachings of the New Testament in particular, completely literally – and women have to keep silent during worship.

When I told them I wanted to be ordained, my parents said, 'It's all right. We won't tell anybody!' And at one level, it felt like I had become the black sheep of the family. On another level, I suspect they were quite proud of me.

It says something for my parents that they came along to the ordination not just of their son – which was shock, horror! – but the fact that it was also the ordination of their daughter-in-law made it a double whammy for them.

LB: *This is Bridget's story, but you can't really tell Bridget's story without letting Kenny come into it. He must be allowed to interject his angle here and there. They are 'Bridget'nKenny' or 'Kenny'nBridget' to everyone I've spoken to in Edinburgh – two very different personalities who have formed a compelling unity.*

Bridget and Kenny are part of a younger generation of priests. As time goes by, the generations will increasingly find it hard to believe that women were ever discriminated against or treated as not equal. To some extent Bridget herself walked through an open door. But as Canon Lucy Winkett told us, there are people who will keep on giving women priests a tough time. 'There are plenty of people out there who still find women priests abhorrent and will use very strong, unpleasant language. It's also not over, in the sense that Roman Catholic women are not yet ordained. There are plenty of them with vocations still waiting, and we must keep on with the struggle for them. It's not over.'

I believe that it's the witness and ministry of women like Lucy and Bridget and all the women in this book, more than any intellectual arguments, that are going to win in the end. What immediately struck me about Bridget, when we went to a Eucharist conducted by her at Old St Paul's, was the intensity she puts into the words of the liturgy. She makes you pay attention. It's not a big voice, nor is she a big person, and yet you are compelled to listen carefully to words spoken with such emotional authority.

Bridget

A little girl in a sea of men
I really admire the women who have gone before me, because it has been such a hard struggle. I wasn't part of that struggle – it had all happened before I knew I wanted to offer myself for ordination. Often the women felt that the only way they could fight this battle was to fight as men do. I know that to do that is at a huge cost to women. We aren't men, and we can't become men. We have to find a way to grow to be women priests, and for that to develop naturally in its own time and in its own way.

I had this very powerful image once when I was doing Evensong. I have to wear these big copes, and they are so heavy and they are always at least a foot too long for me as they are designed to sit on men's shoulders. One day when I was celebrating Evensong and Benediction, I was coming up the aisle in this cope, just feeling weighed down by this beautiful, intricate thing. It felt like I was carrying this mantle of tradition of a male priesthood that's been with us for centuries, and it's a beautiful thing. A beautiful, ornate and rich thing – so this is not knocking what has been – but I got up to the front where there is the really good, strong, *male* choir. I'm not knocking that either – it's beautiful. But I'm not confident about singing in church, and I heard this little girl's reedy voice coming out of my mouth. I sang Evensong in this heavy cope, and then I went and sat down in the sedilia and I wept. I wept for the whole service. I got myself through it, but I was nearly overwhelmed by the feeling that women's priesthood is like being a little girl in a sea of grown men.

I realised that this is what I feel about my place in women's priesthood, here, at this time, *now* – that women's priesthood is still in its girlhood. It has this girl's voice in a male voice choir. It's almost as if we're trying on men's clothes and they don't fit, and that now we have to find a way for the girl to grow into womanhood.

Meeting Kenny

Kenny and I met in Cornwall in 1991. I'd gone home for the summer during my second year at Trinity College in Bristol. I was trying to earn a bit of extra money by doing a locum in occupational therapy, which was my original training. Kenny was doing casual labouring and building work. He worked in Edinburgh during term-time with a charity called the Navigators, doing chaplaincy work with university students, but because he wasn't paid a salary, he always had to get jobs in the summer vacations to give him a bit of a buffer for the following academic year.

Kenny: My Dad became a teacher, but he was a joiner by trade and always practical and I like that sort of work. I find it very therapeutic. Working with people all year, you are always worrying and wondering, 'Am I doing any good? Am I having any influence?' So to work – say, cementing a gable end – is wonderful.

I'd declared a man-free zone for the summer and didn't want anything to do with men for quite a while. I'd been a bit hurt by someone at college. I look back on it now and don't have any regrets. But Kenny and I met through a mutual friend, and we ran about in the same crowd in Cornwall for about ten weeks during the summer of 1991. And rather conveniently,

Kenny had been involved with someone, too, and that hadn't worked out either, so he was feeling the same as me.

So it was fine. It was safe. Kenny and I just got to know one another as friends and then he went back to Edinburgh and I went back to Bristol for my final year.

We kept in touch. Kenny was working from home, a shared flat with students, and he was running study groups and doing a lot of one-to-one spiritual direction stuff with students, helping them work through their doubts and anxieties. He was doing the kind of work that really interested me. It encouraged me to think that there were other ways of exploring ministry; it didn't *have* to be ordination.

1986 Lee Abbey

My original training and career had been as an occupational therapist – which I loved – but I became increasingly frustrated by how difficult it was to approach people holistically because there were certain restraints on you, both of time and resources. And the spiritual side of life – well, you had to be very careful how you spoke about that within the National Health Service.

In 1986 I took a year out and went to live and work at a place called Lee Abbey by the sea in North Devon. I joined the Christian community who run it. I'd once been there on holiday and had been very taken by it. There was a wholeness to their life that really drew me. Work flowed from living and worshipping together.

I stayed there for over a year as a community member. I worked in the kitchen and I led a visual arts group, and was generally just a bod. Living in this community which offered hospitality all the year round to visitors on holiday or on retreat.

'I do not want to have to serve another tea cake and smile – I'm facing major life issues!'

Life there was a shared experience that could at times be very intense and painful. Because you couldn't escape from people, you had to deal with your differences and problems more or less in public. There were times when I felt, 'I do not want to serve another tea cake at four o'clock and smile at people – I shall go mad!' You wanted to say, 'Please can I take an afternoon off because I feel as if I'm facing major life issues?' But you couldn't.

It was all so intense. I look back at it now and I can laugh at myself, but I was less able to at the time. And there were one or two times when I really felt I couldn't keep up the front – I was just too close to tears to be able to do it. But we all went through that, and that was what was lovely about the community. There was a strong sense that people were there for each other.

Incredibly deep friendships were formed, and some of my closest friends now are from that time. It was almost as though we all lived through the seasons spiritually while we were living through the seasons on the Lee Abbey estate. You saw that at certain times people were going through winter and needed extra support, love and care. We were loving to each other. Irritating and frustrating as well, of course, but that's the whole experience of community.

The spiritual hothouse

That year was my first step towards thinking I might be heading into a different line of work, or at least a different way of using my occupational therapy. At Lee Abbey I had fourteen months of probably the most intense experience of my life. It was a bit like a spiritual hothouse. There was a great breadth of spiritual backgrounds and expressions of faith and approaches to prayer all living together. And there was something about the wholeness of work and home and worship being all bound up together that I felt was like coming home. It was like a re-creation of something that I'd experienced in childhood.

A Baptist childhood

There were times as children when we felt that we were a bit in a goldfish bowl. My father was a Baptist minister and we lived in a flat that was attached to the church, in Bognor Regis, West Sussex. Everything to do with the church happened on our doorstep. It was all mixed up. Our home was where the church was and it all happened in the one place.

There are some definite disadvantages to being a clergy child. You really are expected to be always good. People would phone up my mother and say, 'Do you know your children are setting fire to the garden?' Or, 'Do you know your children are climbing on the roof?'

But my parents were careful to keep boundaries, and I grew up with a positive experience of living in a church community. I think more than anything was the feeling that Jesus could be my friend. That was very real for me as a child.

To rebel or not to rebel

When I was a teenager I joined the Baptist youth group, and that gave me the sense that church was a good place to be, rather than something I wanted to get away from. I did think – Shall I rebel? It was the thing you are supposed to do when you are a teenager, and I had the seeds of rebellion in me as much as anybody. I don't think I was an easy child. But I remember thinking – But I know that it's true. I *know* that Christ is alive, and I know that Christ loves me and that I have a relationship with Christ, so what is the point of going through with a rebellion when I know I'll have to come back to it in the end anyway? It was all very clear.

The Baptist youth club was fun to belong to, and we did all sorts of things – sailing weekends, camping weekends and so forth. It also gave me a chance to think and talk about what I felt was right and wrong. We were quite black and white about it – things were right or they were wrong. It seems funny now. But I'm very grateful for that as a starting point. It gave me something solid to stand on.

Finding a new spiritual home

I went away and trained as an occupational therapist in Oxford, and had my first real exposure to the Anglican church at St Aldate's, which was in some ways a very easy introduction to Anglicanism, because it was low church and accessible. But there was something about the rhythm of the liturgy and the centrality of the Eucharist that moved me very much.

It wasn't so much a decision *against* the Baptist Church; it was more a decision *for* the Anglican Church. To begin with it was social – there were lots of things going on for students at St Aldate's, and I wanted to be part of that. But when I got there I felt – increasingly – that that's where my spiritual home was, in that evangelical Anglican tradition.

A time to doubt

Lee Abbey, in 1986, was where I first allowed myself to doubt and challenge the basis of my own faith. It was a very, very important year for me, but it was also a strange, disturbing time when I went through great questioning about the whole thing.

I began to have major doubts about whether God was good. For all sorts of reasons I had had my share of angst and frustration as a child, but hadn't ever doubted then that Christ was my friend. It was that year at Lee Abbey when I really thought – I'm not sure whether I like God. I may believe in him, and I may not be able to escape him, but I'm not sure that I like him very much.

My father has always suffered from depression. It comes in cycles, and it was a very hard thing to carry as a family. Now I found that I had many unanswered questions about that. I started to think – How does God allow it to keep happening?

My father has had lots of different help over the years, from drugs to counselling to prayer counselling to all sorts. These things have helped, but not totally removed it. It's part of our family experience and one of the things that have meant that our faith has had to have a deeper level. I get impatient with people who give black-and-white answers, and have very slick answers to things, because my own experience doesn't live up to that.

But somehow through that I never lost a sense of God being with us in it, and that's influenced my understanding of faith. I can't explain it away. I can't say why it happened. I can't say why it doesn't get better, or why God doesn't heal my father. But of one thing I'm very sure, God is with us in it, and is also big enough to take the range of emotions that it brings up for those of us who are closest to it. I've had my times of being very angry with God, and I've come out the other end of it, and have known that that's been all right to do that, and to express that anger and to have all those real doubts and questions and so on.

That sense of having a relationship with God was so strong, right from being very, very young. You kind of deal with the horrible stuff, it's out there, it's not something you can pretend isn't there. And if our relationship with God can't have that kind of humanity and earthiness about it, it's not fit for much, really.

So there were all those sorts of things I had to work through to know that God was *mine*, and not just what I'd inherited, or what I'd been told was the way.

Lee Abbey was my introduction to catholic spirituality and a theology of suffering that at the time I needed and found very helpful. I did a lot of reading, and a lot of exploration of different ideas. I loved Thomas Merton. I became very intense about his kind of spirituality. It made a lot of sense to me at that time.

So that was my rebellion – to move away for a while from my evangelical background and to become an Anglo-Catholic with a vengeance!

The call to . . . what?

While I was there I had a very strong sense that God was calling me to . . . something – but I wasn't sure what it was. I didn't know where it was going to lead. I suspected it *could* lead to ordination . . . but I was not very keen on ordination, I have to say. And women couldn't become priests then in any case.

Because I had this strong sense of community I thought it could even be a call to religious community. The only things I was sure of were: first, that I wanted to study theology and second, that I needed to go back into the health service for a while and test these feelings out. I was aware it had been such an intense experience, living in that kind of spiritual hothouse environment, that I needed just the ordinariness of a nine-to-five job to test it out.

Just see what happens

So I returned to work in the health service for the next two years, in the Scilly Isles, Truro and Penzance. I moved down to Cornwall, which is where my mother's family comes from and where I feel my roots are. I lived in Penzance, on my cousin's farm, sharing a self-contained flat in the basement with a friend from Lee Abbey.

The conviction that I had a call didn't go away during that time. Some friends and I were thinking of buying a big house in Penzance, to live in but also as a centre for doing youth work in the church. I took a day out to go and pray about it, because it felt like a big decision to make. Some very dear friends have a home that they open as a house of prayer where people can go and take time out, so I went to see Dennis and Anna to have a quiet day with them and think.

Dennis said, 'What's in your heart to do? What do you really want to do?'

I said, 'You know, what I really want to do is study theology.'

So he said, 'So why are you buying a house?'

I said, 'But I can't. I'd never get a grant to study theology. I've already had a bursary to study occupational therapy. I've had my chips as far as further education is concerned.'

Dennis and Anna are wonderful people of great faith. They said, 'It will come. Go through all the normal routes you would go through to get the money, and just see what happens.'

So I applied to the local education authority, and amazingly – I still can't quite believe it – they gave me a grant to study theology. So I went and took a degree at Trinity College, Bristol.

I didn't want to talk about ordination – I wanted to talk about lay ministry – but nobody would

I was there and studying until the summer 1992, just before the vote to ordain women in the Church of England was passed. Obviously we had lots of debates about it at college. There were a lot of women at the college that it had a very serious, significant impact on, but not me. I didn't want to be a priest. I was aware of the issues from those around me, and thought it just had to happen, but it didn't make any personal impact on me, because I wasn't thinking of ordination for myself.

While I was still at college I started to talk to the Diocese of Truro about the possibility of lay ministry. But nobody really wanted to talk to me about it. It was always, 'Oh, no, you need to go and be ordained if you want to work in the church.' It was strangely frustrating. I didn't want to talk just about ordination; I wanted to talk about lay ministry as well.

Then the diocese said that they wanted to recommend that I went forward for Selection Conference for ordination, and I began to be swept along with this. Deep down I knew I wasn't ready. It got to two weeks before my Selection Conference. I telephoned the people in Truro and said I was very sorry, but I just didn't feel I could go forward. They were very gracious about it, and responded very constructively to me being so muddled.

I came out of that experience thinking, 'Oh, my goodness, what have I done? I've almost got my degree in theology. I know I want to work in full-time ministry of some sort. But how on earth am I going to do this? How on earth am I going to find a context that can allow me to explore ministry without being ordained – and find a way of earning a living?'

Kenny: She pulled out because she really thought there was something else that she wanted to pursue. It was ministry, yes, but she wasn't sure about all the church stuff. So when she heard about what I was doing with the Navigators, this chaplaincy and spiritual direction work with students, she thought it might be possible for her to do the same thing.

1993 Marrying Kenny

After that summer of 1991, when we had first met, Kenny came down to Cornwall again at New Year. Then he came to visit me at Bristol, and I went up to see him in Edinburgh at half term. We went on holiday together the following Easter. By that stage it had become a bit more than being 'just friends'. We were spending hours on the telephone together. Everyone at college, in Bristol, was going, 'Ho! *ho???*' But I said, 'No, no. It's not happening, we're just good friends!'

We got engaged in the summer of 1992, just before the General Synod vote. Part of my realising that I didn't want to go ahead with the ordination thing was that Kenny was doing something in lay ministry that really motivated me, working with students on their spiritual search.

I moved up to Edinburgh, and Kenny and I got married the following summer. We worked with the Navigators together from our own home in Marchmont for the next five years. I guess you could say we were job-sharing from the beginning.

The Navigators

We ran a student group of between twenty and forty people. They came to the study groups at our house and we had individual contact with them – we did a lot of one-to-one spiritual direction and discipleship. Part of what we were doing was leadership training, encouraging young people to get to the point where they could lead house groups and build up their local church, or perhaps just to be a pal to somebody who was younger in the faith, and encourage them. And the group itself was a very strong support and had a life of its own. Many of the members still live in Edinburgh and are very loving and supportive of each other. So those friendships that were born around that time are still very current. We see a lot of them, and love them very much.

We weren't paid. We basically depended on gift support and doing a bit of summer work. So it was a great challenge to our faith. But actually there was a great quality of life doing that – and we never went without.

We had what we needed, and we had an incredible sense of being supported by the community. People gave to us in all sorts of different ways. Students who had been through the group and had then started working would come back to us and say, 'I want to support you.' They might give £20 a month to the Navigators, and the charity would manage the funds for us.

We have the same heart and the same vision, but we are very different as people

If you use terms like 'introvert'/'extrovert' rather than words like 'shy' or 'socially confident' or whatever – if you define 'introvert' as 'somebody who needs to have solitary time in order to re-energise' – then that's me. And if you talk about 'extrovert' as 'somebody who is energised by being with other people', then that's Kenny.

Kenny: We bring such a different approach to situations, and as people we are very different. I think we spark one another off in what we are doing. It's not that we always discuss everything and there has to be a kind of committee meeting about everything – but obviously working in the same area, we kind of know what's going on. I often have half an idea of what I am thinking about, and talk to Bridget about it and in the talking something will clarify and I will come away with a new idea and pursue it. She has lots of ideas, she's much more creative than I am, but I think I sometimes have a practical sense of what would communicate and what wouldn't.

I think there is something about the partnership between male and female that is pretty fundamental to what I feel priesthood is about – something about working different gifts together, and different strengths and weaknesses together. Actually it's quite helpful, because in a very tangible way it's possible for me to be who I am, without having to be everything to everybody, because Kenny is who he is.

Two for the road

After I had been with the Navigators for five years, we got to a point where we began to question whether we would be working with students for the rest of our life. We were thinking of having a family, so we were wondering about our lifestyle. We were living hand to mouth, and at times it was pretty faith-stretching. It required a particular sort of energy. There were times when it was plain uncomfortable, but there were other times when it was so amazing how we were provided for, that it balanced out. It was a mixed experience. But really we felt our time with the Navigators was coming to an end, but we didn't quite know what we were going to do next.

We decided to take a little sabbatical, to take time out to think things through, about the future and the way we wanted to go. We wanted to be open to all possibilities. We had both at different times thought about the ordained ministry, and although we had both in the past decided against it, we thought it was important to be open to that possibility, among others, now.

So we went off in a camper van. We were two ageing hippies really, and just wanted to have the camper van experience before we settled down and were sensible and middle-aged. To give it some kind of structure, we set out to explore Celtic roots and centres. So we travelled about on the West Coast of Scotland, in Iona and the Outer Hebrides. And then we went to Ireland.

Yes

When we got to Northern Ireland, I stayed with some Catholic sisters in a convent in Larne for a few days, while Kenny went off in the camper van on his own and did a bit of exploring round Donegal. We had done a lot of talking about it together, but we felt we also needed to be separate in our thinking as well, and see where that led us, and to see if that matched up.

So Kenny took himself off to an island. But he somehow arrived on a different island from the one he thought he was on. When he was there, he came upon a fishing community, where the Catholic priest was doing a Blessing of the Boats service for the fishermen, and organising the local ceilidh. That really impressed Kenny, and he thought that if that was what priesthood could be about, being part of the community and being really involved in peoples' lives – then yes, he could go for that.

Kenny: I have a sort of swinging view of what the priesthood is, because of coming from this very functional background belief that each one of us is a priest, and some days I wake up and think this whole priest thing is just an invention of the church. Then on another level I think it is good that certain people are given this high calling, and there is a purpose for a representative ministry. So I swing between those two views.

I suppose I had done a lot more thinking about ordination before, in a way, so it was easier for me to think of it as an option. While I was at this convent I had a very strong, very powerful dream of Kenny and me celebrating a mass together. When I woke up I thought – Yes, I should give this more thought.

Salt and light

We both came back from this time apart, thinking that we wanted to look again at the possibility of ordination. When we got back to

Edinburgh we went to a Vocations Day, run by the Director of Ordinands. A chap came up from London and talked to us. He talked about how he felt that the most important role of the priest was to help people to be the church in the world. Whatever they were doing in life, whether they were at home looking after kids or high-powered businessmen, the priest's role was to encourage and support them to be salt and light in the world.

I loved that image of salt and light. It is something that sends away the darkness and is somehow a presence of light and warmth. But salt is also sharp to the taste. It can be counter-cultural and challenging. We both thought that if that's what ordination could help us to be, then yes, we'd sign up for it.

They could have said 'Yes' to one of us and 'No' to the other

We had to go through the process separately. We couldn't go through as a married couple. It was a journey for each of us. But that was quite a nerve-wracking time, because they could have said 'Yes' to one of us and 'No' to the other, in which case we would have had to think quite hard about it. You make yourself very vulnerable.

It was a funny kind of situation, because we felt we had to submit ourselves to the process. It was important to go into it saying that we sensed that this was where God was leading us both, individually and together, but the church has to endorse that. It is the church's calling as well as God's calling, because it is to serve in the church.

We had to go through a series of interviews. And then they sent us separately to an Anglican Board of Ministry selection conference. Kenny went first, and was recommended. A few months later, I went, and thankfully they recommended me as well.

Writing my final essay while eight months pregnant

We trained at the same time. The course stretched us. It was a very rich time. It was done part-time, so we did other things alongside it as well. People brought their work experience to the course. I worked at and sold my artwork. I'd done art at A level, and really loved it. At Lee Abbey I had started to see it as a way of expressing faith. I had a couple of exhibitions and did quite well. So we were studying theology and Kenny was painting and decorating and I was painting pictures. (But Kenny made the most money!)

By the end of the course I was expecting Kayna, our first baby. 'Kayna' is a Cornish saint's name. It means 'beautiful' or 'fine'. I was writing my final essay while eight months pregnant.

Having Kayna influenced my thinking about priesthood a lot. It made connections for me, this human experience of getting fatter and fatter and about to produce a baby, with what I was preparing for and about to go into in terms of calling and work. I felt that pregnancy and childbirth were good analogies of the way the Spirit works in our lives. I wrote: 'We may find ourselves awkward and heavy with the demands that mission and living the life of faith in the world can make upon us. We may be frightened as to the nature of the "child" that is being born among us. Is it going to change our experience of life beyond all recognition?'

There are things in there that I go back to and will keep going back to. I think that's what I feel about my priesthood – its roots are in who I am as a human being, a human being before God. That's why I think all of us have a priesthood of some sort to explore. It's where we encounter God in our experience of life. Ordinary, seemingly haphazard things can have a great significance when you look for it. I see my role as an ordained priest to be one of encouraging other people to explore that. Whether that's through contact with people who are preparing for baptism, or people who are dying, or whether it's just people frustrated at work, or wondering how to preserve a prayer life when they are a busy mother. That to me is what it's about, helping people to live reflectively, to reflect on their experience and to see that God is at work within it.

Gob-smacked

We wanted to do a job-share, and we wondered whether anyone would be willing to let us. Kenny was doing a placement with Ian Paton at Holy Trinity, Haddington, but Ian knew he was soon coming to be rector at Old St Paul's. He said to Kenny, 'I was wondering whether you and Bridget would be interested in doing a job-share at Old St Paul's?'

Kenny came home and told me and we both laughed for about ten minutes at the thought of Kenny and Bridget at Old St Paul's. All the time we had been living in Edinburgh we had been part of the congregation and community of St Paul's and St George's, an evangelical church. Nothing could be more different than Old St Paul's, which was more or less at the opposite end of the spectrum.

But the more we thought about it, the more we thought we should do it. We had a great respect for Ian and felt that we could learn a lot from being there with him. Also, although we've both come from and worked in the evangelical tradition, we've always wanted to stand for being willing to cross bridges and to be a connection between different theological stances. Although I hadn't stayed with it, I'd had some exposure to Anglo-Catholic worship and spirituality at Lee Abbey and then in Cornwall. We were both committed to dialogue. So crazy though it seemed, and because Ian had seemed so keen on the idea, we felt that if he was willing to risk it, then we were as well.

Friends threw up their hands in horror and said, 'My goodness me!' I think everybody was completely gob-smacked. But in 1998 Kenny and I were ordained as the curate of Old St Paul's.

Oh, poor Bridget!

There are times when I wish I had Kenny's self-confidence. For instance, neither of us is musically trained, and we've had to do things like singing the eucharistic prayer, singing Evensong and Benediction, when we haven't been brought up in that tradition. It demanded a lot of us to do that, initially, because we hadn't had any training. We thought we would learn by getting people to put it on tape and copy it, because we don't read music either. In a situation like that, I've sometimes felt crushed by it. Talk about a public humiliation! I've really had my confidence undermined by getting it wrong and feeling it was so public. Actually people are very accepting and can live without musical perfection. But you still feel everyone must be thinking, 'Oh, poor Bridget!'

Kenny equally finds it difficult, but he's able to shrug it off much more than I am. So I've come back home from Evensong sometimes and said, 'That was just awful!' And he's got me to the point when I can laugh about it. So I can say that my ministry doesn't depend on singing a perfect Preface.

And Kenny gets to the end of writing a sermon and he says, 'I just never know how to finish a sermon! I just never know . . .' He always says that. I enjoy words and think I have an ability to draw strands of thought together. But Kenny's got an ease in communicating with people, and I really love that in him. So he's helped me in my delivery sometimes, and I think I've helped him in thinking an argument through.

I think we have not to envy each other's gifts. Recognising that we have different gifts and celebrating our own gifts rather than envying each other's. Both of us have to work at that. That's one of the things that working in partnership is about – it's about your own growth as people as well.

The good companions

We both feel very strongly that it's really important that we invest time and energy in our marriage. In a sense our marriage is the bedrock out of which our ministry grows. Our human experience and the struggles that we have in our relationship can be the contact point we have with people, but they can only be that if we are prepared to face them and work through them. We've had to work hard at communicating effectively with each other, hearing each other and respecting our differences.

We feel it's important to have a day off each a week, and to be committed to that within the boundaries of what's possible. Obviously sometimes things come up when you can't. It's a very difficult job for that – you can't fit this work into nine to five. It doesn't work like that and yet I think it's important that we see the importance of our commitment to time with each other and the family, to be good companions.

Representing Christ

In the Anglo-Catholic tradition the priest is sometimes seen as a representative of Christ. Some people therefore find it very hard to recognise a woman as a representative of Christ – because she's a woman, Christ was a man. But to me there's a much more important question. Not about how can female priesthood represent Christ, who was a man, but how can any priesthood represent the whole of humanity if men and women aren't doing it together? It means to be human before God, and it takes both men and women to do that, because we are male and female in our humanity. That's what we are bringing to God, and that is where God meets us.

I don't want to be disrespectful of anybody else's view. There are one or two people that wouldn't come to Communion at Old St Paul's when I am celebrating, but they don't make a thing about it, they will just absent themselves. One or two have made a point of saying, 'This isn't personal to you, it's about my convictions about priesthood.' And I respect that. I think people should live by their own convictions, even if they are different from mine. But I've had a very positive experience of being a woman priest. I know that some other women have had some very difficult experiences and have even had to work with rectors or vicars who haven't been supportive, and have been undermined in very subtle ways.

Kenny: I guess that although I am in an Anglo-Catholic parish at the moment, I still have the 'priesthood of all believers' view. We obviously do now have a specific role in the church, a kind of representative role when we are celebrating Mass, for instance. But I'm thinking more about the practical, everyday things we do, when we have influence on one another. Or the sort of things we did before ordination, with the Navigators. I don't think Bridget being a priest, or for that matter me being a priest, makes any difference. We help each other as people, and for me, that's an expression of priesthood.

I think that's the one way to be a representative of Christ – if you can offer something of the love of Christ to people as you meet their eye and speak to them the truth, that this is Christ himself, offered for us. I know for some the priest is the go-between between them and God, but that doesn't sit very happily with me. I think God meets you wherever you are, and you don't need a priest for that to happen. Yes, we're a focus in some way, but if we represent anything it is humanity.

Let them flow

There are times when I'm administering Communion when I feel very, very moved by seeing people come up and kneel and hold their hands out. There is such an openness about people like that, and it often moves me to tears. I've got to the stage when I think, 'That's all right. Just let them flow.' I don't feel I've got to be this strong person all the time.

I think the type of ministry that Kenny and I are naturally drawn to – because of our types of personality – is very much about relationships and using who we are rather than what we do as the starting point for encountering people and encouraging them to meet with God. I think that's just the way we are. We see the strength that there is in relationships and the way that working with a small group of people to quite a level has a power of multiplication. In the established church there are times when you have to spread yourself more thinly, but that's not the easiest part of this job for us. We're much happier working with smaller groups of people to a depth, as we did with the Navigators.

These poor children with two priests for parents!

We feel the next move is the crucial one, because it will see the children into school. During our time at Old St Paul's we've had our second child, Chirstin. Some of the congregation may have questioned the wisdom of letting an eight-and-a-bit-month-pregnant woman preach and celebrate on Pentecost Sunday, as I did in June 2000! Particularly remembering the coming of the Holy Spirit in powerful and unexpected ways . . . and especially as the alternative epistle reading for the day spoke about 'groaning in labour pains'! But the next day my maternity leave began, and I took a break from the more public aspects of ministry for a few months.

We'd like to have more children, probably. So we'd like to carry on doing a job-share, but we might have to change the percentage of it. Kenny would do a bit more, and I'd do a little less perhaps for the next wee while. We are committed to always having one of us with the children. So maybe something small. Something down-to-earth. A group of people we could work alongside and encourage. I think now that I'd like somewhere that had a sense of the importance of liturgy and doing that well, but perhaps more simply, less richly, than at Old St Paul's.

We'd love to stay in Edinburgh if we could. We've established friendships with people who knew us before we were ordained. If people first meet you as an ordained person, then the boundaries between normal friendship and your relationship with them as a priest – sometimes it's difficult to know where you are with that. So it's good to have friends who have known you before you had those bishoply hands laid upon you!

Some of the old student groups we had from the Navigator days have stayed on in Edinburgh, some have married, some have started careers, and we really value the contact we still have with them. Not least because they are a good source of babysitters! No, they are friends who are really important to us. They telephone us sometimes and say, 'Have you finished your services? We're coming round now with a bottle of wine.' To go somewhere new and have to start all over again and build all that from scratch would be hard.

And these poor children, with two priests for parents! We're saving their child benefit to pay their psychiatry bills later on!

REVD (SQUADRON LEADER) ELEANOR RANCE

12

Let's Go! Let's Be Priests!

REVD (SQUADRON LEADER)

ELEANOR RANCE

Chaplain, RAF Linton on Ouse

I went home, walked in the door, put the television on and the vote had already happened. Someone on the television was saying, 'There will be quite a few people upset about this . . .'

I still didn't know who had won. I picked up the telephone and rang home. Immediately my father and my mother answered the phone at the same time and they both spoke together – '*Hello?*'

So of course I knew at once what had happened.

Introduction

LB: Eleanor joined the RAF as a chaplain in 1999, and has served on RAF bases at Cosford, Kinloss and since August 2000 at Linton on Ouse in the parish of Newton on Ouse. She shares her officer's accommodation with her large friendly cat, Boy. We wandered round the base to see her chapel and office – after a horrendously unattractive photograph of me had been taken and pinned to my coat like a warning.

In her twenties, Eleanor is the youngest woman priest we interviewed.

'*I have to say I did gulp rather – I think it was probably about the day after I was ordained deacon. I had my letter from the Church Commissioner saying that the number of years of pensionable service is like . . . forty years. I thought – Oh, my goodness me – that's a very long time!*'

But since her ordination soon after leaving university, she has had, as all priests do, to minister to people facing the extremes of tragedy. My journey to meet her at RAF Linton was across the wide plain of the Vale of York, not long after the Selby train crash. In the aftermath of that disaster one of the aircraft hangers at RAF Linton had been turned into a temporary mortuary, and bodies were laid out in Eleanor's chapel when families came to say goodbye. She had sat with them and held their hands while they struggled to come to terms with their grief and loss.

I liked Eleanor immediately. She's attractive, friendly and easy to talk to, and if I were to include the whole of our conversation in this chapter it would take up the whole book. I hope I've chosen the bits that give you the fairest portrait of her. I was surprised and interested by how early her sense of being called by God came to her.

The chief thing that I think would strike most people about Eleanor is how she holds together two strongly contrasting impressions. She is not only young, she is also very youthful in appearance and attitude, and has a witty personality, and yet it is immediately obvious how seriously she takes her vocation. This isn't expressed merely by her liking to wear her 'clericals' as she calls them, but in her way of conveying great seriousness and thoughtfulness behind a beautiful and cheery countenance.

Eleanor

Things fall apart

I was born in Reading, and my parents split up when I was very small. My father had pretty much left the family home before I was aware of him. From an early age my 'family' was my mother, my two older sisters, Anna and Emma, and me, and our grandparents – both sets of grandparents. We were a very strong family unit. I didn't really think about the fact that there was anything different from other families. When I was eight years old my mother went back to teaching and met David Rance and they married when I was nine.

I immediately decided that this was my father, and that was lovely. He was called 'Daddy' pretty much from the word go. He had two children from a previous marriage so we gained a stepbrother and stepsister, Matthew and Stephanie. We became a family of seven in the holidays and had wonderful times together.

We had become known as the Rance family. I liked being a Rance. I was a Nice when I was a little girl, until I was seventeen, and then I changed my name by Deed Poll, just before I went to university. My sister Emma had already changed her name to Bridgman, my mother's maiden name and Anna stayed a Nice. So my mother has three unmarried daughters with three different surnames. She just goes with the flow!

I didn't ever know my biological father very well. I don't still. We go to see him sometimes; he has remarried and I also have a half-brother and half-sister, which is lovely.

I think that this was something I learned from experience, and that I've taken into adult life and also into my ministry. Things do fall apart; and they are painful and hideous and even catastrophic sometimes. But there's time and there's space and there's a creative God to make it different.

We're all happy now. In my family, each different group of people involved in it, are happy.

Robes and not robes, adult baptism, infant baptism and all sorts

My mother always took us to church, and church was very much a second home when we were small. Jim Spence, the then vicar of our church in Reading, Greyfriars, was hugely supportive. We used to go to the morning service and to Sunday school and on church outings and all those sorts of things. I enjoyed it all and I've still got very close links with people from those days.

When I was about seven or eight, I started having piano lessons and was asked by the teacher if I'd like to join the local parish church choir – which wasn't our normal church on a Sunday. I like singing, so I said 'Yes'. So then I was singing in the choir of the parish church for ten o'clock Parish Communion and then going to join the family at Greyfriars for eleven o'clock Morning Prayer, arriving just after it started usually. And then back to the parish church for 6.30 Evensong. That became a routine and I loved it. When my mother married my stepfather, he was a member of a Baptist church in High Wycombe, so then I had three churches to go to.

It did make life quite hectic. But it gave me, from an early age, quite a wide understanding of the church. The family church in Reading I grew up in was a traditional, low Anglican, evangelical Church, focused on teaching and mission work. The church where I sang in the choir, St Peters in Caversham, was a high-church, or at least a middle-of-the-road Anglican, and my stepfather was the organist in his Baptist church, so we had experience of a variety of ways of doing things: robes or not robes; choirs, vestments, processions and candles or no processions and plain tables; adult baptism, infant baptism and dedications; and all sorts of different traditions.

Prayer was important at home. We all shared a bedroom, us three girls, and in the evening we'd get ready for bed and say prayers together with our mother. We'd think about the things that had happened and the things that were going to happen and things we were worried about. In December we always had an Advent candle and we'd sing, 'Oh come, Oh come, Emmanuel'.

My mother is great. I found – especially as I got older, when I was at university and looking to be ordained – that she was someone off whom I could bounce ideas about spiritual things; which she still is.

Definitely by the time I was thirteen I had decided I should be ordained

I first thought that I should do something for God when I was about nine or ten. I had read Paul Brown's book – *Ten Fingers for God* – and was inspired by it and thought that I should be a missionary doctor or something like that. But when I got to secondary school I realised that I was absolutely useless at science, so that wasn't going to happen. I also realised that I was more interested in people as personalities rather than in their bodies falling apart.

By the time I was about twelve or thirteen – definitely by the time I was thirteen – I decided that I should be ordained. That was what I was being called to do by God, and that was a very urgent and definite thing.

At school there was quite an amused reaction to this, and a careers adviser said, 'You could always be a secretary in a church.' That was just so off the plot. I didn't speak to him again. My mother and family were supportive, as they always are, but most of my friends just thought I was mad. Mostly people laughed.

That was in 1985, and women couldn't even be deacons then. But a little later, when I was choosing my A level subjects, another careers adviser said, 'I think the way ahead is to read theology at university.' By that time it was 1988 and women were being made deacons and it looked as though they would be made priests in the not-too-distant future. I thought – OK, I'll read theology. Where's a good place? King's College, London? OK – that sounds all right.

'Yes, Eleanor. You are'

At school I had read mostly languages through to GCSE, then at A Level, I read ancient Greek – although I was useless at the grammar – French and religious studies. Then I got a place and went up to King's and did an introduction to biblical Hebrew and New Testament Greek – this time I learned the grammar.

While I was at university in London I went along to see the vicar in the church in Tooting Bec where I had become a Sunday-school teacher, and said that I wanted to be ordained and that I'd wanted to do this for years. He said, 'Good. I'll write to the Diocesan Director of Ordinands.'

So after all those years of saying 'I'm going to be a priest' and everyone laughing or saying, 'Don't be ridiculous', this vicar said to me, 'Yes, Eleanor, you are.'

Suddenly I was being taken seriously and it was quite a shock. It became very real and exciting.

We all got the giggles

There was a group of us at King's all wanting to be ordained. We all supported one another and although it was before the vote, there wasn't any sense of 'You're a woman, so you can't.' There was a chaplaincy, and I got involved in that and I also became a server at Westminster Abbey. So I was getting into yet another tradition, Anglo-Catholic spirituality, and I went on retreat for the first time. We went along to the Sisters at Wantage.

It was a silent retreat. Of course we all got the giggles, as you automatically do when there are seventeen of you sitting in silence, looking at each other in the sitting-room. But it was wonderful as well – a terrifying and an exciting experience.

And then, not long afterwards, it was 1992, there was the vote.

There was this deathly hush

11 November 1992. That day I was at a lecture at college and someone had come in to talk about working with people with HIV and AIDS. Afterwards I went home. I was living in a flat in Vauxhall, so I was only across the river from where the great discussions were going on. I walked in the door, put the television on and it was the end of the debate. The vote had happened and someone on television was saying, 'There will be quite a few people upset about this . . .' but I didn't know which group they meant. So I picked up the phone and rang home – and I knew at once what had happened because my father and my mother both immediately picked up the phone at the same time. They both said together, 'Hello?' So it was obvious what had happened. I was excited and happy, but not exactly surprised. I knew it would happen.

But when I went into college the next day there was a peculiar hush, because there were some people who didn't want to know. They had decided – and I suppose it was a sensible idea, but it felt very odd – that they weren't going to talk about it. At all. So there was me wanting to bounce off the ceiling, because I'd been wanting to be a priest for so long . . . and there was this deathly hush.

How can I tell anyone they are wrong? I can't

When it comes to those who disagree with the ordination of women – I guess each person approaches it in their own way. I have made friends with many who oppose the idea, or who haven't made up their minds. To me it isn't about right or wrong, it is about giving one another space to change and grow. I've met people who say, 'I don't agree with women priests, but I know you – and you're all right.' Which is mad when you think about it, but I think it shows how for some people the subject isn't just theological or even based on principles. It is about how we feel deep down, and what our lifelong experience has been.

For example, I knew one guy who didn't approve of the ordination of women. From time to time he would come to a mid-week service, but he never knew who was going to be conducting it. So sometimes this poor man would turn up to church and discover that it was me taking the service and he'd have to go away again, because he didn't want to come to Communion with a woman priest.

I had not really talked to him much, because I never really got the opportunity. One day he came to church for this service and I saw him come in through the door and I said, 'Oh, I'm sorry, it's me today.'

And he said, 'Oh dear.'

Of course, he was quite unhappy that he felt he couldn't receive Communion. So I said, 'Look, I don't mind if you want to just sit in the church and be here.'

I went off to get ready and he did stay. I started the service and we got to the Confession and he joined in and all the way through the service he was still joining in. I thought, 'This is interesting. I don't know what's going to happen, but we'll just see.'

He came up to receive Communion from me.

At the end of the service I went to the door to say goodbye to everyone and he came out first, and he thanked me and I thanked him. It was an incredible moment, a very moving moment – one of the most moving moments of my ministry.

I've always felt that people who don't agree with the ordination of women, for whatever reason, that that's where they are, that's how they feel and it's OK. It's the same as those who feel that even if their knees are giving in, they can't stop kneeling down for Communion, because that's the way they receive Communion, the way they have always done it. They can't stop saying the Lord's Prayer with the traditional words because it's so much part of them and part of their relationship with God that they can't change it. How could I tell them that they're wrong? I can't.

I also feel that I cannot *not* be a priest. That's what I'm made to be and that's what God's given me. I can't apologise for that, because it's right for me. So there is never a question of having a big discussion with people, and arguing it with them or anything like that. It's our church, our place, our space with God. So I feel happy and pleased that, quite often, without having any great debates, people do feel that they can make that step.

That's what I've always found with people who I've encountered who have had problems with the ordination of women. Of course, it's never really been a big issue for me, because the battle was over by the time I came along. And by and large people don't suddenly wake up in the morning and say, 'I don't think Eleanor should be a priest.' They might do, in which case perhaps they should tell me. But it's a much bigger thing than that, and it's quite arrogant to think it all hangs on your own ministry.

Adventure and enthusiasm and a desire to make new things

I was ordained deacon in 1996, in Southwark Diocese, where a third of the priests were women, which is an outstanding figure when you consider the percentage in the country. It was just brilliant.

I worked as a curate in the Barnes team ministry. It was the first parish I was shown round, and it felt right. I liked the diocese as well. I've always felt at home there. I still do and I'd like to think that I could go back there one day. I like its attitude and I like the people I worked with there. There's always been a sense of adventure and enthusiasm and the desire to make new things.

I absolutely loved working in Barnes. I worked in three different churches. They had all sorts of different traditions within themselves. I worked with young people, old people – absolutely everything. I was involved in working with Youth Apart, teaching Old Testament for a reader's course, general parish work, and I loved all of it.

But coming to the end of my second year, I was reading the *Church Times* (as is my wont!) and there was an advert for a chaplain to the RAF. It just said: 'Are you interested in chaplaincy in the RAF?'

It wasn't for one specific post – it was just a recruitment poster really. My mother's father was in the RAF, so she grew up with it. For the past two years I'd been chaplain to the Air Training Corps at home, and that meant that I had already had access to the RAF in a little way. And that summer I'd already agreed to go as an extra adult on their summer camp at RAF Benson, which is about half an hour from my parents' home.

It was a nice leisurely summer afternoon and I thought, 'Oh, that looks interesting. I wonder . . .' So I cut it out. But I didn't do anything straightaway.

How many women priests would be at a point in their lives when they could say, 'I'm going to join the RAF'?

I thought – with this little piece of paper tucked away in my study – 'I'll go on the camp this summer and I'll see what it's like and then I'll think about it when I get back.' I didn't have much time to think about it when I was there, because we were always out doing mad things like navigation exercises and pretending to be warriors, which was quite entertaining. I was wearing my clericals most of the time but people we met on the station didn't believe that I was a priest. They thought I was having a laugh.

So, the end of August came and I thought, 'Well, that wasn't so bad. It was interesting.' It had given me a little tiny image of what it could be like living and working on an RAF base, but nowhere near enough. So I thought I ought to follow it up a bit further.

I wrote a letter in response to the advertisement, saying that I'd like some more information. Two days later, I had a telephone call – which was so quick it rather alarmed me. They said, 'What can we tell you? It would probably be a good idea for you to meet a chaplain.'

They had had a Church of Scotland minister who was a woman in the branch, but she had left. There weren't any other female chaplains.

But really that wasn't so surprising. It was only a couple of years since the vote to ordain women priests, and you couldn't be a chaplain without being a priest or minister. How many women priests would be at a point in their lives where they could say, 'Yes, I'm going to join the RAF'? You'd have to be young. You'd have to be fairly free, or at least have a family who could move around from place to place with you potentially.

I went off to meet the chaplain at the station in Bracknell, which was one of the nearest stations I could go to on my day off, without telling anybody what I was doing. I knew that if I mentioned the idea of joining the RAF to my mother, she would think it was brilliant. I knew she wouldn't try to direct me in any way, but I still needed to think it through myself first. So I went to Bracknell without telling anyone, and spent a day with the chaplain and found out more about the life and work of an RAF chaplain.

'Oh dear. There's nothing holding me back now'

Afterwards I thought, 'OK, I haven't heard anything that's terrified me.' Even then it took me quite a long time to finally get round to saying, 'OK, I'll go for it.' I just left it.

But they telephoned me a couple of weeks later and said, 'Well, what do you think?'

I said, 'Mmm . . . I want to talk to my archdeacon.'

That was David Gerrard, Archdeacon of Wandsworth. David is wonderful and I really liked working for him. I thought – If I'm going to do this, I need to feel that I am not being mad, that this really is what God wants me to do. I don't want to go off on some completely ridiculous tangent. I don't think of my priesthood in terms of a career but I suppose a bit of me was thinking, 'I don't want to make the wrong move.' So I went to talk to David and we had lunch together. I said I was thinking about joining the RAF.

He said, 'Oh, that sounds like a sensible idea.'

As we talked about it, it did seem quite good. The commission that you had to take when I went in was for four years. (It's changed now to six years.) So it's not a huge amount of time, and I could look at it as a second curacy. I'd still only be thirty-one when I came out. Most people aren't even ordained before that age, and I'd have had seven years of experience in two very different environments. So the green lights were shining and that was a bit worrying really, because I thought, 'Oh dear, there's nothing holding me back now!'

'I'm not sure how you'll fit into the military – pushing boundaries!'

I filled out the application forms. It then takes quite a long time, because they have to do all the security checks and medical forms and so on. The selection process is similar, though not exactly the same, as it would be for anyone else joining the RAF. I think I sent the forms off the first week in December, and I went for an interview with the chaplain's branch at the end of April. They said they would be happy to sponsor me to join the RAF.

About two weeks later, I had my Officer's Selection Board, which is – in a curious way – very similar to ABM, when you are being selected to be a priest. You turn up on a weekday lunchtime, have some aptitude tests in the afternoon and then an interview the next morning. It's almost exactly the same.

In the RAF you're supposed to be well up on current affairs. So there's me, sitting there saying, 'Well, I read the *Guardian* when I've got time and – oh, yes – I read the *Church Times* every week.' They must have thought, 'What on earth have we got here?'

They asked questions about aircraft and where we were working in the world at the moment and the sorts of things that had been happening in the world. I remember saying at one point that I liked to push boundaries and challenge people's preconceptions a little bit. I was really only thinking of things like wearing my clerical collar when I go to do my shopping at the supermarket. People still seem amazed to see that women priests have to eat. But this chap looked a bit startled and said, 'I'm not sure how you'll fit into the military – pushing boundaries!'

The 'bleep' test

Then you have the medical and fitness tests. The military fitness test is known as the 'bleep' test, because you run up and down a gym between two marks, and there's a machine going 'bleep'. It bleeps and you set off and you have to get to the other end before it goes bleep again; but if you get there before it bleeps, you have to wait until it bleeps again before you can go back. The bleeps are fairly far apart at the beginning but then they get closer and closer together and you run faster and faster. But you're not running very far and you're turning round all the time, so it's quite exhausting – or it is for someone like me, who isn't very fit and is a bit asthmatic. It's also quite confusing. I'm totally useless when it comes to anything like that, at getting a grasp of what you're supposed to do.

They split us up into two groups and we dropped out when we'd had enough. So they then made a note of the level you'd got to and that is where you are at in terms of fitness, and what your potential is. They don't say, 'Oh, you're nowhere near fit enough, you can't join.' So it's not too bad.

I got through that, and then we were given some leadership exercises as well. You have to try to get to a certain point without falling off a log, and put barrels together to reach something, to retrieve an object. The sort of thing you'd expect for people going on active service. You take it in turns to lead those exercises. You're divided up into syndicates and when it's your turn to lead, you tell the others in your syndicate what to do.

Vicars and tarts

I somehow got through the selection, left the parish in Barnes and joined the Royal Air Force on 5 August 1999. Then I went off to Cranwell, in Lincolnshire, to do the training. You're issued with everything, full RAF uniform, the very first day.

When they come into the RAF, most officers do twenty-four weeks of training. They have a lot of drill, a lot of fitness exercises, room inspections and all that sort of thing. As clergy, we cram everything into eight weeks. Clergy and doctors, dentists, lawyers and anyone transferring from other armed forces go through this intensive eight weeks SERE course, as it's called. (Specialist Entry and Re-Entry.) Also known as 'the vicar and tarts' course!

I kept telling myself, 'It's just a funny adventure holiday you're spending, Eleanor. It'll all be OK'

A lot of it was learning how to be an officer and how to command people. We went out on these leadership camps. You're given a job and for three hours you are in charge. So we did all these 'three-hour leads' and I was useless at it. Instead of saying, 'Move that over there. Now!' I would say, 'Please would you move that over there.' I kept getting told off for saying 'please'.

But chaplains are not given the same commission as normal officers. We do hold the Queen's commission and therefore our rank is acknowledged, so we're saluted, because that's acknowledging the Queen, it's not acknowledging us. But we're not called 'ma'am' or 'sir'. We're called 'padre'. And we can't give orders, because it would be ridiculous, wouldn't it, if the chaplain was telling people what to do or was charging them when they misbehaved themselves? So we don't have that part in our commission that the Queen gives us.

But there I was trying to do all this ordering people about – and being useless at it. And running great distances in big boots and getting out of breath . . . Or we would be given a task to do like: 'Over there is a bomb. You must defuse the bomb, but if you get within X metres of the bomb it will detonate.' So we had to fit up some sort of rig so we could go over the top of it or move things with poles and rope.

I kept telling myself, 'It's just a funny adventure holiday you're spending, Eleanor. It'll all be OK.'

But of course, the thought of failing the course and having to come back in six months' time . . . I wouldn't have done it. I'd have said, 'No, I've got to leave the RAF and go back to parish life.' Because for me – I'm a priest first.

Being a priest is the thing that matters

There were moments in that eight weeks when I was quite unhappy and uncomfortable about what I was doing. I felt that I wasn't being a priest because I was being moulded into an officer and I felt quite torn, I suppose.

But there were good things, too. There were the three other clergy training at the same time and in the evenings, when we'd come in after a long day running around learning to be officers, we all used to dress formally for dinner, as you do in the mess. I would put on a clerical shirt. We all would. We were saying, 'This is what we are. Priests.' That was nice.

Mind you, the first time *I* did it, about 100 young officer cadets turned round and stared because they hadn't had a clue that this was what I was!

Exercise Peacekeeper

All the same, I didn't feel I was learning anything very useful until the last week. The very last exercise you do before you graduate from Cranwell is called Exercise Peacekeeper. You go to another area. You set up a camp of tents and you have a temporary mess tent and temporary unit and you all live there. What you do is you learn to be a commander in different situations.

It was the first time that they'd had a number of chaplains together at SERE for a while, so for this last week our SERE squadron, including us four chaplains, was attached to the main graduating squadron of about eighty people who had done the full twenty-four-week course. There were about 100 of us altogether, divided into two shifts. You'd do a twelve-hour night shift or a twelve-hour day shift, and two chaplains were assigned to each shift.

You start off the exercise in your normal combat gear, but by the end you're running around with your full protective equipment on, the stuff that protects you from an air attack, a chemical or gas attack. You always have your respirator with you. You'd go to bed at midnight and could be woken up at two or three in the morning by the air-raid siren, and you'd have to get to the trenches with your respirator on and in your proper kit. We were learning how to survive.

You might be put in charge of the guard or you might be running the whole operation, or you might be looking after the day-to-day running of the camp. Or you might be part of the enemy contingent, coming in and doing dodgy things, like trying to break down the barricade at the front gate.

But for this particular week, we chaplains weren't doing any of that.

We were being chaplains. We set up our own tent. It was a normal tent with clear windows and one day we jokingly said to one of the chaps who was working with us, 'It would be great to have some stained glass windows.' And he came back the next day with different coloured sheets of acetate and we stuck them on the windows.

We were there for a week, and on Sunday we held Morning and Evening Services. We felt very strongly they shouldn't be compulsory and people should only come if they wanted to. No church parade. No 'jolly yourselves along, chaps' sort of thing. And lots of them did come. We were there for Battle of Britain Day as well, and held a service – but being the RAF, that was compulsory.

We put chairs and tables in our tent, and people would come in for their lunch and sit with us. We filled our pockets with sweets and wandered round the camp and gave them to people and chatted to them. And once it became known that there were four chaplains training, we found that people would want to come and chat with us. People who'd had a bad lead when they'd been in command, and felt they'd failed would come and talk to us about it. So we were being priests. We were doing the pastoral work that we are called to do.

We were also given some make-believe scenarios to deal with. Once there was somebody who was holding someone else hostage, and we had to go and deal with it. Someone else decided they didn't want to shoot people anymore, and we had to have words with them. I went out one day with a crowd of people who had to retrieve the body of a member of an aircrew whose aircraft had crashed. We had to go out under enemy fire – all blanks, obviously – to find this dummy, hidden in the bushes somewhere. I, obviously, am non-combatant as a chaplain, so I was unarmed, wandering around like an idiot, having to be protected by the others.

But over that week there was a growing realisation that we were there, that we had a purpose, and that we would be there in a real situation. We felt we were becoming padres in reality, as well as in the role play.

Sometimes the edges got rather blurred. A couple of times when we were off-duty and sleeping in the tent, there was an air-raid. People would go round kicking the tents and shouting, 'Get out, get out, go to the trenches' and people would come running past us and go, 'Oh sorry, Padre!' even though we were just as much part of the exercise and training as they were. It was all a very good experience and it meant that we made a lot of friends.

If I hadn't had that week on Exercise Peacekeeper, I'm not sure if I'd have felt I'd make the right decision in joining the RAF. But having done that I thought, 'Yes. This makes sense. This is what I thought I was coming to do.'

I've had about eighteen months in the RAF since then. Obviously there are huge differences between this sort of ministry and parish ministry. That's what you'd expect really.

And here am I, single, certainly without children, and a priest – a priest in the RAF

It's also different from life in general. I do sometimes think, 'Ooh! This is different!' I've got a crowd of friends from school – there are about seven of us – who I keep in touch with, sporadically. I wouldn't say we meet every week or anything anywhere near that – but each year we manage to catch up.

The last one of that crowd – except me – is getting married this year. All the others have got children. And here am I, single, certainly without children, a priest, and a priest in the RAF. And yes, that is quite different. And I sometimes think – Oh goodness, what on earth's going on?

Because I'd very much like to be married and have children. I've always wanted that and I've always felt that that would be very much 'me'. The thing I have to consider really – especially when I was in the parish – is I feel I live in a goldfish bowl. You do, doing this work, being in this sort of life. I remember once at theological college someone saying, 'You don't live "above the shop", you live in it.' I think that's true. Now that's fine, but that's fine if it's just you. That's not to say it's fine for anyone you meet, and sometimes I think people are maybe a bit put off by the idea that I'm a priest. There's pretty much a major limit on what I would allow to compromise my role and my future.

A lot of guys – and people in general – say to me, 'But you're a priest!' And they're still trying to come to terms with what that actually means. Are you allowed to drink? Are you allowed to smoke? Are you allowed to have boyfriends? Are you allowed to marry? And all those questions that people don't dare ask but they want to know the answer. So I try to show them that I'm Eleanor. Yes, I can go into the bar and have a drink and yes, I can have a boyfriend. And that's absolutely fine. But yes, I'm also a priest. I'm going to go into the bar and have a drink, but I'm not going to get rolling drunk and start dancing on the bar or gossip or . . . well, there are boundaries.

If I do marry and have children, I would want to stop working full-time until my children were at school, but I would still want to exercise my ministry in some way. Once you are a priest, it's something that you are, and you don't, can't switch it off and switch it back on again.

I sometimes kid myself that I'll wake up one morning and think, 'Right, OK, this is all sorted, and the plan is this . . .' But it's never going to be that straightforward and I do sometimes think that maybe that's one of those things that may not happen. You see other women – men too, but women especially – who are in the early years of their professions who end up being single because there was no real space or time for relationships to develop. The job became their whole life.

But I don't see that that's a necessary thing. I know a vast number of women priests who are married with families. Some are married to other priests and some are even married to normal people who have normal lives! But it's something that I think about – I suppose, inevitably. You just have to let these things fall into place and be open to the future.

My mother and stepfather had their wedding blessed in the Baptist church by the Baptist minister, because they couldn't have a wedding service in a church. And for me, at nine years old, it was a very significant moment because he blessed my parents, but he also then blessed the whole family – two sets of children and two sets of parents, a new family. And for me it was a very important symbol that God makes new things – even when those things appear to have already been created. There were already a mother and children and a father and children, and yet here was a new family.

That has influenced hugely my adult understanding of what God can do and my understanding of marriage. Yes, there can be mistakes and cruelty, but there is always space for new things. So I hold those two things in my mind when I think about relationships and the future. You don't ever know what's around the corner and that's true for everybody. I'm a hopeful traveller anyway.

The world is much, much bigger than you allow yourself to think, and God is much, much bigger. He has all sorts of other things going on, like a safety net beneath you, that you don't even think about 90 per cent of the time. But it's there when you need it.

Padre

I came in as a flight lieutenant because of my educational qualifications. In the RAF, if you've no other professional qualifications you start as a pilot officer, then you're flying officer, and then you're flight lieutenant and those three officer ranks are known as junior officers and then you go squadron leader, wing commander, group captain and so on.

After my first year of satisfactory service, I was given the rank of squadron leader. That means that I have the relative rank of a senior officer. I don't give commands and orders, but I have the right, as a chaplain and an officer, to go in and talk to the station commander or anyone else on the station, if I feel that there is something going on that I am not happy about. I've never done it, but as a chaplain I have the right.

In the RAF the chaplains look after everybody on the station. Here, I suppose there's about 1,500 personnel. Some of those are civilians employed by contractors or by the MOD, and we're responsible for them too.

The difference between the RAF and the other forces, in particular the Army – I don't know so much about the Navy – is that we care for everybody, including the families and children of civilians. The Army chiefly care for their soldiers. The army chaplain goes on detachment with the regiment. We usually stay rooted with the people at the station. It's important because it says that our community life is important. I suppose it also reflects the different way our forces work. The RAF tend to fly out from station and back to station, whereas the Army have to go away for long periods; and the Navy are away on their ships for months at a time.

The RAF has a different way of looking at rank, too, from the Navy. I salute people who are senior in rank to me and anyone junior ranked to me salutes me. The Navy says that if you're a chaplain, you assume the rank of the person you're talking to. So in the Navy, if you're talking to the most junior, insignificant person, then it's as if you are junior too. And if you're talking to the most senior person, then it's as if you are senior – you're on a level footing. But our rank structure gives us the freedom to go in and make things right for people. I think it both helps and it hinders, having rank. I much prefer for people to see my collar than my rank.

Where is God in all this?

I am involved with a lot more welfare issues than I would be in a parish. People who don't ever come to the church will come to me because they're told when they join the RAF, 'If you've got a problem, go and talk to the padre.' It's mainly family problems. They expect us to be able to sort things out for them. I find sometimes that I can spend a whole week dealing with what I suppose the rest of the world might see as social issues or welfare issues.

You might ask, 'Where is God in all of this?' And I would say that the reason that they come to me is because I'm here for them, whoever they are and whatever their situation is, and the reason I am here for them is because I believe that God is here for them. I put it into that context, even if they don't. Sometimes I'll say, 'I'll be thinking of you, I'll be praying for you.' But that would make some people feel very uncomfortable, so then I don't. It doesn't mean that I don't pray for them and remember them, just that I don't say it.

My church community here is small and it's mixed. It's military and it's civilian. It's old and it's young. You get that feeling of a real family parish. I always go to the new arrivals brief and say, 'There's a church here, it's yours, it's your space.'

I preach here every week. It must be very hard for the congregation, as it is for me, because sometimes I finish a sermon and I think – I'm sure I said that last week! I suppose, at the end of the day, that the story of faith *is* the same every week. God loves you, he forgives you, he has immense compassion for you and he died for you. All we need to do is say to God, 'OK, I'll let you come and sort me out, I'll let you renew me, mend those bits that I've broken and damaged.'

Hello, everybody

Women work in every branch of the RAF, except for the RAF Regiment, so no one has ever expressed much surprise at seeing a woman chaplain. Some come from nonconformist backgrounds where they'd have been used to women ministers; or from no church background at all, so they've not even heard all this big discussion that's been going on and they've not picked up on the fact that this is anything different or new.

I'm the only female chaplain in the RAF at the moment, so when we go to conferences together, which we do once a year – the Anglicans – it's me and the men. There are other women around from other denominations, but when it's the Anglicans, it's just me and the men. We had a visiting speaker at this conference last summer, not a serviceman, and he said to me one morning, 'I don't know how to address you all, Eleanor, because I don't want to put you in a funny position. But you see, I don't want to say, "Good morning lady and gentlemen," but if I say, "Good morning, gentlemen" then I'm missing you out. I don't know what to do.'

I said, 'Well why don't you just say, "Hello everybody"?'

No flying bishops in the RAF

Another interesting thing about the RAF is that there is no provision in the chaplain's branch for flying bishops. There are no Resolutions A, B and C, no flying episcopal oversight, no Act of Synod. They don't effectively exist in the RAF. If a chaplain doesn't like the fact that there's a female chaplain working on the base – and some of them don't – then they are told, 'Tough. That's just the way it is.' Women priests are allowed and they belong, and that's how it is. And that's true of all the armed forces.

Just pootling along

Probably 90 per cent of the time I'm doing my own thing and not really thinking – Am I being a good priest? Am I spending enough time for God, allowing God to guide me in prayer and being reflective about what I've done? I'm just pootling along.

There are sometimes things that you have to do that are hard and painful and you fail. I remember at theological college, my overwhelming feeling was, 'I am inadequate. I am inadequate at this.' But that doesn't mean to say that you shouldn't be doing it, and that you can't develop and grow. I have never once regretted being ordained, never once and I've never even thought – Oh, if only I'd never done this.

I'm only twenty-nine. I've been ordained just under five years. I've got my whole life and my whole ministry ahead of me and I don't know where it's going to take me. God has that space to plant, that time for me to develop and grow. I feel happy that, you know, it fits. It fits me.

Let's go – let's be priests

I'd never wanted to be a priest because it was my right as a woman. I wanted to be a priest because I've always felt that that's what God wants for me and that it's the most fulfilling thing he could offer for me to do and be. So it wasn't ever about my rights as a woman, it wasn't about the fact that we should be liberating something or expressing some other side of our faith or developing some new kind of feminine spirituality. It was about me, and others like me, being free to be what God called us to be, full stop. Male or female doesn't matter.

Until we're twenty or thirty years down the track and we look back along the path of history, we won't really see what difference having women as priests has made. I don't think I could articulate what the special things are that women bring to ministry. I know some male priests who are so wonderfully good at what they do, so totally good at it, and I don't think they lack any special qualities a woman might have. I'm inspired by them.

I always felt that it was right for me to be a priest. I do remember once when I was still at school thinking – Oh, this is driving me mad! I had been having a nightmare about Greek grammar or something – which is totally understandable – and I did think – Whatever am I doing? But I remember feeling very strongly at the time, 'If this is what God wants for me, it's the best possible thing that I could do with my life. I can't say, "All right, God, that was your idea – but I've got a better idea." '

I suppose my world as I was growing up was a bit insular. I didn't think about the others outside it and what they were experiencing. On that day, when the vote went through, when all those women were standing outside – those who were already ordained, those who had been waiting for years to be ordained – I wasn't part of that group of people. I was in a different place in terms of my experience and my understanding, and when my turn came, I walked through an open door.

I've never had to beat the door down. I may have had to encounter a few raised eyebrows as a teenager but that's nothing compared to what some of my colleagues have experienced. It means that I don't have the feeling of battle-weariness. I almost expected it just to happen for me.

It's going to have a new look in every generation. I think a different dimension to women's ministry has begun now, and that we need to make sure that we are respectful of one another. Because the real danger is that the people who have battled so hard for so long will see people like me just walk in and think, 'Hang on a minute! We fought hard for this.'

I acknowledge that, but I also want to say, 'And now we've got it, let's go! Let's be priests. That's what we're here for.'

2001—50 AD: Florence, Archbishop of Canterbury?

Warning: Men in the middle of the road

If any explanation is still needed for why we called this book '*Jobs for the Boys?*', the road sign that Andrew and I kept passing on our travels north and south seems to give the complete answer: Warning: Men in the middle of the road. Or as one of America's first woman priests, Revd Nan Peete, said – to prolonged applause – at the 1988 Lambeth Conference, referring to the parable of the labourers in the vineyard, 'There is always grumbling by those called earlier, believing that the new arrivals are taking what is theirs.'

Here are a few sample examples of men in the middle of the road – and some of their grumbling:

> I went to offer the peace. He shouted at me 'No' and folded his arms and turned his back. It was a public humiliation for me, but what was worse, we were two priests in the Church of England, and one was refusing to receive the peace from the other in front of the whole congregation – it was pretty extreme behaviour . . .

> *I mentioned to my husband that I thought I had a vocation to be a priest and he and my then parish priest, laughed. And for eleven years after that, I shut my mouth . . .*

> Three people, two women and a man, left the church as a result of me coming here . . .

> *One of them made it absolutely clear that he was not going to support my application under any circumstances . . .*

> They wrote me a letter and in it they said that they had changed their mind about having a woman. They didn't add the black bit to it, but I already knew that that was being said . . .

The Archdeacon led a morning on City churches, and three of us who were recently arrived were invited to speak. One church had absented itself because I was going to speak.

One man came up to me and said, 'Prove to me that you have been called by God.'

I am afraid, because it has become clearer that those who oppose us are becoming more vociferous once again, especially as the prospect of women bishops comes into focus.

There are people here that won't come to communion when I am celebrating; they will just absent themselves. One or two have made a point of saying, 'This isn't personal to you, it's about my convictions about priesthood.'

I decided that I should be ordained. That was what I was being called to do by God, and that was a very urgent and definite thing. At school there was quite an amused reaction to this, and a careers adviser said, 'You could always be a secretary in a church.'

So sometimes this poor man would turn up to church and discover that it was me taking the service and he'd have to go away again, because he didn't want to come to Communion with a woman priest . . .

When they saw me with the keys in my hands going into church, they would say, 'Are you the new caretaker?' And I would say, 'Yes, indeed.'

There were people who were jealous, and there were people who were really very cruel. I didn't feel I belonged. Some people thought I'd ratted on lay ministry, and called me a poacher turned gamekeeper . . .

I wasn't allowed to take funerals. I remember the priest explaining 'Well, we want to give people the best care at this time.' And what he meant by 'best' was: not a woman . . .

I made a banner saying, 'Twelve years in the ministry, but only the dog gets the collar' and I took along my dog, Delilah, in a clerical dog-collar . . .

Somebody came up to me and said, 'Well I hope you are pleased with yourself now. You've just unchurched your husband. You have just undone his entire ministry' . . .

One person wrote to me, 'You will of course no longer be welcome at Walsingham.'

The bishop said to me, 'As far as I can see there are only two problems. One is your gender, and the other is your age.'

I can remember one young man saying to me, 'I don't know, it's not only because you're a woman that we find you so difficult – but you're so old as well.' I was just forty . . .

They didn't seem to notice at college that it was all the men doing everything. It wasn't malicious, it was just not noticing . . .

Finally the priest said to me, 'I am really sorry, but it isn't going to work. You seem to be a strong woman, and I just can't cope with strong women – please don't tell the bishop.'

We had had this wonderful gift given to us, and we couldn't celebrate. It was like you had had a baby and you had to keep taking it upstairs in case it upset the visitors . . .

I have never been so consistently patronised as I have since taking up this job. One man said to me, 'Oh! You're far too young and pretty to be the rector!' I said, 'I hope you tell your male priest that.'

At the end of it, after you have shown your authority and conducted the service, there's always somebody at the reception afterwards who will tell you that they, of course, don't think women should be priests.

We didn't interview the Vicar of Dibley

When we told people we were preparing this book almost everyone asked, 'Are you interviewing the Vicar of Dibley?'

The Vicar of Dibley must be the most famous religious woman in Britain. She is comical, but also compassionate and quite a powerful figure in her community. She's a full-blooded, sensible person surrounded by very odd, eccentric people, and she just gets on with the job. Not a bad summing-up of the life experience of many women – and not just women priests. Some women priests have an ambivalent view of Dawn

French's creation, but Canon Lucy Winkett believes it is not at all a bad stereotype.

'Why farces always seem have to have a vicar in their completely nonsensical world is another question, but if vicars *have* to be made figures of fun, and I think they do, then better the Vicar of Dibley than the Derek Nimmo, asinine, male stereotype in *All Gas and Gaiters*.'

Working in the very public arena of St Paul's Cathedral since she arrived there in October 1997, Lucy Winkett is in a good position to gauge the reaction of the non-churchgoing general public to women priests.

'Right now, where we are in the story of our ordination, women priests must never underestimate the shock of a congregation at seeing a woman in a pulpit for the first time, or taking a service. I live in a world where the debate about women's ordination is huge, and you forget that there are plenty of people out there who haven't got a clue that the whole thing has happened.

'I get an overwhelmingly positive response from visitors to St Paul's if they see me leading worship, particularly from women. It is often an annunciation moment for them. A kind of "Yes!" Women see me, and respond to something that they had probably never thought of before. And that is hugely affirming for me. I think for most women who come here, it is more like an annunciation, or a revelation – it's a gut thing more than a worked-out logical position.

'I don't want to keep on reinventing the wheel. Why should I and other ordained women have to keep trotting out the arguments about why we should be ordained? I don't want to take part in debates. It's a given. It's over. It's not right for us to be continually called upon to justify what we are doing. I've been ordained for five years as a priest now, and I love it. I really love it and I don't want to do anything else.

'But there are still people who will give you a tough time. There are people out there who still find women priests abhorrent and will use very strong, usually sexual language. So it's not over. It's also not over, in the sense that Roman Catholic women are not yet ordained, and I believe there are Orthodox women too, with vocations that haven't even begun yet to get any recognition. It's not enough for us to say, "Oh, great! We've done it." There are plenty of women with vocations – still waiting.'

Costing the earth

'I was personally mortified when the BBC television programme was shown about St Paul's, but I can see now, much later, that there was some good coming from it, and don't wish it away any more. It has been a costly business for all of us who were up front, and there are people who, having gone through that process of being filmed, still believe that this is not an appropriate role for women to take in religious life, or in society, and never will be . . .

'I've found that I am able to form relationships with people who are "the other side". But they are quite uncompromising relationships. What I don't want to be is constantly an appeaser. Women are always in that role – making sure that everybody else is OK, making sure everything is fine and happy. The relationships that I have forged are *forged*. They are hammered out on an anvil of "You are profoundly wrong." I really believe that. But with that very clear, you can still have a relationship. I want us to disagree in the context of knowing who we are, and knowing the other person. I think you can disagree more profoundly and more fundamentally if you know each other. To me, that's a stronger position. It costs you the earth to keep the channel of communication open sometimes, it really costs, but I want to do it in the faith that it's costing the other person the same.'

Muddy waters

For nearly 2,000 years the universal Christian church ordained only men as priests.

Yet at the very beginning, it was not so. The little group around Jesus did not consist only of twelve men. There were many women, including his own mother, who followed him as closely and faithfully as 'the twelve', and had as important parts to play in understanding and revealing his mission to the world. Mary Magdalene and the sisters, Mary and Martha, were every bit as much apostles as Peter, James and John. It is clear from the letters of St Paul that there were several women in authority in the churches he was writing to.

It must have been some time after the death of Jesus that the church he founded changed. It decided to abandon the liberation and equality that had been his gift, to follow and emulate the model of the secular authority of those days – men only in charge.

We asked Una Kroll if she thought women had always felt called to the priesthood, or if it was only in the last 100 years.

'In the second century, a sect called the Montanists thought men and women were both baptised in Christ, and therefore were equal in Christ, and they ordained some women priests. But they were condemned as heretics by the wider church. Through the Middle Ages, if women did have vocations to priesthood, since it was impossible as it were, they usually became nuns. Many of these nuns lived a priestly life, a eucharistic life. They didn't talk about priesthood, they just acted in a way you would expect a priest to act. A rare few did attain positions of power and influence, just as a rare few did in the secular world . . .

'It wasn't until the twentieth century, and after 1919 when women

first got the vote, that the Anglican Church started thinking seriously for
the first time about women's ordination . . . Unfortunately the waters
were mudded by the simultaneous growth of the secular feminist
movement . . .

'Ours was not a movement from within the church institution – not
initially. We were outsiders. What we were doing was looking for leaders
within the church who would be brave enough to stick their necks out.
But necks sticking out were not, for many years, things you saw many of.
There were bishops who would say to you privately, "I believe that this
is right." But they wouldn't come out and say so publicly. The only
people who stuck their necks out were idiots like me, and we were very
ordinary housewives, not politically experienced and absolutely naive.

'I was in general practice in 1967. I was quite a lively woman in
society when I went along for the first time to a meeting of the Society
for the Ministry of Women. These incredible women! I mean, they were
battle-axes, but I think I fell in love with them, partly because it seemed
as if they were banging their heads against brick walls.

'Women in secular society were also encountering difficulties, because
as the feminist movement got going in the 1960s, so opposition grew,
and at that time, for example, there were no women broadcasters of the
news. A woman might break down if she had to report something awful!
And the only women in religious broadcasting in those days were people
like Mary Stocks and Elsie Chamberlain – who had both got very deep
voices. And that was also true for the women doctors. When women first
became doctors in the 1920s, the only way they felt they could operate
was like men, so they wore masculine-looking suits, spoke in deep voices
– and all these women were huge in personality.'

One argument the church had in the 1970s and 1980s was that you
couldn't use the fact that all over Europe and America women could no
longer be discriminated against on the grounds of their gender in the
professions, as a reason for allowing women into the priesthood. That
would be to use a secular model for what is a sacramental matter. And yet
having men priests only had itself been a matter of following the secular
way of doing things. Jesus had called both men and women.

However, until 1994, the Church of England kept its jobs for the
boys, and because even now it still will not ordain women bishops, it is
the only remaining organisation or institution in English society that
legally discriminates against women.

'Why don't you just resign now and let her get on with it?'

In July 2000, Archdeacon Judith Rose sponsored a private members
motion at the General Synod, to discuss the theology of women bishops.

'Mine was a very mild motion. It wasn't asking that we have women bishops. It was only asking that we start doing the theological background to it. One proposed amendment (by Bernice Broggio) was very radical, saying we need to move to have women bishops now. I deliberately resisted all the amendments. I think we need to do our homework first . . .

'Once women were ordained to the diaconate in 1987 there was quite a psychological shift. For the first time they wore dog-collars, which have a visual impact and a psychological impact. The church suddenly woke up to the fact that it had women in holy orders . . . We've only had women priests for six years, which is a short time in the life of the church, a traditional institution that encompasses change only quite slowly for all sorts of reasons, and some of those are good reasons . . .

'Christian faith is about peacemaking and reconciliation. There's a lot to be said for the Christian principle of holding diversity together, and the church has tried to hold within it people who hold diametrically opposed views. We have women priests, and we also have a respected place for those who oppose the ordination of women. But I believe for the most part, they are asking the women to carry the price of that. The men who are opposed to the ordination of women are still recognised and respected by all the bishops as priests. The women's priesthood is not recognised by some priests and by some bishops . . .

'Whether women should be bishops will undoubtedly be back on the agenda within the next five years. I don't think we shall have women bishops for seven years, and it's more likely to be at least ten years. But things might go quicker than I think. It may have a positive effect in reunion with the Roman Catholic or the Orthodox Church if we don't have women bishops yet, but a very negative effect on relationships with the nonconformist churches.

'It is unlikely that our relationship with the Methodist Church is going to get very far if we can't recognise their senior women. I would be very surprised if they are going to be prepared to have serious talks about reunion with the Anglican Church until we do have women bishops. I mean, if they're going to accept bishops at all, which they may or may not do, then they certainly won't want them to be exclusively male.

'I see no reason why the Archbishop of Canterbury couldn't be a woman in the next – less than fifty years.'

At the July 2001 Lambeth Conference, Andrew and I were invited with other members of the press to the dean's house and garden for a drink after the Sunday Eucharist in York Minster. I was introduced to George Carey, who told me that he had recently been talking to some children and they had asked him if a woman could ever be the Archbishop of Canterbury.

He had said, 'Oh yes, I am quite certain that will happen'.

To which one of them had retorted, 'Well, then, why don't you resign now, and let her get on with it?'

So this is our prediction:

2050 AD Florence, Archbishop of Canterbury, born July 2001 AD

LIZ AND ANDREW BARR
NOVEMBER 2001